T0367815

THE MONEY CLUB

Is Your Financial Future Safe? What Every Woman Should Know

MARILYN CROCKETT

and

DIANE TERMAN FELENSTEIN

with Dale Burg

A FIRESIDE BOOK

Published by Simon & Schuster

FIRESIDE
Rockefeller Center
1230 Avenue of the Americas
New York, NY 10020

First Fireside Edition 1998

FIRESIDE and colophon are registered trademarks
of Simon & Schuster Inc.

Manufactured in the United States of America

10 9 8 7 6 5 4 3 2 1

Library of Congress Cataloging-in-Publication Data

Crockett, Marilyn.

The money club: Is your financial future safe? What every woman
should know / Marilyn Crockett and Diane Terman Felenstein with Dale Burg.

p. cm.

Includes index.

1. Women—Finance, Personal. 2. Investments. 3. Finance, Personal.
I. Felenstein, Diane Terman. II. Burg, Dale, III. Title.

HG179.C747 1998

332.024'042—dc21 97-23184 CIP

ISBN 0-684-83719-6
0-684-84605-5 (pbk)

CONTENTS

THE MONEY CLUB

INTRODUCTION

Facing the Fear: Diane Terman Felenstein

For me to be talking about finance is a little like Steven Spielberg giving advice about fabric softeners. For most of my life, I had been cautious about money—I kept track of spending and saving—but I had no concrete plans. The future always seemed very far away.

As a kid growing up in Manhattan, I was so happy-go-lucky that they called me the Mayor of the West Side. I never dreamed life would change. Then I turned eleven and my father lost his job. In one moment, everything my twin brother, David, and I had always taken for granted vanished.

I'll never forget that summer. My girlfriends were shopping for camp, getting their yellow slickers and Milkmaid's "Pixie Pink" lipstick at Saks Fifth Avenue. I was devastated that I couldn't be part of this yearly ritual.

I prayed that my parents could somehow find the money to send me back to Camp Scatico. But they never did.

My father went on chasing his dreams and my mother went to work. Although she had grown up in a home with a chauffeur and a butler, Mom was not too lazy or too proud to sell table pads door-to-door and table-to-table at flea markets. (Over the years, she became everything from a model to a stockbroker.)

There was no way I could go to one of the better private schools with my friends. The one I attended was definitely second-rate. David passed the rigorous test for Stuyvesant, a selective public high school, and eventually went on to Syracuse.

I went to a local college, New York University. But every few weeks I would have to march into the bursar's office and swear that "the tuition money was in the mail." The academic priority in our family was David, who was doing well at college and went on to medical school. The investment paid off. Today he is a renowned doctor involved in groundbreaking cancer research.

After one semester at NYU, I dropped out and got a job. My pay, in cash, was put in an envelope marked "New Girl." I was insulted that they didn't even use my name. One week later, I was fired. Frustrated and miserable, with all my friends at college, I moved on to Mercury Records, where I saved up for a trip to the Virgin Islands. It turned out to be the most important trip of my life.

I met a woman named Claire Orson who told me about a position as public relations director at Audio Fidelity Records, where she had worked. When I applied, my prospective boss insisted I was too young, but I talked him into a two-week trial period at $75 a week, $15 more than what I was making. Although I had no idea what the job entailed, I wanted it desperately. I knew I would have to get the company's name in the newspapers. What I didn't know was how to do it.

Determined to be a self-taught publicist in two weeks, I created my own Diane Terman Public Relations crash course! I figured if I was going to be fired I might as well go for the top. So I called *The New York Times* and naively asked for the "records" department. Payroll connected me to Personnel, and from there I was shunted off to Accounts Payable. I finally reached the Music Department, where I confessed to a staff writer that I had only eight more days to prove myself. He was so stunned by my revelation, he agreed to see me.

Hurricane Donna and I arrived at the paper at the same time. The wind was howling through Times Square, I was drenched, and I had no clue what I was going to talk about. In the middle of our conversation, I suddenly heard myself telling the reporter our company was going to be recording the sounds of the hurricane. He seemed interested, so I made the story even bigger. I said we were sending engineers to the roof of our building. The reporter promised to cover the big event.

I rushed back to my office and demanded a meeting with my boss. When I told him what I'd done, he roared and hit the roof—with engineers. We added the sounds of toilets flushing, hearts beating, phones ringing, and other effects. We had no scheduled date for releasing this album, but when the story appeared in the *Times,* we were swamped with calls from record distributors all over the country. Radio stations were actually asking to buy the record for their special effects libraries. Seeing there was a real market, Audio Fidelity quickly produced the record and, eventually, an entire line of sound effects recordings.

The company offered me a choice between a raise and a pension plan. A pension plan? A ridiculous idea! I took the raise. Audio Fidelity offered Claire and me office space to establish a public relations company. We would sift through the Yellow Pages and cold-call prospective clients. Every time we landed an account, we would frantically brainstorm public relations strategies for the new client's specialty. As we learned, the firm grew.

Meanwhile, I got married. My husband had left his family millinery business and was manufacturing a dress that my father designed. I look back on it now, and it sounds like something from a Carol Burnett sketch: a dress that, depending on which buttons you unbuttoned and which pleats you released, was either a day dress, a culotte dress, or a bowling dress. My husband needed my help to rep this unique item, a situation complicated by the fact that since it sold in three different categories (dresses, casual, and sportswear) it had to be shown to three types of buyers. Early each morning, I would arrive at the garment district with my valises and visit buying offices and department store buyers. Then at 9:30 I'd head to my public relations job. I spent my days and nights juggling appointments between my office and the garment center.

We had a baby, but the marriage didn't last. I divorced my first husband and moved our company to my apartment to be near my daughter, Deborah. As a single mom, I was paying all the expenses. Since I had no idea how to balance a checkbook, once a month I would go over to Chase Manhattan Bank, where Mr. Badenhagan would sit down with me to straighten out the mess I had made.

Things were looking up. I became engaged to a man named Marshall Felenstein. We had been married only two weeks when he took me to meet the family lawyer to discuss our wills. At the time, I didn't realize how responsible and considerate he was. All I could think about was the lawyer saying, "Let's talk about your estate." My estate? I had two charm bracelets and a diamond ring from my first marriage plus about $1,000. I was humiliated by my lack of assets. Marshall told me he didn't care. He was just relieved that, unlike his first wife, I didn't come with a huge dental liability.

Marshall turned out to be a take-charge person, which was okay with me. I was raised in a generation where women counted on men to handle the finances. Having money one day as a kid and losing it the next had only turned me into a careful spender, not a careful planner. I considered personal finance, even my own, to be the world's most boring topic. When we met with an accountant or insurance agent, usually because my signature was needed, I zoned out and doodled.

I wasn't just bored. I was uncomfortable. I didn't participate. I barely understood the conversation, so I didn't know what questions to ask. I never thought about—and certainly never questioned—whether these professionals had my best interests in mind. Ashamed of my lack of knowledge, I always prefaced any remark with "Please forgive me," "This is probably silly," or "I'm sorry to ask again, but I just don't understand." To his credit, our accountant, Ross Kass of Jablons, Kass & Greenberg, persisted in his belief that I would eventually "get it." But like millions of other women, I left everything to my husband.

Not anymore.

Today, I'm not the same person I was just a short time ago. What changed me? I formed what turned into a financial self-help group for women. Today, I am increasingly involved in managing the family finances. I have taken charge of my own stock portfolio. Marshall and I have already reorganized our personal insurance and our estate plans. The process is ongoing—learning a new language takes time—but now I am a genuine participant. In the past, I had no input. Today, I notice things Marshall might not have noticed. He's grateful that we can share financial opinions; that our interests have broadened as a couple; that he has my help. And believe it or not: this is fun!

For my last birthday, I asked for (and got) several financial newsletters as presents. I spent part of a recent vacation on a cruise ship picking the brain of an expert on mining and gas exploration, and I faxed a message from Mykonos—at about $1 per word—telling a friend in New York not to sell her utility stocks based on that information. (I was right!)

What happened? People who change direction in their lives can often pinpoint the very moment of the "click"—the moment when they decided to make the change. For me, it happened on a plane. I had been reading an article about the Beardstown ladies, the group of Midwestern women who wrote a best-seller about their investment club. When I finished, I thought about these women who were focused on looking ahead, while I was not. I thought about Ross, who insisted that I was capable of taking charge of, and furthermore of understanding, the entire scope of my financial future, though I did not think so. I thought about Marilyn Crockett, the broker I had recently met, who suggested I could be making better investment decisions, though I had not thought so.

I do my best thinking on my feet. That night I was pacing up and down the aisle for hours. I thought about how I'd become a successful career woman. I ran my own firm. I attracted many major clients, among them Ultra Slim-Fast (which I launched), Prestige Cosmetics, The Tova Corporation, Handi Wipes, Bob Hope's Birthday Benefit, United Cerebral Palsy, Fred Joaillier, Schrafft's Ice Cream, *Self*, Salvador Dali, the London Festival Ballet. I had lectured about my field at Cornell and Syracuse universities (where I was proud to have my daughter, then a student, in the audience). In the course of doing public relations for so many different clients I had been exposed to every kind of business. I could track every dime my company spent. But while I was concentrating on the day-to-day details, I wasn't planning for the future. I had left that job to my husband.

And yet I had seen more and more close friends becoming widowed and many divorced. How could I assume my husband would always be there to take care of me? Statistics showed there was a pretty good chance

I would be left to make my own decisions someday. That idea was almost too frightening and overwhelming to contemplate. Thoughts and ideas and impressions spun around in my head long into the night. And before morning, I'd come up with the idea for The Money Club.

Once I got home, I had only to place a few phone calls to confirm that my situation was fairly typical. "If anything happens to your husband," I would ask a friend, "could you keep living in your present home?" I knew that was everyone's big concern.

"I'm not sure," my friend would say.

"Is your money invested?"

"Oh, yes."

"Do you know what your three largest investments are and how much they are worth?"

"Not really."

"Do you know what you can expect from a pension plan?"

"No."

"Do you know how much life insurance you have? Or if it's enough?"

"No."

"Have you made provisions for complicated medical and living problems for your elderly parents and in-laws who live far away?"

"No."

"Do you understand what's in your husband's will?"

"No."

"Do you know how much money you'll have if anything happens to him?"

"No."

"Do you know if your medical plan covers Alzheimer's disease?"

"No."

"Do you feel comfortable functioning at work and running your household? Do you know where to have anything repaired and how to manage your children's sicknesses? Could you manage a charity event for a thousand people and feel comfortable that it would run smoothly down to the last detail?"

"Yes."

These replies were typical of the responses I got over and over again. Like my friends, I had found time to raise a child, be a companion to my husband, take care of my home, pursue my career, keep up my appearance, volunteer for charity work, oversee our social life. The only thing none of us found time for, it seemed, was the boring and difficult task of managing our money—the very thing that made our existence secure.

I assured my friends that I wasn't putting them on the spot to humiliate them; that I didn't know any more than they did; and that I was going to get professional help for us. As a public relations person, I am very sensitive to marketing and packaging. When my company introduces a product line, we spend a great deal of time coming up with just the right approach, and we follow through down to the tiniest detail: the right paper in the press kit, the right box to send it in, the right day and date to send it out. I decided to package my idea as well.

I thought the best approach was to announce that I was forming an investment club. If I'd called it a pension plan club, or a long-term-disability club, no one would have joined. The term "investment club" would bring women into the tent even though I knew making money wouldn't be our major priority. Many of my friends already had money or could reasonably expect to inherit some, from either parents or a spouse. What they needed to know was how to manage and protect these assets.

Marilyn and I worked together to set up the club and invited several women to join. Shortly after we formed the club, *The New York Times* wrote a story about us because the group included so many high-profile women—successful entrepreneurs, highly respected professionals, top corporate managers, outstanding fund-raisers, spouses of top executives. There was certainly no shortage of academic degrees and street smarts in the group. But because we were quick to open up to one another, we soon discovered that as a group we knew astonishingly little about managing our own financial affairs. As a result, we also shared many fears and concerns.

Since we were, in fact, organized as an investment club, we did buy stocks. Marilyn quickly helped us learn how to research companies that were familiar (Coca-Cola) as well as those about which most of us knew nothing (Intel). We never set out to make a fortune in our club investment, which is relatively small, and we're starting somewhat late in life—most of us are only ten or twenty years from retirement. But we hoped to improve our future by what we learned as much as what we earned. In fact, what we have learned—from the experts, from one another, and from our own exploration—has enriched us beyond measure.

We have worked as a group to acquire and share information that has given us power to act more decisively and in our own best interests. We inspire and comfort one another. We aren't afraid to ask "dumb" questions or to say, "I don't understand." *We're not ashamed to go over the same things again and again.*

Making your own decisions and putting your own money on the line are heady propositions. Keeping abreast of business news adds a wonderful new dimension to our lives and opens up new avenues of communication. Best of all, the more confident and secure you become in dealing with finances, the more confident and secure you become in dealing with all aspects of your life. I feel better about myself. We all do.

I am fortunate in that I made changes in my life before I was forced to. I have been married to Marshall, who is the president of a retail real estate and consulting firm, for over twenty-five years. I continue to run the public relations firm I founded in 1971. It's a special thrill to be in business with our daughter, Deborah. Now I seem to have another calling. I'm on a personal crusade to help my friends and friends' friends. Now when we're on the phone, we're talking about investments and insurance. Our reading materials are annual reports and financial newsletters. I find it shocking! And I am so proud that I touched such a powerful chord. I am equally proud that when friends call with questions, I have the answers!

I was in my early fifties before I decided to acquire the tools that would help me make the future secure. Now that the future is almost here, I am ready. So are my friends, and we want to share what we've learned with you.

What we have learned doesn't apply just to our particular group. It applies to women everywhere. How much you have to invest and whether or not you have big assets is secondary. The issue for every one of us, no matter what our means and where we live, is learning how to overcome our fears and take control of our financial world.

I want to tell you something about going through this book. Some of the parts take a lot of concentration. Some of the technical information may seem—okay, I'll say it—a little boring. While we were learning, I felt that way, too. So I can see you putting the book down to make a phone call, or do the laundry, or start that needlepoint project. But I beg you to stick with it. Even if you get only one or two points, they will help make the whole clearer. Pieces will start to fall into place. Give yourself a hug, and keep going. I promise, there will be many moments when suddenly something you never understood becomes perfectly clear. And you, too, will hear the click.

Making Yourself Competent: Marilyn Crockett

From birth to age eighteen, a girl needs good parents, from eighteen to thirty-five she needs good looks, from thirty-five to fifty-five she needs a good personality, and from fifty-five on, she needs cash.—Sophie Tucker

When you're a happily married woman in a certain social stratum, you can usually close your eyes to financial matters. You can leave it to your husband to pay the bills, arrange for credit cards, and oversee the income tax forms so all you do is sign on the dotted line. Many of the women Diane and I know—even those who are established career women—live like this.

But you can't assume that's the way it will always be. On average, women outlive their spouses by ten years. Even if she is not widowed, a woman may see her husband incapacitated by illness. And plenty of husbands will take a walk—if the wife hasn't already given them the boot.

The vast majority of women whose husbands are disabled, pass away, or leave the marriage are completely unprepared for the task of managing their money. That's not my opinion: that's fact. These women are psychologically and, through lack of financial know-how, unable to manage their assets. The statistics bear this out: 80 percent of women are left in financial jeopardy through widowhood or divorce. Seventy-five percent of the elderly poor are women.

Now consider another category: women who, married or not, have grown dependent on the support of their employers. They've held good jobs for years and count on the status quo. But what happens if your job is simply cut, or a new boss doesn't like your face? What if the firm decides it needs younger (and less expensive) managers and you're shown the door? Perhaps you'll find another job. But if you're pushing forty, or have pushed past it, that can be a difficult experience.

In many ways, it's as if you've been divorced. You've relied on the company's support to provide all the necessities—from office equipment, telephone and fax lines to car service and credit cards. The company made all the choices for you when it came to life insurance, health insurance, long-term-disability insurance. It paid your salary and supervised your pension plan. That's all gone.

Many women who have lost a job take a look at their own impressive résumés and decide to go into business for themselves. But they may be overwhelmed by the dual roles of building the business and managing it. So they concentrate on the former, which is the part they know, and avoid the areas where they feel shaky. Result: tax, accounting, and other financial problems. And if the financial underpinnings are shaky, a small business can go under in a blink.

It doesn't take a job loss or a failed business to change your situation overnight. There are other devastating events: the doctor finds a shadow on an X ray, your husband and you decide the marriage can't go on. Change is more likely than not, and once your life has been shaken up, it's never quite the same. But if you feel financially competent, your recovery will be that much easier.

My own personal upheaval came when a long-term relationship—one that I had assumed would last forever—came to an abrupt end. I'd been with the man in question for eighteen years, and I hadn't worried about the future because he was financially secure; I was sure I would be taken care of.

After I graduated from Florida State University in Tallahassee with a bachelor's degree in home economics, I had decided I didn't want to cook and sew for a living. I loved to travel, so I took a job as a flight attendant. It didn't pay very well, but I didn't really need the money—or so I thought. I had become involved in my relationship, and flying was an exciting way to keep busy while my boyfriend pursued his own career.

He appeared to be settled and secure. And I thought I was, too. My business plan was "Have a nice day." I was flying high—both figuratively and literally. But when the relationship came to an end, I came down to earth very fast. Then the airline I worked for, Pan Am, went out of business. I knew I was in trouble, but I didn't know to what extent until I decided to take a look at my financial situation. "Maybe there's something in my retirement account," I thought. I looked—for the first time ever—at my pension plan. At that point, I had been working for the same airline for eighteen years. I was horrified at what I found: when I was sixty-two, I would be getting $100 a month to live on.

I was forty and basically alone, with no job, no vocation, and no money. Fortunately, I knew how to start from scratch. I had done it many times before. Growing up as a military brat (my father was Deputy Assistant Secretary of the Air Force), I never lived in any place longer than three years. My family was always moving, so my younger brother and I had no constancy in our lives. Each time we found ourselves in a new home, we had to start from scratch.

Trying to fit in at new schools all over the country was an ongoing challenge. I learned what a big help money could be. Once I was wearing the right clothes, the right makeup, the accessory of the moment—whatever was in—I felt better. Of course, it wouldn't be long before we moved again, styles changed, and I needed different clothes and different makeup and different accessories.

My parents didn't really understand the importance of funding the ongoing "Marilyn makeovers," so I was desperate to get a job. At thirteen, I didn't even qualify for working papers, but I talked my way into an afterschool spot as a file clerk at a real estate office. My parents chauffeured me to and fro. I loved having my own money, and I continued to work at different jobs through high school and college.

I had personally experienced the benefits of investing in the stock market at a relatively young age. While in college, I was offered a chance to study in Italy. My family didn't have the ready cash, but we did have some stock in the Marriott Corporation. My father graciously sold some of it to fund my trip, and that's how I discovered the beauty of liquid assets. But that discovery was also bittersweet, as we watched Marriott's stock double over time.

I also learned about risk and the value of teamwork—both of which were to serve me well in the future—in what was a highlight experience: performing with the Florida State Flying High Circus. My college was the only one in America with a circus, and I became part of a featured act. While a man rode a tiny bicycle, five other women and I would climb aboard and perform acrobatics. It was scary but exciting. I discovered how much I enjoy a certain amount of challenge and risk.

Fortunately, while I had been basking in the notion that my romantic relationship was going to determine the course of my life, my world had been expanding. As a flight attendant, I worked some of the choicest overseas routes, usually in the first-class section. There was plenty of downtime during those long overnight flights, so I'd entertain myself by reading the magazines my passengers had left behind. First-class passengers, not surprisingly, read business magazines. I became hooked on those magazines. The subject matter fascinated me. And when I had the chance to chat with passengers, I didn't ask where they lived or how many children they had. I asked about their work—what they did for a living, what companies they worked for, and why. I got firsthand information about which industries were booming and which companies were making the greatest profits. And I began following the companies on my own, curious to see how the stocks were doing.

Becoming more and more involved, I started to pick investments for myself and advise friends for fun. Eventually, though I was working full-time as a flight attendant, I began to work as a financial analyst for my then-boyfriend, who was a venture capitalist. I considered it a lark. I hadn't yet realized this investing was a potential career. But when I was forced to look at my finances and reevaluate my life, I started thinking about becoming a stockbroker.

Remember when Scarlett O'Hara vowed, "I'll never go hungry again"? Well, I was a latter-day Scarlett. I vowed at age forty that I would never again put myself in a position of starting from scratch. I would create my own security and stability. I would make myself financially independent. All my early experiences had made me resourceful, and I was able to make that low point in my life into a turning point. I became a woman on a mission. I set out to learn everything I could about taking control of my future, starting with the management of my own finances.

Although I had no sales experience and no financial credentials, I got an interview with a recruiter from a major Wall Street brokerage firm. When I achieved high scores on the qualifying tests, he enrolled me in the company's six-month training program. Since only 6 percent or so of all stockbrokers are female, I was one of the very few women in my training class. I wasn't intimidated. I was inspired. I wanted to show that a woman could understand money and advise others about their finances as well as a man—if not better. That determination paid off. I graduated number one in my class.

I am now First Vice President, Investments, at a major New York brokerage firm, where I oversee tens of millions of dollars in assets. But my favorite aspect of the job is still helping other women, business owners especially, to understand and manage their affairs and to avoid the mistakes I made. It's a very personal crusade for me. Like my distant relative, Davy Crockett, I am challenged by the wild frontier. His was in the wilderness. I found mine on Wall Street.

As a group, women are at much greater financial risk than men. They start saving money much later than men, and they invest their money much more conservatively. They squirrel it away rather than make bold choices. Women also change jobs more frequently, often before they're fully vested in a retirement plan. Because they're generally paid less, their pensions amount to less. And single women save only about one sixth of what they need to live on when they retire.

Most women get information about money as haphazardly as we get information about sex—from friends, who often aren't equipped to give advice, and from books. Our parents, who may have learned something from experience, often don't pass it down: they don't want to reveal how much they still *don't* know, and we don't want to listen to them anyway. Somehow we manage to figure out what to do about sex, but when it comes to coping with money we're less successful. And that can create a lot of shame.

Even though many women feel more or less incompetent when it comes to personal finance, they're unwilling to ask questions because they don't want to look foolish. Being embarrassed in front of your broker or your life insurance agent can cost you your life savings. Out of embarrassment, you can make the wrong choice—or just sit with your money in the bank and make no choice at all, which is worse. I want to help women overcome these feelings.

One way I help is as a licensed representative of the National Center for Women and Retirement Research (NCWRR), a nonprofit organization associated with Long Island University in Southampton, New York. Its goal is to help women become financially aware and competent. I also give seminars on a regular basis at the Learning Annex and to many other women's groups. I always start by telling my audiences about my past. I tell them that not too long ago I knew as little about finances as they do. Then I say that if I could learn what I now know, so can they. And perhaps most important, I tell them, "There's no such thing as a stupid question."

Women who have been on their own for most of their lives, like me, are at least in one respect fortunate. We can't hand the job to a partner, so we have no choice but to learn something about managing our finances. That may save us from being victimized. If she has relied completely on her husband, a woman who is divorced or widowed may not discover until too late that the "investments" have stayed stagnant, the life insurance policy has lapsed, and the money she expected to inherit is going to the stepchildren. Even a loving husband may leave his widow financially devastated out of carelessness or ignorance.

It's paradoxical that women, who are on the whole highly responsible about the maintenance of their homes and themselves, can be so careless and irresponsible about their finances. Just as you perform certain household jobs on a regular basis and go for a yearly checkup, you must make fiscal fitness part of your life. Because in the end, there may not be anyone else around to do it for you.

When I first met the women in our club, I was struck by how all of them seemed to have accepted as fact the idea that finance was an area best left to men, that men had some mysterious powers or special abilities when it came to things like investments and insurance. Even though the divorced and widowed among them were obliged to manage their own affairs, the responsibility made them nervous and hesitant. Even the professional women knew surprisingly little about personal finance, and those who had advisors weren't sure they were being well served. They needed the tools that would put them in charge.

Though we organized as an investment club, from the beginning Diane and I had envisioned something much broader in scope. We planned educational sessions and workshops on subjects that opened up entire new areas of investigation to the women. Some of the club members—a matrimonial lawyer, a trusts and estates specialist, and an insurance consultant—shared their professional expertise. All had stories to tell of lessons learned from prior mistakes. The investment club became our financial self-help group.

Thanks to the club, the women are now active participants in managing their finances. They have taken steps to insulate themselves against financial disasters. When necessary, they have had their portfolios reviewed and have met with estate planners. Most important, they say how profoundly different they feel now that they are comfortable in areas that had formerly been impenetrable and mysterious to them.

Women at every level of society confess to a secret fear of becoming a shopping bag lady—if not literally homeless and penniless, then without resources and not in control. If the women in the club, with their power, their access, and their assets, felt such fears, Diane and I knew that surely they were shared by women everywhere. And that's why we decided to write this book.

The members of the club were generous about contributing help to an effort we all believe in. So were other women who heard about this project. In the pages that follow you'll find all the basic information you need to take control of your financial life, along with many personal stories that illustrate why and how that information is important. Though some of the women preferred to use pseudonyms (their names are in quotation marks), the stories are real. We hope to inspire and educate you as much as we have one another.

CHAPTER I

GETTING IT TOGETHER

Founding the Club

My husband confessed that he was having huge financial problems and hadn't been paying the mortgage. We were in danger of losing our home. We needed new advisors to replace the lawyer and accountant who'd let us slide into a financial chasm, and I wasn't sure how to use my own money to protect the two of us. Thank God I'd joined the club. I had networks to reach out to, people to consult. Best of all, when we got advice, I understood the issues. I had a confidence I'd never had before, and to my lasting pride, I'm the one who got us out of trouble. Every woman should have a club like this one.—Anonymous

From 1985 to 1995, the all-female investment clubs in America—about 41 percent of the total number of clubs—outperformed the all-male clubs (13 percent) by three to one. Today's women aren't meeting to make quilts. They're weaving financial safety nets.

There are many investment clubs in America, but ours is unique. Though at the beginning we spent most of our time on investments, that was simply to lay the foundation. We intended to branch out and educate ourselves about money and everything else that affected our financial lives. And that's just what we have done.

When the women who would become The Money Club gathered in a Manhattan apartment for the very first time, there were eighteen people in the room—married and single, widowed and divorced. Most were linked only through their friendship with Diane. On the jacket of the book are some of the charter members and others who became important to our success. They are:

Top row, left to right:

VIVIAN SEROTA, a glamorous, earthy, effervescent patron of the arts, has a diverse management and theatrical production background. She serves on the board of Daytop Village International addiction treatment centers and the Guggenheim's "Learning to Read Through the Arts." She is married and the mother of a married son and married daughter.

CAROL LEVIN, a women's activist, brings the pixie charm of Liza Minnelli, an offhand humor, and tremendous vitality to her beloved Women's O.W.N. (Optimum Wellness Now) and many other projects. She and her husband, the CEO of Revlon, have one daughter in high school and a married son and daughter-in-law who have followed them from Minneapolis to New York.

CAROL SAFIR, like her husband, Howard, the New York City Police Commissioner, former Fire Commissioner, and onetime Associate Director of the U.S. Marshal Service, has worn many hats, among them real estate agent and international business consultant. An auburn-haired "girl next door," she has a son fresh out of law school and a daughter who is a newly minted FBI agent.

CARLYN MCCAFFREY has a wry wit and sharp mind that have earned her an exalted reputation among trusts and estates attorneys while her genuine concern has earned her the gratitude of her clients. A partner in the New York law firm of Weil, Gotshal & Manges, she has a bicontinental relationship with her husband, who presently works in Europe. They have four adult children.

Second row, left to right:

DIANE STEINER, with a dazzling smile and great determination, blends empathy and intelligence with a passionate commitment to her clients' rights that make her a top matrimonial lawyer in one of New York's premier firms, Sheresky, Aronson & Mayefsky. She is married and the mother of a grown son and daughter.

KATE COBURN, lively and curly-haired, packs a lot of energy and drive into a size-four body. Well known in New York real estate circles as the head of retail leasing for Rockefeller Center, she now advises other owners, developers, and retailers on strategic marketing and leasing issues.

DIANE TERMAN FELENSTEIN.

GLORIA GOTTLIEB, a willowy blonde with a mischievous grin, started an insurance business with her husband just after their marriage. They are now among New York's top agents. Their park-view home is filled with modern art and photos of their grown son and daughter.

Bottom row, left to right:

MARGOT GREEN, dark-haired, trim, and elegant, turned her sophisticated taste into a business asset and founded a custom couture establishment. Known to her clientele as "the fastidious fitter," she is the mother of two adult sons.

HARRIETTE ROSE KATZ, a statuesque blonde and leading New York event planner of private and public celebrations, is also a culinary expert and oenophile who has been awarded the title Conseiller Gastronomique des Etats-Unis and heads the New York chapter of La Chaîne des Rôtisseurs. She recently planned the wedding of her daughter.

MARILYN CROCKETT.

JANE BISHOP SHALAM, a delicate beauty, marshals her abundant charm and formidable organizing skills to get extraordinary results as a community activist and as a dedicated club member. Married and the mother of three sons, she's also helping raise her widowed brother's preteen daughter.

CAROL S. KOGAN combines the cool elegance of a fashion model with the mind of a crackerjack executive. Formerly president of several top women's designer apparel companies including Bill Blass and Oscar de la Renta Studio for Hero and Christian Dior Sportswear for the Jones Apparel Group, she has a business network throughout the United States, Europe, and the Far East. She divides her energies among her own consulting company, her husband's international movie business, her son, daughter, and new granddaughter.

Other founding members of the club, not pictured, include:

DONNA BIJUR and LINDA LIEBERMAN, directors of Service Party Rental. Donna is now a consultant in Sweden, and Linda has also launched another business, "Just Linens."

BAMBI FELBERBAUM, a board member of several hospitals, is a supporter of philanthropic programs that focus on women's, children's, and medical issues. She is married with two adult children.

KAREN FISHER is the president of Designer Previews, a designer referral service.

JOANN JORDAN, a real estate broker for fifteen years, is currently with Ashforth Warburg Associates. Joann, who became the second president of the club, is a widow with an adult son and daughter.

PAT WEINBACH, a designer, heads her own firm specializing in remodeling and renovations. She is married, with three adult children.

We had a lot of experience under our collective belt. Among us, we had traveled the world, met with statesmen and popes, been invited to the White House and the Academy Awards, run volunteer organizations with million-dollar budgets, and demonstrated our competence in executive offices and professional suites.

But those of us who were married didn't discuss money issues with our husbands, to whom we'd left all the financial control. If single, we stumbled along as best we could. Very little stumped us in other areas, but we knew nothing about dealing with our money. We didn't know how to calculate what we had, what to do about it, how to protect it, even how to find and talk to people who could help us. The very subject of personal finance frightened us.

Our group included women with power and access in their own right and/or married to highly placed professionals, some of whom were top executives at leading investment banking and accounting firms. Being generally well connected, we had access to information that others might not. But having money and access isn't the same as feeling in control of the money or knowing how to use the access. As a group, we were as financially unsophisticated as could be.

Even the wives of top-echelon money men didn't know any more about finance than anyone else. Money, investing, personal finance—these subjects are on the dark side of the moon for many women, including all of us. And though on the surface every woman in our group was traveling in privileged circles, we eventually realized that almost all had faced a personal crisis around an issue of money. Our families had struggled, we'd seen fathers and husbands fail, we'd been obliged to support ourselves on our own and been left in a financial lurch when widowed or divorced.

One of our members was just in her twenties when her husband died of heart failure, leaving her with a baby; remarrying a few years later, she was widowed a second time. After her divorce, another member went to withdraw savings from the bank and discovered her husband had drained the account. As a young wife, another had helped her husband write checks for bills each week and later found that he'd put the carefully stamped envelopes into the incinerator instead of the mail slot. Another came home one Sunday to discover her husband gone and the house picked clean. Every piece of furniture and shred of clothing had been stored or sold. She never saw any of it again.

Even after joining our club, some members had to come to grips with devastating changes. Two lost high-powered jobs and all the financial benefits that come with them. When we considered doubling the amount of our monthly contributions, they told us that if the obligation went up, they'd have to drop out, so we kept the status quo. When someone's husband had a business failure that forced him into bankruptcy, we joined forces to help her out during that difficult period. Our second president, Joann Jordan, lost her husband suddenly and without warning. Becoming immersed in club activities was one means of coping. "It was a diversion from my grief and a form of self-protection, because it helped me learn how to maximize my finances." Being in the club has made a big difference to every single one of us, each in her own way.

We are a no-frills operation. There is no coffee served and little socializing. We get right to business and rush off to our offices and duties immediately afterward. Still, because we are dealing with a subject that affected the underpinnings of our lives, we have bonded more closely than any group we'd ever been part of.

At the beginning, we used the words "frightened" and "stupid" to describe how we felt, and we discovered we had plenty of company. We learned not to allow anyone to "pull the ignorant strings," as one woman described it. Everyone was encouraged, given the freedom to ask questions and make mistakes, to receive sympathy and face challenges. That nurturing environment was a huge help.

Learning together makes you feel safe—like Weight Watchers or Overeaters Anonymous.—Carol Levin

In learning how to care for ourselves, we became competent to help each other. In times of need, we can now help choose attorneys and accountants and insurance brokers. We have suggestions of substance. We have grown in competence and confidence and developed the tools and resources to empower ourselves.

From our positive experience came the desire to let other women know that though we might live in the middle of New York City, we are in many ways like women all across America. We have experienced the same fears and feelings of powerlessness, and we know that they can learn to take control just as we did. Starting your own club may be the first step in the process.

Fortunately, our club had just the right people to help us find our way. Diane is the leader-cheerleader who motivates the members with her enthusiasm and keeps our bonds strong. If necessary she soothes ruffled feathers and sifts through complaints to see which have merit and must be addressed. She has an unflagging belief in the importance of the club, and her absolute faith has held it together.

Marilyn has kept the members on educational course, guiding us through the fundamentals of personal finance and eventually acting as a sounding board. She helps interpret the reports on potential investments and connects them to what's happening in the market. She has found a wide range of guest speakers.

The National Association of Investors Corporation (NAIC) is immensely helpful in setting up a club, though we augmented their suggestions with a do-it-yourself approach. Fortunately, we had wonderful assistance from our attorney, Charles J. Hecht; our accountants, Carolyn Specht, CPA, of Pierpoint Associates and Anthony Graci of Grodsky, Caporrino, & Kaufman; and our banker, Philip Glazer at Republic National Bank.

We concluded that the best structure for our particular club would be an LLC—a limited liability company, which combines the tax benefits of a partnership with the limited risk of a corporation. The latter was especially important to those of our members who had significant assets in their own names.

Charles drew up the papers and helped us adopt an initial set of bylaws to govern the day-to-day working of the club. A bigger challenge was in selecting officers. None of us had any experience with an organization of this kind, yet we knew that the first group of leaders would be establishing precedents. Certainly successive officers would modify them, but the first officers would be blazing the trail.

HOW THE MEMBERS RUN THE CLUB

Diane was elected our first president, largely on the theory that she was the driving force behind the club and couldn't quit even if she wanted to!

Kate Coburn was elected vice president, because of her extensive business experience.

Carol S. Kogan served as our first treasurer, primarily because she had had a great deal of bottom-line responsibility in her career. In addition to keeping the club's books, Carol checked over the brokerage house statements and other financial accounts and worked with the accountant. Though the job was extremely time-consuming, she probably learned more than anyone else in the club.

Donna Bijur and Linda Lieberman, who already worked together running one of the city's largest party rental firms, agreed to keep working together as co-secretaries. Taking the lengthy minutes that documented all our decisions proved to be a major job.

These officers and Marilyn constituted our first Executive Committee, charged with developing proposals and policies that could be considered by the membership.

The first set of officers worked much harder than they had expected to. At the end of a year, they handed the torch over to their successors: Joann Jordan became president, Jane Shalam became vice president, and Margot Green became treasurer. Joann personally called many members to ask their guidance in strengthening and improving the club. The members were unanimous in their praise of the guest speakers. They wanted even more of them, covering even more subjects; they wanted to proceed faster and learn about more sophisticated concepts, like convertible bonds and selling short. But Joann and Marilyn agreed not to rush ahead, to proceed at a pace that would allow everyone to understand the basics thoroughly and make sure there was enough time allocated at the meetings to review our investments.

At this point we had determined to make our operating system more flexible, so Margot worked with our professional advisors to simplify the bylaws and overhaul the accounting. Though things were functioning more smoothly, the membership had grown to the point where there was simply more to do, from duplicating, collating, and mailing materials to keeping the networking strong.

COMING TOGETHER AS A GROUP

Keeping the group together that first year was even more difficult than staying on the Cabbage Diet. Reaching accord on every detail, with many different temperaments in the room, was a challenge. Women like Diane who are used to working as entrepreneurs had to adjust to making decisions by committee. The large brokerage firm with whom Marilyn is affiliated agreed to provide meeting space, but the meeting time was the subject of extensive debate. So was the format of the meeting. And of course we debated what type of investments to make and how long to stay with them. Some of our members were philosophically opposed to investing in certain types of businesses.

Some members were more knowledgeable about investing than others. The spectrum ranged from people like Joann Jordan and Harriette Rose Katz, who had dealt with brokers frequently, to Vivian Serota, who had never owned a stock or bond.

And there was some unhappiness with the 7:30 A.M. starting time, especially during the bitter cold, snowy, dreary winter. On the positive side, these minor inconveniences weeded out the women who weren't deeply committed to the club. Our original group of twenty-eight shrank to a hardy sixteen, all of whom earned one another's respect and deep friendship. Having a smaller group was an advantage while we were still getting organized, because it was easier to work with.

After discussions that rivaled anything at the United Nations, we decided in the second year to open the club to new members, including a few who had been "orphaned" by other clubs where the commitment wasn't strong enough to hold the members together. We now invite new members to a meeting each September to see how we operate and what their responsibilities will be. They are given workshops and clinics that bring them up to speed. At the moment, we are thirty-nine. Communicating with and overseeing details for a larger group is more time-consuming for the new officers and makes their burden somewhat greater, but at least the problems are fewer, since at this point we are running so smoothly. On the positive side, having a bigger group means we have more money to invest and thus to diversify.

ANTEING UP

We agreed to put in $1,100 per person at the start—$1,000 for the investment and $100 as a one-time charge for legal fees and printing costs for drafting the partnership papers. Every month afterward, we'd each put in another $100 toward investing plus $15 for administrative and mailing costs such as accounting fees, photocopying, and mailing.

Unfortunately, many members failed to incorporate this item into their monthly check-writing routine. They would forget to bring the checks or come without their checkbooks, and our beleaguered treasurer, Carol, would have to hunt them down. We considered making a once-a-year payment instead. That would have put more money in the kitty and we would have had the money working for us all year. But the majority of people didn't want to write such a large check.

Philosophically, Marilyn was against the lump sum anyway. She wanted us to continue to invest a fixed amount regularly, no matter whether the market was up or down. This technique, called dollar cost averaging, has a couple of advantages. Making steady contributions kept our nest egg growing and helped us develop a habit of investing. We eventually decided to make quarterly payments—$300 for investment and $45 for administrative costs.

We were realistic about our expectations. Putting aside $100 a month, particularly once you're over forty, as most of us were, cannot build a nest egg that will fund your retirement. Financial education was our number one goal, and we felt good about seeing our investments grow by percentages if not by dollars. Meanwhile, we were learning the language of investment and learning to think in a new way.

> *Before I joined the club, I thought you could look at stocks two ways. There was one kind of stock, speculative stock, that you could take a gamble on—like high-tech stocks. Getting into them was like buying a vinyl slicker; it was showy, it was risky, but what the heck! The other kind were the blue chip stocks. Buying them was like buying a camel-hair topper. It might cost a little more, and it isn't so trendy, but it would hold up and be fine for a few years. When I joined the club, I realized the thinking was a lot more subtle than that.*—Carol Levin

LEARNING THE LANGUAGE

At the first meeting, Marilyn said something about reading a balance sheet, implying that we could. She was looking out the window, thank goodness, so she didn't see Diane and the woman next to her exchange a glance. Virtually every face in the room was wearing the same dubious expression. But no one said a word. Not a soul had enough self-confidence to put up her hand and say, "No, Marilyn, actually, I don't know how to read a balance sheet. Could you explain?" No one wanted to make a public confession of ignorance. Diane told Marilyn the next day, and Marilyn knew she'd have to stay with the basics, even with this sophisticated group.

> *At the beginning, everyone was literally hunched over with embarrassment, but as time passed we learned to relax and straighten up. It is important that other women know how much we didn't know, how much we managed to learn—and how much fun we had doing it.*—Vivian Serota

Marilyn introduced us to the basics of investment. At the very first official meeting, she divided us into committees to study different sectors (like transportation or utilities) and prepare reports on specific companies, introduced us to research tools, and gave us guidelines for selecting stocks. Within a couple of meetings, we had already voted to make some purchases and our treasurer had placed the order with Marilyn.

Some clubs invest only in companies that are familiar, which more or less limits them to industrial companies. But it isn't smart to restrict your buying to one sector of the market, since different sectors do well in different economic circumstances. Marilyn encouraged us to think more broadly—and stay flexible. A member assigned to study transportation stocks came in with a report about Nike. She figured that walking was a form of transportation, which led her to sneakers.

We quickly realized that sitting through an hour-and-a-half meeting once a month wouldn't teach us everything we needed to know. We had to do more reading and more learning. When necessary, Marilyn runs extra clinics. We may have to review some difficult subjects three and four times—and sometimes even more—before everyone gets to "Aha!"

We all started to follow the business and world news on TV and in the papers more closely.

> *Now I read the financial pages, and all the news pages, because what's happening around the world and the nation affects all the stocks. It used to take me twenty minutes to go through the newspaper. Now it takes me an hour.*
> —Margot Green

We also subscribed to various newsletters. Diane's favorite is Dick Davis's newsletter, which she says is the most readable and offers many points of view; Harriette likes John Dessauer's *Investor's World* for its upbeat approach. All this information is useful not only for making our reports but also for increasing our general awareness and knowledge.

PREPARING THE REPORTS

Since we buy stocks based on our reports, preparing them is a big responsibility. Each report gives as much information as possible on an individual company: the nature of its business, where it's located, who's on the management team, its past history, and of course, its future growth and earnings potential.

Though we had multiple stock committees at first, we found that researching the reports was very time-consuming. Now we have a single stock selection committee that consists of six to eight members who serve four-month rotations. Though the committee has the responsibility to find and research stocks, any member can bring the committee a suggestion at any time and/or attend its meeting, which many choose to do. (Sometimes they even bring guests.) It is a duty to serve—but we like it. Preparing the reports is how we learn. And the committee members become so close that they are usually reluctant to give up their responsibility to the next team.

For the sake of diversity, Marilyn suggested that the club should own no fewer than twelve to fifteen different stocks—but no more. Following more would be cumbersome.

We do our research in several ways, starting with sources like *Standard & Poor's Stock Report* and *Value Line,* which print complex, continually updated reports on every stock. All brokers have these publications, as do most libraries. We always call the company's investor relations department for an annual report, quarterlies, and any other information that is available. And those of us with private accounts call our brokers to ask for the analyst's report prepared at their firms. Many of our members are also going "on line" for financial and company information and sharing ideas with the rest of us.

Initially, the idea of writing and delivering a report threw some of us into a panic. Vivian Serota tried desperately to dodge the task. The material hadn't come in. She had laryngitis. She'd left the papers at home. She probably would have said the dog ate it, but she didn't have a dog. Though tempted to lend her a hand, Diane knew it was important for Vivian to do this herself. When she finally made her report, Vivian got a round of spontaneous applause. More important, the members voted to buy the stock on her recommendation. Many of us are still anxious about making a report, but none of us worries about feeling stupid anymore. The atmosphere is so supportive; and besides, at this point we have developed some expertise at going about the job.

I'm one of those people who feel, as that ad suggests, that you should "Squeeze the Charmin," which is exactly what I did when I researched the company that makes it. When I was working on Home Depot, I spent a day going down every aisle of the store. When I had to report on a hearing aid company, I went to its office and tried out all of the products.—Jane Bishop Shalam

Now that we have grown confident enough to loosen up a bit, the reports have become more accurate, more interesting, and more entertaining. Harriette Rose Katz, who organizes events, reported on a company that owns funeral homes and provides accessory services from flowers to limousines. She suggested that we think of the company as the party planner of the funeral business. That was perfectly clear to everyone, and we bought the stock. Making her presentation about Tiffany's, Gloria Gottlieb arrived with a "show and tell"—the familiar robin's egg blue box from the world-famous retailer. (She never mentioned whether she had been obliged to buy something new in order to get the box.)

One group became so enthusiastic about the research process that they call themselves the Tipsters and hold their own monthly meeting in addition to club gatherings.

It's a thrill when the group votes to buy a stock on your recommendation. When we invest, we usually buy an amount that's close to a whole number. It used to be about $5,000, but now that the club is larger, we are buying in larger amounts.

In contrast, it's a bit wrenching when the club decides to sell the stock you've "sponsored." Marilyn distributes monthly updates on each stock that include its purchase price, the length of time we have held it, our gains or losses, and the percentage of the portfolio the stock holding represents. Members assigned to follow these stocks (another rotating task) may report on new developments. Then we discuss whether to buy, sell, or hold the stock.

Within a year, the group was very much in charge of its own meeting. Marilyn had become more of a counselor than a teacher. She continues to discuss trends and interpret the movements of the market, helps take the emotion out of our discussions, and may be asked to make the swing vote if there's a stalemate. We have the experience and information-gathering skills to feel comfortable about making investment decisions not only for the group but for our personal portfolios.

WHEN THE MEMBERSHIP CHANGES

We have a three-strikes rule: If you miss more than three meetings, you're out. One member had to reschedule a flight to Europe to be in compliance. We weren't happy to inconvenience her, but our rules stand.

We haven't asked anyone to leave, but some of the original members decided the time commitment was more than they were prepared to make and bowed out. Whether the departure is by request or voluntary, the procedure is the same. We buy the member out. To keep the departure process orderly, we allow only periodic resignations. You must wait until our quarterly collecting and accounting to get a disbursement. This keeps our cash reserve from dipping too low.

Thanks to monthly contributions and the fact that our investments had done well, the original investment of $1,000 by each charter member had tripled by the time we invited our first new members, so they each paid about $3,000. New members continue to buy in at whatever a share is currently worth: our total assets divided by the number of members.

WHAT THE CLUB HAS MEANT TO US

By the end of the second year, we'd worked out most of the kinks and things were moving very smoothly. Our once-chaotic meetings have become symphonic, because the Executive Committee spends a lot of time preparing so that the meeting runs as smoothly as possible. There's so much to cover in an hour and a half that we schedule educational programs for alternate meetings only. And we schedule clinics and review sessions with Marilyn in the evenings, largely for new members but also for old ones. There's always something new to learn.

Choosing and watching your investments is a place to start learning about money. But the real value of the club is that it has made us think in a very different way.

This club empowered me to make decisions about many things. I've begun spending less on clothes and accessories. Today I'd rather buy stock. I'm in a service business that has a limited return on investment. The only way I can accumulate money is through my investment portfolio.—Harriette Rose Katz

We were also exposed to a great deal of new knowledge by a myriad of experts. Our club lawyer, Charles Hecht, gave us the story on insider trading. Peter Schaeffer invited club members to his world-renowned Fifth Avenue gallery, A la Vielle Russie, where he talked about collecting art as an investment. Experts from mutual fund companies, including AIM, Alliance, Oppenheimer, and Seligman Henderson, money managers from Lazard Frères and Provident Capital, leading technical analyst Jeff Weiss, and renowned Wall Street expert Mary Farrell also responded to Marilyn's request to share their knowledge. So did disability and life insurance analysts. *Value Line*'s Richard Sandborne explained how to use this reference tool. After attorney Steven Shanker and insurance specialist Gary Bleetstein led a session on estate planning, club member Carlyn McCaffrey organized a three-part evening program, "What You Need to Know About Your Husband's Estate," drew a crowd that included several of our spouses. Not long ago accountant Anthony Graci came in to explain tax strategies and—at last—how to read a balance sheet!

No matter what age you are or where you are located, there is a great deal of knowledge available to you. If you form a club, you can call on lawyers and brokers and insurance experts and accountants. Perhaps you'd want to schedule a session on financing college tuition or retirement planning. You'll open yourself up to new knowledge and new power. We certainly did. When we look back on that first day, we realize how much we've learned and shared. We're now part of a team, equal players on a level playing field. When we don't know something, we're comfortable about asking. More important, we now see the connections among every aspect of our personal finances. Our investments are part of our overall financial planning, which in turn is related to asset allocation, which involves retirement planning, life insurance, and estate planning. And that's what we cover in this book.

We won't promise that all the material will be easy. We do promise that all of it is important. The book will speak to you in the many voices of the women who shared their stories, on and off the record. Some of the women are club members. Others are women who heard about our book and volunteered to be a part of it, motivated by a desire to have other women learn from their mistakes. Once you've learned the lessons they have to teach, you won't feel dumb or frightened again. You'll be in charge of your personal finances and able to help make your future secure.

After the club was formed, a small group of us spoke at an adult education program at the Learning Annex. We wanted to share our experiences and assure other women that they can take control of their financial lives. We hoped our listeners would think, "These women are intelligent, capable people—and yet not too long ago, they were insecure about their finances. If they needed help, then I guess it's not so strange that I do, too." We were amazed that our audience included women from so many different backgrounds, from a CEO to an astrologer. It was an enormous thrill to have them look to us for inspiration. Even better was to run into one or two of them long afterward and have them come up to us and say, "You've changed my life."

Now we hope to change yours.

CHAPTER 2

ENTERING THE COUNTING HOUSE

Asserting Yourself

The king was in the counting house, counting out the money. The queen was in the parlor, eating bread and honey.—Traditional nursery rhyme

We women spend our lives counting. We count calories. We count fat grams. We count the number of ounces our babies drink and the number of rows in our knitting. We count the flights on our Stairmaster, the inches of hems, and the tablespoons in recipes. Why do we have such a hard time counting our money?

I coulda, I woulda, I shoulda, and I didn't. In comparing notes, the club members—and the women we interviewed for this book—told similar stories, all with the same theme: "I didn't deal with the money." "I didn't take control." "I left everything to (my husband) (my father) (my accountant)." When the human race began, women cultivated the crops and men were hunters and gatherers. Why do we assume they are therefore better qualified to understand whole life insurance and municipal bonds better than we are? The professional advisors we've talked to assure us that they aren't.

Even when relinquishing control is clearly a mistake, women hand over the reins.

I was an officer of my husband's wholesale florist business, which was already collapsing because of his drinking problem. Sometimes I co-signed checks and sometimes I wrote them myself. Finally, at thirty-nine, he landed in the hospital in an alcoholic coma. He had no living will or life insurance. We needed a court order to pull the plug. He lived another eight weeks. His medical insurance had been unpaid for months; luckily, he had sent in a single payment that the company had cashed, so it had to cover him. Because I had signed checks, the government considers me responsible for withholding and sales taxes, payroll taxes, and bank debt. I have no insurance and I can't get a job. I hope some woman learns from my experience. Don't take a backseat role.
—"Marion Layn," 41, retailer, widow, two children

STAYING IN CHARGE

When men don't have the answers, by default they make decisions anyway. When women don't have the answers, they're ashamed. The only thing that is shameful is simply ducking the issues. But if money isn't your strong suit, and particularly if you're burdened with many responsibilities, it's tempting just to hand over the money matters to someone who appears to be qualified. This is risky behavior. Your money is never as important to anyone as it is to you. We've heard many financial disaster stories from women who relinquished control.

I was too busy getting my new company off the ground to deal with the IRS and the Department of Labor. Instead, I would put mail from those agencies into a folder. My friend did my accounting and bookkeeping, and each week his associate would come to do the payroll and leave with the folder. I'd think, "How wonderful! It's gone!" and ignore the fact that I never saw any of it again. Then the IRS started sending notices that quarterly taxes hadn't been paid for two years. Worse, all the documentation was missing. I had sunk my life savings into a business that was now at risk. Although I have now resolved the issues with the IRS, it was at great financial loss. I had to get burned before I took any of this seriously.—Laura Geller, 38, owner of Upper East Side Manhattan makeup salon, single

It never occurred to me to doubt the integrity of my CPA. Then one day I got a statement from an account I'd left dormant for a while and discovered there was only $10 remaining in it. I subsequently found that my accountant had forged my name to withdraw the money. I learned a great lesson: don't take anything for granted.—Beth Dozoretz, 45, senior vice president, FHC Health Systems, married, one young child

I left everything to the bookkeeper. But she happened to be out the day I took the call from American Express saying my partner and I had exceeded our credit limit. On investigating, we learned that the bookkeeper had been charging everything from computers to Christmas gifts to our business. She even had her family members on the company health insurance plan. Somehow, in the course of juggling all our responsibilities, we had made a practice of signing checks without looking at the bills. That will never happen again.—"Deborah Burns," 35, office relocation expert, unmarried

MARRIED . . . WITH MONEY

Where women are most likely to relinquish control, of course, is in a marriage. We would like to believe that you can be more trusting in a marital relationship than a business relationship, but unfortunately, that's not always so. You must be aware of what's going on, whether or not you're contributing money to the marriage.

Women who don't work sometimes think they don't have any finances to handle. Wrong.—Gloria Gottlieb

Not long ago, a New York tabloid covered the story of a young woman in terrible trouble because her ex-husband had cheated big time on his income tax. Her only misstep had been to marry the guy. She had absolutely no knowledge that he was cooking the books. But she had signed the joint income tax return.

They divorced and he disappeared. Then she learned that even though she was no longer married to him, she was still married to his debts. New York is a state that considers marriage an economic partnership. By co-signing a tax return, you take equal responsibility for its contents. Since the ex-husband was unreachable, the government was looking to the ex-wife for payment of the penalties and fines. And now her current fiancé was postponing their marriage until he knew how it would be affected by her financial status.

Moral: what you don't know *can* hurt you. Do not sign income tax returns unless you understand them. It's not acceptable for your husband to present them to you at midnight on April 14 for signature because they have to be in the mail the next day. If you need time to review them and someone to help you understand them, say so, and get an extension. Taking that position may be hard for you, but it's a small problem compared with facing down the IRS.

I am alarmed by how many women are loath to confront their spouses about financial matters even at the risk of their own financial peril.—"Claudia Roper," 36, banking officer, married, one child

If you think your husband might be underreporting income or have any other concerns about your taxes, ask someone other than your husband's accountant to review them or recommend someone who can. A review may not uncover anything illegal but may alert you that the return involves a certain degree of risk. For example, the accountant may be very aggressive about claiming deductions that might ultimately be disallowed. In such a case, tell your husband that this approach might save money in the short run, but if the IRS prevailed, as a couple you could lose a great deal.

One solution is to file separate returns. The assets in your name wouldn't be vulnerable to a lawsuit or tax obligations and would be protected for both of you. A spouse who has concerns about liability—for example, a doctor, who might face malpractice suits—might welcome the idea of filing separately. And a husband who has concerns about his wife's welfare wouldn't want to leave her in a precarious situation.

> *Shortly after the government notified us of a tax audit, my husband died of a heart attack. The IRS disputed some of his deductions, and I had to pay off the debt. I used up the money from the marriage, then my inheritance from my parents. Since I couldn't afford to maintain our house, I had to uproot the kids and move. If only I had discussed our finances with my husband, perhaps I would have known enough to have fought this more successfully. I certainly would have known how to manage. Instead, our world fell apart.*—"Gail Fisher," 52, teacher, widowed, two teenagers

If there's a family business and you're a working partner, you have a special right and duty to understand what's going on. Women who simply trust that their husbands have everything under control may be disappointed.

> *My husband and I worked with other partners in the retail business. I had no say about the financing, but I thought he was keeping close watch. Using borrowed money, we opened store after store—and then came the crash. We had believed that our partners were doing everything by the book, so we had signed personal guarantees for the loans. We lost our shirts. Next time, I'll question every detail.*—"Lanie Sanders," 29, craftswoman, married, mother of twins

> *For twelve years, he managed the business and I was sales manager. We'd built a $200 million enterprise, but his management tactics undermined my efforts. Twice we were at the brink of collapse. Now I realize that if two people are involved, you need two sets of advisors. Two sets of eyes are better than one. Hiring your own advisors is the best investment decision you can make.*—"Clarice Evans," 41, housewares manufacturer, married, mother of two

TALKING MONEY WITH YOUR HUSBAND

When the only "discussions" you've had about finances have been along the lines of "Honey, our household account is low" and "What do you mean, I'm spending too much?" you may have some difficulty starting a real dialogue. There are several reasons:

- You're flying in the face of a few hundred thousand years of tradition. Women have historically been passive nurturers and men have been the providers. Now you're trying to move into traditionally masculine turf.

Several years ago, I was the only woman working in sales and marketing for an investment management firm. We were told to advise clients not to tell their wives how much money they had. At that point in my career, I was happy to be considered one of the boys. Now I look back and I can't believe where my head was.—Rita Robbins, 39, sales and marketing specialist, married, one child

- He may regard your questions as criticism. Maybe he doesn't want to be second-guessed. If he had always left the grocery shopping to you and suddenly started inspecting the bills, you might become irritated and suspicious. Similarly, if you have always left all the financial decisions up to your husband and suddenly start questioning him, he may be surprised and uncomfortable.
- It's also entirely possible that he knows very little, has in fact done a terrible job, and doesn't want you to find out.

My husband reluctantly agreed to meet with a financial planner. His records were messed up, half the papers were missing, and he'd made some terrible investments. When his mistakes were revealed, he lost control. "You're just doing this to embarrass me!" he screamed.—"Bonnie Green," 53, travel agent, married

- You're talking about his mortality. Life insurance and wills are sensitive topics.
- And finally, you are talking about his money. *His* money. Yes; even if you think the money belongs to you both, he may think of it as his. He made it. And he'll decide what to do with it.

One client told me that he wasn't "getting enough" from his wife so he was putting his bonus money into a new account that she didn't know about.
—Melissa Levine, 35, financial planner, single

For one or more of the above reasons, he may very possibly become angry when you start talking about money. Don't be put off. If you can't talk openly about money, your entire marriage may be headed for trouble. After all, it is perfectly reasonable for you to start this conversation. It is not wrong for you to try to take control of your future. You are entitled to make sure you're properly informed and properly taken care of. You *must* learn about money. In all likelihood, someday you'll be left alone to handle it.

Club members, like many other women we interviewed, found these conversations difficult but passed along useful suggestions. So did marriage and family therapist Donna Laikind, M.S., some of whose suggestions came from PREP, a structured form of communication skills developed at the University of Denver.

Start slowly

Do not try to go from soup to nuts in a single conversation. If you start questioning the life insurance, the pension plan, and the investments all at once, the red flags will definitely go up. Talk about one area, perhaps leading up to it with a news item from the paper or your own life: so-and-so is hospitalized and his wife is concerned about the medical coverage, or somebody's brother-in-law has managed to put away enough to support a very comfortable retirement.

Prioritize the issues

Talk about lower-intensity topics first. Bring up stock investments before you start in on estate planning. If the life insurance issue will be a hot button, start by talking about property insurance.

Reassure him

If out of the blue you suddenly announce your intention to review the life insurance policies, your husband may feel as if you're checking his pulse. Tell him you'd like to share the responsibilities for all your financial planning. Maybe he's needed some help all along but didn't know how to ask.

> *Try to keep his ego intact. Say, "You're doing a great job providing for us. But there's so much to keep on top of. Let me help by gathering more research. Maybe what you've bought is fine, but I'll see if there's anything new."*—Judy Schindler, 49, former investment banker and estate planner, married, three children

Put yourself in the picture

It's not just his mortality and his life insurance you're dealing with. It's yours, too. Remind him that your planning involves both of you, your children, and your grandchildren.

Avoid sounding suspicious or accusatory

Don't in any way suggest that your husband is underhanded or inept. You don't want to send the message that he's going to be steamrollered—especially if you're going to recommend seeing a financial planner.

COMMUNICATE YOUR CONCERN ABOUT THE FUTURE AND YOUR DESIRE FOR HIS HELP

Use whatever words you feel comfortable with.

- "I would like you to explain to me how to handle our finances, because I don't understand."
- "I am anxious about how to protect myself (and the kids) if anything happened to you, and I would like to know what you've planned."
- "You may not want to talk about our finances now, but it's very important to me that you do, and I would like your cooperation."

LET HIM KNOW YOU'RE SERIOUS

When I asked how he'd invested the wedding money, he replied, "What are you worried about?" I said that since the money was half mine, I thought I should be involved. Wall of silence. Then I started to watch business shows on CNN and CNBC, and I began to read books on investing every night. When he saw I really meant business, he finally said, "Okay, let's talk about this."—"Betty Hyatt," 29, nurse, married, no children

THINK ABOUT TIME AND TIMING

Don't bring up money on the day he's gotten bad news from the IRS or his competitor landed the big account. Don't start this discussion when the phone is likely to ring or your son is going to ask for help with his homework or just before the big game. Go for a walk, or go to a coffee shop for a *latte grande*—someplace where you can spend uninterrupted time together.

Have the conversation face-to-face

No matter how nervous you are, don't hide behind the phone for this (or any other) discussion. The phone distorts what is happening and the conversation seems less real. Besides, on the phone, he's free to doodle or fidget with something on the desk instead of focusing on what you're saying.

Don't kitchen-sink

"Kitchen-sinking" is bringing up every bad thing he ever did: he forgot your birthday in 1978, he wasn't nice to your parents in 1982, it was his fault you were late to that wedding in 1991. Stay on the issue.

Don't universalize

Never start sentences with "You never . . ." or "You always . . ." These accusations are *never* entirely accurate and they are *always* very provocative.

Don't take over

Once you think you've gotten his ear, try to work collaboratively. Try sentences like these: "How does this sound to you so far?" "Is this something you've thought of yourself but didn't want to talk about?" "What are your ideas for getting to the bottom line on this?"

Try to raise the issues, not your voice

Nagging and shrieking are common irritating female tactics. According to therapist Laikind, researchers have found that in response men's bodies are flooded by chemical reactions that actually make talking physically difficult for them. They withdraw. They say, "I don't want to talk about this now." Besides, yelling makes you seem irrational. So try to keep your voice down.

Offer a solution

Use the magic words "If . . . then." For example, "If I cut back on expenses, then maybe we could buy more (life insurance) (mutual funds), etc." It's hard to ignore someone who's offering something positive as a starting point.

Share the burden

Your husband may be uncomfortable that his financial planning isn't as good as it might be and/or daunted by the prospect of dealing with all the chores. Make yourself the facilitator. Offer to sort out the papers and make files. Offer to do whichever of the preliminary steps you're comfortable with: getting names and references of a financial planner/insurance agent/estate lawyer; scheduling an interview; doing the pre-interview yourself; or even attending an initial meeting on your own to gather information.

Have a backup plan

If you can't get him to talk, tell him you'd like to arrange a meeting with your accountant for the purpose of finding ways to save money, which should get his attention. He may then be surprised at what he hears. Maybe it's his boat—and not your spending—that's sending your budget over the top. From saving money, you can move on to other topics at subsequent meetings—life insurance, estate planning, and so forth.

Postpone, but don't cancel

If he still won't talk, table the conversation, but bring it up again within forty-eight hours. If that doesn't work, try again—soon. Think like a salesperson: every sale begins with a no.

KEEP AT IT

Don't have the fantasy that just because he loves you, he's going to say, "Yes, darling, whatever you want." It doesn't work that way. You have to get his attention. I would post headlines on the bathroom mirror and in the sock drawer: "SO-AND-SO DIES: WIFE DESTITUTE" or "SECOND WIFE OF TYCOON LIVING IN CARDBOARD BOX." It took two years, but finally he agreed to go to the estate lawyers. This is what I consider originality and long-range planning.—Vivian Serota

Handling all the financial chores and making all the decisions is a huge responsibility. Ultimately it's likely that your husband will be grateful that you want to share it.

At first, whenever I asked questions, my husband went bonkers because my lack of investment knowledge made it difficult for him to give me answers I could understand. He's come to like it. When he's thinking about the future, he doesn't have to worry that I'll be unprepared to make sound investment decisions if he goes before I do. Now he's more confident that what he has worked very hard to achieve in his lifetime won't be squandered because of my lack of investment savvy.—Jane Bishop Shalam

PUT YOUR HOUSE IN ORDER

My husband had a pain in his leg for two years and the doctor shrugged it off. When we finally went to a specialist, we learned he had advanced cancer and only weeks to live. We were in the worst possible emotional shape and our personal finances weren't in order. My husband had to resolve issues that ranged from dealing with two children from a prior marriage to terminating his business partnership. I was making trips to the safe deposit box. The accountants and lawyers were faxing documents from the hospital. My husband was signing papers with a morphine drip in his arm. And all the while, he was dying.—"Stephanie Barber," 40, graphic artist, widowed, two children

You probably know where to find every single holiday ornament, sheet and pillowcase in the house, and are the Sherlock Holmes of missing underwear, book bags, and garden tools. It's equally likely you have no idea where to find the will or locate the life insurance policy. Worse, you may not know what's in them.

Too often, we don't think about these things until there is a crisis—an accident, a hospitalization, a theft, or perhaps a divorce, an incapacity, or a death. In such moments, you should be free to deal with your stress and grief without the additional burden of confusion and helplessness that come from unresolved questions and missing information. Dealing with financial paperwork is time-consuming and emotionally troublesome, but you can't wish the job away.

Maybe your husband already has your financial files in order. If so, ask him to show you where everything is and go through it. If not, work together to organize and store all your important papers. That's the best possible way to be fully informed about your finances. If you're single, you also should set your paperwork in order and let family or friends know where it is and what to do in the event something happens to you.

So get out the file folders and the marking pens. Clear out enough space to store all the files. If you allocate one teeny drawer, your organizing will just get sloppy. Go to a furniture or office supply store that carries practical, reasonably attractive, and inexpensive storage units for this purpose. Plan with the same care you took with your linen closet and the kids' toy storage. At the end, you'll have accomplished several goals:

You'll save yourself a tremendous amount of anxiety and hassle if you know where everything is. It's particularly important to have this information when you are going through a major transition. Ask any woman who can't get the financial information for her divorce lawyer or who's been widowed and doesn't know where to look for anything.

You'll find out what's missing in advance of a crisis. It's best to discover the gaps in your disability insurance when you're looking through your files, not in a hospital corridor. You need to know your property is under-insured (and clear up the problem) *before* the fire.

You'll have everything in writing. Don't rely on anyone's oral promise to "take care of it"—and that includes your husband's. Changes made to any document should be initialed, or you may be counting on protection that isn't there. Make photocopies of any faxed material, since faxes fade.

Papers that are organized are easier to review. Look over everything at least once a year. A tiny change—the name of a beneficiary—can have a major impact.

You'll know where to consolidate. Having multiple CDs and IRAs makes it harder to keep track. Try to move most of your investments into one brokerage house.

You'll never need to pay for a paper chase, which may be very expensive and time-consuming.

You'll know nothing has been overlooked. When you and your husband, or you alone, make your plans, or you consult with a professional, you'll have anything you need instantly available.

In the Resources section of this book, you will find a complete list of all the information and documents that should be in your home financial files and your safe deposit box. The material is not at the end of the book as an afterthought but in order for you to focus on it when you have set aside the time. Photocopy the lists, fill them out, and gather the information as directed. This may be one of the most important tasks you ever complete. Doing it will give you a tremendous sense of relief and satisfaction. Then, every year, review and update the material.

IF YOU'RE SINGLE

You can't wait for "Mr. Right" to arrive before you have a plan. You need to start taking care of yourself immediately.—Kate Coburn

Too many women procrastinate about dealing with their finances until Mr. Right comes along. This is a huge error. He may be very late arriving. He may come and then go. Or he may not show up at all. It's very easy to find excuses for not dealing with your money.

"I'm too busy making a living," I would say. Or "I haven't enough money to start investing." Of course this is a Catch-22. If you don't invest because you don't have the wealth, how do you plan to get the wealth? You can start modestly, with just $100 in a mutual fund. But you have to start.—Barbara Laskin, 40s, media trainer, married, one young daughter

Just because you're on your own doesn't mean you have to take care of everything alone. There are many places to go for help.

THE EXPERTS YOU NEED

Ideally, you should have a financial planner and/or broker to help you make money, an accountant to help you save it, and an attorney and insurance broker to help you protect it. Professional help is not just for rich people, nor is it necessarily a very expensive proposition. By shopping around, you should be able to find help in your price range.

Though you can reduce commissions by using discount brokers and buying no-load insurance, we feel that if you're a novice, you need the advice of a full-service broker and an insurance agent. Either can serve as an overall financial advisor until you are in a position to hire someone especially for this purposes. Since a broker and agent are paid by commission, they do not charge to consult with you.

As for estate planning, if you have under $600,000 in assets,* you need

*As we go to press, the government is considering raising this figure.

only a simple will and—to cover ill health and incapacity—a living will and health proxy. You may be able to pick up the forms at no charge from a local hospital. Only with a larger estate do you need an estates and trusts specialist, and at that point you can surely afford one.

Even in the interest of economy, don't rely on one-stop shopping. Accountants may do some basic financial planning, but most are not investment experts; a financial planner is not a lawyer, a lawyer is not an insurance expert, and an insurance expert is not an accountant. Avoid anyone who professes expertise in many areas. Also avoid helpful but nonprofessional family members.

> *My friend said her father was her financial advisor, but I persuaded her to put some money in a mutual fund. When her father died, he didn't even have enough assets to pay the burial costs. She wound up liquidating her mutual fund investment to cover the fees.*—Melissa Levine

If you have more significant assets, planning and investment services are available from a variety of money management firms and other specialists, and it's probably worth paying to have your attorney, accountant, and broker meet once a year. Your attorney may report some new twist in estate law that will trigger your insurance broker to make a recommendation for coverage, and so on. Even if your assets are smaller, encourage your team to compare notes by phone when possible.

Also take advantage of the tremendous amount of information available free these days. Many brokerage firms hold seminars and give lecture series designed just for women, whom they want to attract as customers. If you don't have enough assets to automatically land on a mailing list, call the companies in your area and ask if they will be offering any programs that you can attend. There are also inexpensive adult education courses. Not every lecture will be equally valuable, but you will always come away with something.

When you do have enough extra money to get personal, expert attention, make the investment. Women are sometimes shortsighted about paying for professional advice. They'll find the money for a special dress or to hire entertainment for a child's birthday party but claim they can't afford to pay the people who can help protect their money and their financial future. Money for professional help is very well spent. If ever your marriage falls apart, you will certainly need it.

> *If contemplating divorce, a woman should not take on a spouse single-handedly. In addition to an attorney, of course, she should consult one or more of the following: a professional financial planner involved in the couple's finances, a stockbroker, an insurance consultant, a banker.*—Christina Rizopoulos Valauri, 41, senior securities analyst and former banking officer, married

DO YOU NEED A CHANGE?

Many married women feel that their accountants and/or advisors act as if the husband is the client, not the couple. If this is true in your case, tell your husband you'd like to meet individually with your advisor to review last year's returns or the current stock portfolio because you plan to take a more active role in family finances. Then make an appointment. In a one-on-one meeting, you can ask any questions you may have been hesitant to bring up with your husband present. Also, you can establish a more personal relationship.

Ask for material to take home and read. Once you've reviewed it, call with any further questions. The response to that second call is a good indicator of how you will be treated on an ongoing basis. Most people are cordial at an initial meeting, but the follow-up is what is important. Does the advisor take or return your call promptly, brush you off, or refer you to an assistant?

If you don't have positive feelings about your advisor, you should make a change. Separating from someone to whom you've entrusted confidential information often creates anxiety and even fear that perhaps information will be used against you or material will be withheld in retaliation for your departure. In reality, this won't happen. Financial professionals are subject to regulations that require them to return your papers on request, and it's extremely unlikely that they'll become vindictive if someone leaves their practice. Turnover is inevitable.

Your husband may be reluctant to make a change, but you should have advisors with whom you are as comfortable as he is. When you tell him this, also remind him that often change brings a fresh perspective and new enthusiasm. Keep pressing. When you've decided to make a change, try to make it at a logical time. For example, if you switch accountants right after the tax returns are filed, you have months for the new person to become familiar with your records.

HOW FINANCIAL ADVISORS WORK

A financial advisor or planner who helps you manage your money may be trained as an accountant, a lawyer, a stockbroker, or an insurance specialist. Financial advisors may be sole practitioners, members of a small firm, or associates in a large company. Find one through personal recommendations or from a professional organization and interview several until you find someone with whom you feel comfortable.

The major distinction among them is how they are paid. About 25 percent earn money from commissions, 25 percent from fees, and the rest from some combination of the two. Many consumer advocates have concerns about commission-based planners who work for an insurance company or brokerage house. Is their goal helping you make the best investment choice or selling you the product with the highest commission? Commissioned advisors, for their part, argue that a one-time commission cost may ultimately be less expensive than ongoing management fees. Also, many today handle "wrap accounts," charging annual fees for managing all assets and trades. And it is true that planners associated with a large brokerage or insurance firm have access to research information not available to a fee-based planner in a small or solo practice.

An advisor who receives a combination of fees plus commission might be thought to favor products that pay a higher commission. Some planners deal with this by deducting any commissions from the annual management fee.

CHOOSING A FINANCIAL ADVISOR

The biggest hurdle for many women is making the initial decision to go for help.

> *My biggest mistake was compounding my mistakes, making one after another. By the time I realized I needed advice, I was too embarrassed to ask for it. A good friend really helped by pointing out, "You don't have to have all the answers. You just have to know where to go to get them."*—Erma Bressler, 55, originator of kosher weight-control program Start Fresh, married, three grown daughters

Whether you're looking for a financial advisor or other type of professional (a new accountant, insurance broker, and so on), get a recommendation from another professional, preferably one who deals with money. Or contact a professional organization (see pages 60–61). Accountant Steve Greenberg of Jablons, Kass & Greenberg advised club members never to select a professional from the Yellow Pages, especially not a professional with a very large ad. Needing to advertise is a sign that not enough business is coming in by word of mouth. The large ad signals that you may get assembly line treatment.

Once you have a recommendation, call to check the person's qualifications, background, and years of experience.

> *Personally, I wanted someone my age who could grow up with me—someone with experience beyond my area who could go through different life stages with me and understand where I was.*—Laura Pomerantz, 49, corporate executive, married, three grown children

You should also ask all of the following:

- Whether the person specializes in a particular area—retirement, insurance, whatever. Make sure the specialty fits your concerns.
- Whether the compensation will be fee-based or commission-based. If the planner is commission-based, make sure he or she sells products

from two or more companies so you can comparison-shop. Also ask what the commission is on any specific recommendation. If you know that buying a $20,000 annuity may enrich the planner by $2,000 but a mutual fund investment will bring him only a 4 to 5 percent commission, you will want to get a second opinion on the purchase from your lawyer or accountant. If the planner is fee-based, ask whether you will be charged a flat fee, an hourly rate, or a percentage of the assets, if you'll get an hourly breakdown of the charges, and whether some of the work can be performed by a less expensive associate. There will probably be no charge for a brief introductory meeting, but then the meter starts running. Some fee-based advisors make recommendations only and won't supervise purchases or keep the paperwork.

- Ask to see two or three plans and follow-up reports from past clients.
- Get the names of two or three references, preferably from clients whose age, marital status, and financial situation are similar to yours. When you contact the professionals, ask about their working style, strengths and weaknesses, and track record. If you are pleased with what you hear, make an appointment.

DIAL-A-RECOMMENDATION

Financial Advisors

The International Association for Financial Planning (IAFP) will give you five names of planners in your area. This is the largest trade association for financial planners in the United States, and parties registered with it will have passed a qualifying exam (800-945-4237).

The Institute of Certified Financial Planners (ICFP) will give you the name and number of one to five planners in your area (800-282-7526). CFPs have passed a very rigorous exam.

The National Association of Personal Financial Advisors will give you a list of planners in your region who work on a fee-only basis (800-366-2732).

The National Center for Women and Retirement Research will refer you to people who are licensed and approved by it to help you in planning (800-426-7386).

Certified Professional Accountants (CPAs)

We have used the word "accountant" several times; in most cases, we are referring to a CPA. A CPA holds a license, is subject to peer review, and is required to take extensive annual training. An unlicensed accountant can do the work of preparing a tax return but cannot represent you to the IRS.

The National Conference of CPA Practitioners (NCCPAP) at 888-488-5400 has a registry by area of expertise.

The American Institute of Certified Public Accountants (808-862-4272) can also give you a lead.

Also, every state has an association of certified public accountants, though in some states they're organized as the Society of CPAs and in others as the Institute of CPAs. The library can help you track down the association you need.

SIZING EACH OTHER UP

Make sure that you are satisfied that the planner meets your criteria in the following ways:

- ***Qualifications.*** Being a CFP (certified financial planner) is helpful, but more important is solid experience at a good firm or a good track record over time that can be confirmed by someone you know. Also ask about: credentials and years of experience (if you haven't asked already), any special training and continuing education the advisor pursues, and what licenses the planner holds. A qualified investment advisor must have a Series 65 license and needs additional licenses to sell stocks (Series 7), mutual funds (Series 63), insurance, and so forth. If the planner doesn't hold such licenses, what broker and/or insurance agent does the planner work with? What resource services will he/she use? All but seven states and the District of Columbia require most planners to register with the state's security department. This doesn't guarantee honesty or competence, but it does indicate the person knows the law.

• ***Expectations.*** When clients are disappointed by their financial planners, it is almost always because they weren't on the same page from the beginning. The client didn't ask enough questions and had unreasonable expectations. Tell the advisor what kind of returns you expect, and don't believe anyone who offers you a specific rate of return. Even the Psychic Network doesn't promise that.

This is what the candidate will ask of you:

• ***Investment history.*** Don't come empty-handed. Like a medical specialist, a financial specialist needs information to arrive at a diagnosis and course of treatment. He or she needs your financial history to determine what you have to work with and how much risk and diversity you like. Plan to bring at least two to three years of back income tax returns and a list of your assets and information about what they cost you, and ask if anything else will be needed.

• ***Your goals and time frame.*** Do you want to buy a house within five years, or are you primarily thinking about funding your retirement? If you want the house, your financial plan will probably involve short-term investments that involve some risk. If you're planning for retirement, you can think long-term.

REVIEWING YOUR IMPRESSIONS

Consider all the following when you decide whether to hire this person.

• ***Attitude.*** Did the person seem interested and sympathetic to your needs? Did you get unrushed, undivided attention? Did the person talk above you, patronize you, talk only to your husband? Are you comfortable with this person?

Whatever the amount of money you're talking about, to you it's substantial. You want to feel the expert is responsive to your needs and is communicating with you. When an expert starts talking financialese, you have to ask him or her to speak to you in words that are understandable. Your attitude should be "If I can't understand you, it's because you're not being clear."—Kate Coburn

• ***Preparation.*** Was the person ready on time and with material that had been gathered specifically for you?

• ***Fee.*** Do you know what the fee is? What is and what isn't covered? If this is not clarified, you may have later problems.

The CPA sent me a huge bill for some minor work. When I questioned him, he said he didn't realize I was so "fee sensitive." When I said, yes, I was "fee sensitive," he suggested I pay what I thought his work was worth. I did, and I never heard from him again. Don't be intimidated.—Betty Broder, 48, executive, electronic retailing, divorced

A professional fee can *always* be questioned if you have legitimate concerns. You may be surprised at how often the bill will be reduced. Word of mouth from a dissatisfied client can be very harmful. A professional knows that a reduced fee may not satisfy you completely but may reduce the amount or likelihood of your complaining publicly.

• ***Support services.*** Who are the backup people, and what duties do they perform? Does the firm appear to be well organized? Does the financial advisor's firm offer additional services? (A brokerage firm, for example, may offer help with mortgages, insurance, estate and retirement planning, a line of credit, and/or seminars.)

• ***Preparation.*** Did the person present a variety of options and explain them all thoroughly and clearly? If you found the explanations confusing, perhaps the consultant—not you—was at fault. Were you given material written in a language you could understand to take home and review? (Call with any questions, as suggested above, and see how you are treated.)

• • •

Financial planning is as much an art as a science. There are no guarantees, and no one's right 100 percent of the time. Go with a track record, and go with your gut.

The members of our club had a double advantage when it came to financial planning. Our guest speakers helped us become more savvy about money matters and comprised a network of people to whom we could go for advice. Though the club gave us entrée to the world of personal finance, the next step for each of us was to deal with investments, retirement planning, insurance, and estate planning on our own.

CHAPTER 3

MAKING A PLAN

Investment Basics

The prevalence of bag-lady fears, particularly among professional women who are beyond economic dependence on a man, is really quite astonishing. It emerged time and again as I talked to hit movie-maker Nora Ephron, best-selling author Gloria Steinem, superagent Joni Evans, former Planned Parenthood director Faye Wattleton and others. They, just like me, harbor fears of finding themselves old, alone, forgotten, homeless.—Gail Sheehy, *Money*, November 1996

Ephron, Steinem, Evans, and Wattleton are baby boomers. So are most of The Money Club members. We grew up in the years following World War II, a period of enormous economic growth and affluence, when spending was more than acceptable. It was encouraged. Our parents were rewarded very well for their efforts. If they worked for a large company, they had job security and a big pension. If they bought homes in the '40s or '50s, their investments grew to ten times what they paid, sometimes more. The Social Security checks they collect today typically represent several times the total of their contributions.

Things have changed. Our parents expected the achievements of their children to eclipse their own. To us, the future seems a lot less certain. We confide to one another our concerns that our offspring—as talented and ambitious as they may be!—will not be able to match our success. They are moving back home after college because they can't find jobs. They are finding it difficult to accumulate the down payment to buy a home.

We also worry about our own prospects, being at special risk because we are women. The average age of being widowed is just fifty-six, possibly after a spouse's medical and/or nursing home bills have eaten into the savings. Seventy-three percent of women die single, often isolated and far from family members. We don't feel prepared. Like women everywhere, many of us in the club became used to leaving money management chores to someone else—a parent, a brother, a husband, or maybe an accountant or lawyer—even though 80 to 90 percent of us will at some point be responsible for making all our own investment decisions.

No wonder the bag lady fear is pervasive. Though in our rational moments we assure one another that there is virtually no chance we will someday be on the streets, all our possessions in a shopping bag, some of our fears may be more realistic: that we will have to change our way of living or have to move from a home that we can no longer afford. The rules of spending are different from the rules of gravity. Going up is much easier than coming down.

The experts who spoke to us in The Money Club made us aware that if we wanted to keep the status quo, we first had to figure out what it was. Until that point, most of us had never made a serious attempt to calculate our net worth. If anyone asked what we spent each month, we'd just say, "Too much." We have realized that this kind of denial is true at all economic levels. According to one estimate, half the women in America pay the household bills. But look at the other side of that statistic: nearly 50 percent do not. Why?

> *So many women tell me how stressful it is to have to deal with their money—but I look at how much they're handling in the course of their everyday lives and it seems to me that financial stress is nothing compared to the other problems they face on a routine basis. These women are smart, but they don't see their own potential.*—Audrey Landau, 44, owner of Madison Avenue Maternity and Baby, married, three children

We believe that anyone who is reading this book is capable of figuring out what she's got and how much she spends. *If you don't know, it's because you don't want to know.* It's like putting off a mammogram: you're afraid you might find out there's a problem. The fears should motivate you, not stop you.

> *My father lost all his money. It was always a possibility in my mind that it could happen again in my lifetime. Were I more in control, I could have put my fears to better use.*—Lucy Feller, 61, artist, widowed, two grown daughters

FINDING A STARTING POINT

Set aside time in the evening or on a weekend when you and your husband—or you alone—can copy and fill out the Yearly Income and Yearly Expenses sheets that follow. Last year's income tax form should have all the information you need about your income. To calculate your expenses, gather last year's checks and monthly bank statements. Sort the checks according to the categories we've listed. (Some of the categories may not apply to you, and you may want to add some that we haven't included.)

Break down your credit card expenses by category and add the totals to the subtotals on the Yearly Expenses sheet. You should use separate cards for business and personal expenses to make record-keeping easier. You may also save money by tracking credit card interest for business expenses. Interest for business expenses is tax-deductible.

Though you may have written a few checks to cash, more probably you took most of it as withdrawals from a bank machine. Look at your bank statements to find those amounts. Add up the total and insert under "Miscellaneous/cash."

> *The only way to know what you spend is to write it down. Otherwise, you have no idea. Keep a small notebook to mark down your expenses daily for two or three months.*—"Gladys Stern," 60, designer, divorced, two adult children

To help track expenses, some of us found it useful to open an asset management account at a brokerage house. The costs range from zero to

$150, depending on the firm. Many of them provide checks with the letters A to Z printed above your signature. You assign a letter code to each category of your expenses and circle the letter when you write a check. A computer groups the checks for each category on your monthly and year-end statements.

YEARLY INCOME

Income	*You*	*Spouse*	*Joint*
Salary or self-employment income			
Dividend income			
Stocks,			
Mutual funds			
Interest income			
Bonds,			
Savings accounts,			
CDs,			
Money market funds			
Rental income			
Alimony and/or child support			
Bonuses and commissions			
Total Income			

YEARLY EXPENSES

Expenses	*You*	*Spouse*	*Joint*
Home ownership			
Mortgage payments/rent/ condominium fees			
Real estate taxes			
Property/liability insurance			
Electricity/heating/fuel/water/ sewer/gas			

Expenses	*You*	*Spouse*	*Joint*
Telephone			
Property repairs			
Home furnishings			
Appliances/repairs			
Domestic help (if any)			
Gardener/yard care (if any)			
Transportation			
Car payments			
Insurance			
Repairs/maintenance			
Gasoline/parking/tolls			
Public transportation			
Personal expenses			
Clothing			
Hair/nails/beauty salon/barber			
Dry cleaning/laundry			
Food/liquor/household supplies			
Newspapers, magazines, books			
Entertainment (movies, games, etc.)			
Dining out			
Health club/YMCA			
Sports equipment/activities			
Vacations			
Club/organization dues			
Dental			
Medical (including eyeglasses)			

Expenses	*You*	*Spouse*	*Joint*
Health insurance			
Gifts/tips			
Unreimbursed business expenses/ professional dues			
Pet Care			
Charitable contributions			
Organized charity/church			
Support of relatives			
Child/parent care			
Day care			
School tuition (if any)			
College savings			
Other			
Insurance premiums			
Life			
Disability			
Long-term care			
Loan payments			
Student			
Credit card			
Other			
Income taxes			
Savings and retirement			
Company plans (vested portion)			
IRAs, Keoghs, SEPs			

Expenses	*You*	*Spouse*	*Joint*
Other corporate plans: 401(k), stock purchases, thrift savings			
Miscellaneous/cash			
Total Expenses			

Once you've come up with your totals, subtract your total expenses from your total income. The results may (a) astonish you, (b) make you feel guilty, (c) convince you that you've added wrong, or (d) all of the above. Whatever the number, it is the amount you have available for savings and investment. It is your starting point.

Most likely, you'll have to raise that number. You may be as shocked as we were to learn that in your twenties and thirties you should already be saving 10 percent of your gross income, more as you get older. By the time you're in your late thirties or forties, if you have no savings plan, you should begin putting aside 15 to 20 percent.

> *Women have to learn to put aside money for taxes (if an employer isn't withholding it) and for savings—and never touch those funds. Kids should know this from the time they are old enough to earn a dime. I wish I had.*—Lynn Frankel, 50, management consultant, married, two children

If your figures come up short of those percentages, you'll have to figure out where to cut your spending. Divide your expenses into "necessities" and "optional" and look for ways to trim what you don't absolutely need. Whatever you're spending, someone you know is spending less and still managing to live well. You can do the same.

> *What helps me keep spending down is that every time I spend, I add up the amount of jewelry I have to sell to make that much money. I take this very seriously. I consider it being a "value engineer."*—Judith Ripka, 54, jewelry designer, married, three grown sons

Spend less, and save more. The most important message the club members learned was this: pay yourself first. In the past, paying our department store bills was our top priority. Now the first check we write every month goes into our investment accounts.

Vivian Serota said making a commitment to investing is like making a commitment to exercise. The results, not the activity, are what count. The easier you make it on yourself, the more likely you'll do it: with exercising that means finding a gym near the house and setting aside regular exercise time. With investing that means sending the check at the beginning of the month. In both cases, it helps to work out (or invest) with a friend (or a club). If you need an additional incentive, a good financial advisor can serve as your "trainer."

> *My advisor changed my life. He would actually get on the phone once a month and say, "What did you save this month? I haven't seen a check from you. Where is it? What are you doing?" He stayed after me to make sure I was disciplined about savings.*—Betty Broder

In both cases, set realistic goals. At the beginning, you won't be going to the gym seven days a week. Neither will you start out saving 25 percent every month. The most important thing is simply to get started, the younger the better.

Just look at this example: At thirty, Lucy begins to save and invest $40 a week, about $2,000 a year. At forty, she gets married and never puts aside another penny. (We think that's foolish, but that's what she does.) She leaves her accumulated $20,000 in investments that return an average of 9 percent annually. Her friend Ethel, on the other hand, is divorced at forty, with nothing in the bank. She decides to make a $40-a-week commitment starting right now. After twenty-four years, she's put away around $48,000, also earning a 9 percent return.

Where does that leave them both at sixty-five? Lucy has about $285,000 waiting in her investment account. Ethel, who put aside $28,000 *more,* has about $100,000 less. The lesson is that (a) life isn't fair and (b) the early bird gets the bankroll.

You can dither around about commitment when it comes to romance, but not when it comes to investment. It's very, very easy to say, "I'd rather have the suit or that pair of shoes. I can't live without them. So I won't save money this month." But the only way to ensure that you can have the suit or the shoes in the future is to invest regularly, diversify your holdings, and stay in for the long haul. *Today would be a good day to start.*

But before you invest, you should have an emergency fund in reserve, enough to cover three to six months of household expenses—less, if you're a two-income family, since it's unlikely you'll both be out of work at the same time. Emergency money can be parked in a checking account, a savings account, or a money market fund—places where it grows slowly, if at all, but is accessible on demand.

If you have other sources for emergency funds, you don't have to tie up a great deal in cash. For example, you may be able to borrow against a 401(k) plan at work; or you may have a whole life insurance policy that has a loan feature. You also may be able to get a home equity line of credit if you own your home. This allows you to borrow up to 70 or 80 percent of your home's market value. The rates are relatively low and the interest on the loan is tax-deductible. (Even if you have no plans to borrow money, it is a good idea to get approval for a line of credit while you have a job. If you can't show a steady source of income, getting a loan may be difficult.)

One of the club members said she thought most women think more about organizing their closets than their assets. Having a long-term goal (to buy a house, finance tuition, support retirement) and a specific dollar target helps give you a purpose. But plans have a way of expanding (and they should). We believe you should put aside as much as you think you can—and then a little more. The best thing about having money is not having to worry about having money.

DEFINING YOUR GOALS

All investing has the same purpose: to preserve capital (so your hard-earned money doesn't go down the drain), to generate income for current use or reinvestment, and to make money grow. How you work toward those goals depends on your individual circumstances.

- How old are you? How many years of investing do you have ahead of you?

- What's your time horizon? How long can you wait for the return that you want? If you need money available for big expenses within the next five years—tuition, a wedding, a car—don't put that money into stocks. You should be prepared to leave money invested in stocks in place for at least five years.
- How much risk are you comfortable with?
- What's your tax bracket? Tax-free municipal bonds might be more appropriate for you than other investments. (Check "What Tax-Free Means to You" on pages 108–109.)
- What are your needs? Are you saving for retirement, education, and/or supplemental income?

ASSET ALLOCATION

One very basic investment concept should be familiar to you from other life experiences: don't put all your eggs in one basket.

> *I went for financial help and told the advisor I was already diversified. I had my money in five separate bank accounts. I soon learned that that's not what she meant by diversity.*—"Sarah Campbell," 32, telephone company supervisor, divorced, one child

Diversity means dividing your money among a variety of investments in the hope that if one doesn't work out, another will. If telecommunications stocks aren't doing well, maybe utilities stocks are. If the entire stock market is on the decline, then you can count on a steady income from bonds.

Experienced financial people believe that *how* you allocate your assets may be a lot more important than *what* you buy. This is like the old story that if you set enough monkeys typing, by random chance in the course of infinity, they'd create a book. Over time, if you bought any five randomly selected stocks, chances are your holdings would turn out to be more valuable than if you bet exclusively on any one stock. (This fact should take some of the anxiety out of your decision-making.)

Even before you select specific stocks, you must decide what proportion of your assets should be in stocks, how much in bonds, and how much in anything else.

Many people have the bulk of what they own tied up in their home, for practical and emotional reasons.

> *Until I owned my residence I didn't feel psychologically secure and grounded. Only afterward could I move forward with my professional goals.*—Yue-Sai Kan, 40s, television producer and hostess, China's National Network (CCTV), and chairwoman of Yue-Sai Kan Cosmetics, single

However, as a purely practical choice, real estate isn't the best investment vehicle. If the real estate market goes into a slump, it may stay there for quite a while. Even in a good market, it may take you months (and sometimes years) to sell a house or other real estate.

Other types of investments involve long-term commitments (like collectibles) or involve major risk and expertise (like commodities), which is why most people typically divide their investments between stocks, for growth, and bonds, for income.

STOCKS VERSUS BONDS

Did you ever wonder why these are the two primary forms of investment? Brad Burg of *Medical Economics* has a very clear explanation. Suppose your friend was running a business and needed money. Either she'd borrow the money from you and pay you interest, or she'd sell you a piece of the business.

If you buy a bond, you are in effect lending money to a company (or to a municipality or the government). You are a creditor. But if you buy the stock of a company, you are a part owner and participate in the risk of the company's operations. Since equity means ownership, stock is sometimes called *equity*.

If the company goes belly-up, the creditors are paid off first, so bondholders have a more secure investment. If the company does extremely well, owners get the bulk of the benefits, so stockholders have potential growth in their holdings.

THE IMPORTANCE OF RISK

Before you decide on what investments you will make, and in what combination, you must know something about risk. Maybe you have heard the saying that "Men want to make money and women want to save money." Most of us in the club were initially terrified at the thought of losing money. When you fear making a mistake, the most obvious tactic is to make no decisions at all. Many of us had taken this route. We appeared to be uninterested. We were really afraid.

> *Because I don't want to think about money, I give more thought to what color I'm going to paint my nails than to what investments I should make.*—"Connie Otis," 46, restaurant hostess, unmarried

Now what we have learned is that investing isn't a game, but it has the shape of a game. If you're a player, your style may be to start cautiously or jump in with both feet. Either way, you can get hurt. But if you're not on the field, you can never be a winner.

A key concept in investment is the risk-reward ratio—the relationship between the possibility that you will make a lot or money or lose it all. The greater the potential an investment has to exceed the expected return, the greater the risk you must take.

There is no such thing as absolute safety. For example: if you have $100,000 or less in a savings account in a bank insured by the FDIC, the government guarantees that money cannot be lost, even if the bank fails. But is that money really "safe"? Money in the bank usually earns interest. But the interest may grow very slowly. Suppose Christopher Columbus put $1 in the Old World Bank paying 5 percent simple interest, which means a straight 5 percent interest per year. At the end of one year, he'd have $1.05. At the end of two years, he'd have $1.10. To celebrate New Year's Eve 1999, he'd have accumulated a little over $25.

But suppose he had put the money in the New World Bank, which pays 5 percent compounded daily. By year two, he's got $1.11. By year three, he's up to $1.65. That constant increase mounts up rapidly. With the accumulated money from the New World Bank, Columbus could afford a multi-billion-dollar blowout to usher in the twenty-first century.

Still, even when the interest on your money is compounding, inflation—the rate at which prices are going up—may drive up costs faster than your earnings. Inflation is measured by the Consumer Price Index (CPI), which is based on data collected in eighty-five cities regarding the cost of 400 goods and services in broad categories including food, clothing, medical care, and entertainment. (Another, similar gauge, the Producer Price Index, or PPI, measures the change in prices of goods that are primarily used by business.) If you can't keep up with the CPI, you're constantly losing purchasing power.

TYPES OF RISK

When it comes to personal finances, women define risk as losing their money, but the loss of purchasing power represents a bigger risk. Over the past quarter century, inflation has been growing steadily at about 4 percent annually, meaning that a dress that costs $100 this year costs $104 next year. If you put $100 last year in a bank where the interest rate lags behind inflation, today you have less than $104 and the dress is out of your reach. The cost of some necessities, like food and fuel, has been rising faster than the inflation rate. Private education for example, has been going up at the rate of 6 to 7 percent a year.

Generally bonds, which are like a loan to a government, a municipality, or a company, are considered relatively safe investments. During the time the loan continues, you get paid a certain amount of interest. If you hold the bond until the agreed-upon term is over, when it is said to have matured, you get back your original investment. But if the interest paid on the bonds can't cover both rising costs and the tax you'll have to pay on the interest, you're subject to inflation risk.

All bonds are rated to indicate their riskiness, as we will explain in the next chapter. But even with the highest-rated bonds, which are virtually guaranteed to return 100 percent of your original investment, some risk is involved. If you need cash in a hurry and have to sell right away, you may not recover your full investment. If you bought a $1,000 bond paying 8 percent and interest rates are now 9 percent, why would anyone pay $1,000 for your bond if he or she could get an extra point investing the money elsewhere? On the other hand, if interest rates go down to 7 percent, of course, your bond is worth more than $1,000. The possibility that your bond can't be resold at the price you paid is called *market risk.*

If your money is tied up in a long-term, low-income investment, you may lose the chance to make a better investment. This is called an *opportunity risk.* Here's another example:

> *I told the broker to keep me in "safe" stocks. The economy had been doing very well but when I looked at my portfolio a year later, my stocks had grown only a small amount. When I spoke to the broker, I discovered we had a misunderstanding. To me, "safe" stocks were solid, growing companies. To him, "safe" meant nonvolatile stocks like utilities that paid dividends and were unlikely to drop much, but wouldn't necessarily experience a lot of growth. I should have asked more questions.*—"Ronda Kaye," 34, physical therapist, married, one child

When your bond comes due (or, as happens occasionally, pays off ahead of time), you may face *reinvestment risk*—the possibility that you can't move the money you get back into something paying the same high rates.

Some big risks have higher failure rates. In the commodities market, where people buy and sell things like pork bellies and peanuts, many trades by novices are unprofitable. On the other hand, some risk-taking pays off. For example, very conservative investors avoid companies that are vulnerable to legal action, that have assets located in politically unstable areas, or that are not diversified. So they would have missed out on the huge stock success of such companies as Philip Morris, Amgen, or Coca-Cola.

Because stocks are riskier than other investments, the potential for payoff is greater. If you bought fifty shares of Columbia Pictures stock in the early 1970s for less than $2 a share, a decade or so later, when the company was taken over by Coca-Cola, you got Coca-Cola stock in exchange. By the mid-1990s, for each $100 you originally put in, you'd have many thousands of dollars.

YOUR PERSONAL RISK TOLERANCE

When we were first learning about risk, most of us associated the term with, say, skydiving. But jumping out of a plane is a thrill-seeking activity. As you will see, taking some risk in financial terms is actually a cautious thing to do.

Your *risk tolerance* tells your broker how long you're willing to watch your investments go down without panicking and selling. A serious investor should be able to withstand seeing the entire stock market depressed for at least two or three three-month periods in a row. If you're a very anxious investor, look at the Beta rating of a stock before you buy. (It's listed in *Value Line*.) A Beta is a measure of volatility. A stock with a Beta of 1 goes up and down at approximately the same rate as the market. With a Beta of less than 1, it fluctuates less than the market in general, but with a Beta of 2, it has twice the market's volatility.

You should find it reassuring to learn that the chances of losing money in the market drop dramatically the longer you're in. According to Ibbotson Associates, a widely quoted consulting firm, if you invest money in stocks in the Standard & Poor's 500-stock index (S&P 500) for any one year, you have a 27 percent chance of losing if the market goes down. The odds drop to 10 percent if you stay for any five years and 4 percent for any ten years. If you stay in for any twelve-year period, your chances of suffering a loss falls to zero. (Over the twenty years from spring 1976 to spring 1996, stocks averaged a 14.2 percent rise per year.)

Take the case of IBM, a solid leader for so many years that it was nicknamed Big Blue. When the stock slipped from around $150 to $100, bargain hunters snapped it up. But when the stock fell to under $50, a lot of buyers dropped out of the game. Within three years the stock rebounded, and by the beginning of 1997 it had totally recovered. Buyers who'd never lost faith kept purchasing the stock regularly. They wound up paying the lowest price for some shares, the medium and top prices for others, but kept their average cost per share relatively low.

Sometimes stocks recoup even faster. Intel in September 1995 was selling in the $60s and had dipped into the $50s three months later. Nervous investors got out by June 1996, when it was at $70. Too bad for them: six months later, it was at $136. Within a year it was over $150.

The market is a constant cycle of ups and downs. If circumstances in your life change so that you become less willing to take risk, have your broker update the *account holding page* that she or he fills out when you open your account, to indicate that you have become risk-averse, recognizing that your money will grow more slowly.

In certain circumstances, you can afford greater risk. When you're under thirty-five, you can stick your neck out and even invest in a few high-fliers; you have years to make up any losses. You can also afford investment risk if you have a lot of money, since you'll never have to sell in the middle of a bear market to pay your telephone bill.

People in the age range of our club members, forty-five and over, are usually advised to balance their investments almost equally between stocks (risk) and bonds (income). But many of us prefer to be more aggressive.

> *Some people say to subtract your age from 100, put the equivalent of your age into bonds and the remaining percentage into stocks. Once you're past fifty, the majority of your holdings is in bonds. That approach isn't for me. My business is thriving, I'm still productive, and I want to see my money grow. I'm willing to take more risk.*—Margot Green

As you become a more experienced investor, you're more willing to take risk.

> *I used to keep 80 percent of my money in fixed-income investments, which is not in anybody's pie chart. But that's what I needed to sleep at night. Now, I've begun to develop the flexibility to take sufficient risk and the confidence to ride out the ups and downs of the market.*—"Dana Landis," 52, art gallery saleswoman, married, two grown children

> *When other people did my investing, I would look at the reports and not know anything. I didn't know what the company did or what it made. Now I have a portfolio of companies, and I understand all of them. If you do your research and understand the company and its long-range prospects, you can be more comfortable about hanging in there for the long term.*—Margot Green

If you find even conservative stock investment too nerve-racking, you may have to confine your investments to CDs and Treasury bills and high-rated, insured municipal bonds. But while taking physical risks may be hazardous to your health, avoiding all financial risk may be hazardous to your wealth.

RATING THE RISKS

In increasing order of risk (lowest to highest), this is how investments are *generally* rated and why.

MONEY MARKET FUNDS

Banks, mutual funds, and brokerage houses all offer money market funds: they use your money to make short-term investments, and you share in the profit. Because there is virtually no risk in bank money market funds insured by the Federal Deposit Insurance Corporation (FDIC), they pay only about half what you get from other money market funds.

BANK CERTIFICATES OF DEPOSIT

Issued by banks and savings and loan companies. Guaranteed to a limit of $100,000 if the bank or savings and loan is insured by the FDIC.

TREASURY BILLS, NOTES, AND BONDS

Backed by the "full faith and credit" of the U.S. government.

GOVERNMENT SAVINGS BONDS

The most widely held form of investment.

Agency bonds

These bonds come from various government agencies. Government backing is implied, but you don't have the absolute guarantee you get with Treasury bills, bonds, and notes.

Corporate bonds

Backed by the corporations that issue them. Corporations must pay interest on bonds before any dividend is distributed and, in case of company failure, must repay bondholders before stockholders. The stronger the company, the higher the bond rating and the lower your risk.

Municipal ("tax-free") bonds

Backed by the cities or states that issue them to raise money for local projects such as roads, airports, schools, hospitals. The higher the rating, the lower the risk. Resale may be problematic.

Zero coupon bonds

Issued by the U.S. government, corporations, or municipalities. Resale may be problematic. The principal is guaranteed to be returned at date of maturity.

Preferred stock

In between a stock and a bond. Preferred stockholders are paid dividends before holders of regular ("common") stock, but preferred stock doesn't grow as fast as common stock.

Large-company blue chip stocks

These are stocks of the largest companies in the country. They have leading positions in their industries and long, unbroken records of earnings and dividend payments.

All other domestic stocks

Other stocks are less stable than blue chips, with less predictable earnings.

Foreign stocks

Riskier than domestic stocks simply because they are foreign. Currencies abroad may fluctuate, political situations may be unstable, and accounting standards may be inconsistent.

Junk bonds

Also called high-yield bonds. Backed by companies with risky prospects. In case of bankruptcy, they may not be able to pay off creditors.

Options and futures

You purchase a contract to buy or sell shares in a company at a specific price in the future. If the price goes up or down contrary to your expectations, you may find that your options or futures are worthless.

Penny stocks

If you can't find it listed in the paper, it's probably a penny stock. Companies that sell unproved products (for example, biotech stocks) or have no earnings history. Cheap but high-risk.

COLLECTIBLES

A specialized form of investment—jewelry, art, antiques, stamps, coins, and so on. The resale market is not predictable.

PRECIOUS METALS, COINS, AND STONES

Gold and silver haven't been "treasures" for years. Just holding gold and silver doesn't produce income. Also, the resale market is not predictable.

A one-year Treasury bill and a one-year CD are good baselines to judge the riskiness of an investment. The greater the discrepancy between the one-year T-bill and/or CD rate and any other investment you're considering, the greater the risk involved.

KEEPING YOUR INVESTMENTS BALANCED

You should review your portfolio twice a year, and certainly every September at a minimum, in connection with tax planning. You can't just buy and hold your investments. You have to react to changes in the economic climate or in the circumstances of a particular company—new management, a problematic foreign political situation, legislative action that is adverse to its interest. In a sense, you're tending a garden, pulling out what isn't growing and replacing it with items that will bloom.

If you have the habit of acting on "hot tips," you may have made a lot of short-term gains and long-term losses. Unload the losers. Don't turn into a financial "battered wife," hanging on to an investment that's too risky in hopes that it will turn around. In the future, stop listening to the source of the tip—an inexperienced broker, your brother-in-law, your friend's husband, or your own husband. In the future, get your advice from experienced professionals and do your own research. (See "Doing Your Research" on page 114.)

At the end of a good year in the stock market, the worth of your stocks may be out of proportion to the value of your bonds, so you should sell off some stocks and put more into bonds. This is called reallocation. Or a particular stock may have grown disproportionately. Investors are usually advised to set a *discipline* of a certain percentage and when holdings in a single stock exceed that percentage of your portfolio to sell the excess. (Our club discipline is 10 percent.) When you're rebalancing, don't forget to take the holdings in your retirement fund into account.

You need some sound information when you're evaluating what you own. Our investment club has been a constant source of stimulation and new ideas. Club members read fewer novels and catalogues and more newsletters, quarterly reports, and financial magazines. Spend time with friends who share your interest, and find an investment professional you can rely on.

FINDING A STOCKBROKER

A good stockbroker is an invaluable source of information. While years ago, brokers did trading only, their role has expanded. Most financial institutions have educated brokers to examine your overall financial picture and use tools like computer software to set goals and customize your investment plan.

Never select a stockbroker who happened to call as you were sitting down to dinner one night, or one recommended by a friend who made a killing in a single stock based on this person's advice. Also don't assume that being associated with a large firm means the broker is top-notch—or even honest—or you could be the one telling a story like this:

The broker was with a reputable firm, though I had no connection with it personally. He suggested I have an account on margin—which is like buying on credit, a risky situation to put yourself in. At first, I was making small amounts of money. Then he started trading without consulting me. He'd say I wasn't available. He started churning my account, sometimes making trades three times a day, which of course gave him a lot of income in commissions. He'd sell something without my permission and, when I'd protest, buy it back, and I'd incur a loss. He was making thousands in commissions, and I couldn't seem to stop him. I didn't realize he needed written permission to act without my consent. Finally I met someone in the firm socially. When I told him what was going on, he put a halt to it and the firm reimbursed me. I've learned that blind trust is your enemy, and you're as powerless as you feel. If you see one thing that doesn't seem right, speak up immediately.—Barbara Bellin Brenner, 56, house portrait artist and renderer of interiors, married, adult daughter

To check out a broker, call NASD (the National Association of Securities Dealers) at 800-289-9999 between 9:00 A.M. and 5:00 P.M. ET and ask for the broker's CRD (Central Registration Depository) file, a database that lists brokers' employment and disciplinary histories. You can also get it on the World Wide Web (http://www.nasdr.com). As of 1997, you should be able to get a complete report, showing all pending and settled arbitrations (even if the charges were dismissed), civil proceedings and customer complaints alleging damages of $5,000 or more, settlements over $10,000, any current criminal or regulatory investigation, resignation or termination as a result of investment-related violations, and more.

Of course, when professionals serve the public, some disgruntled customers are almost inevitable. Anyone can make unfounded allegations, and the report in the CRD may be difficult to interpret. If the record shows something negative that isn't criminal behavior, give the broker a chance to tell the story from his or her point of view.

Opening a brokerage account is like opening a bank account. You have to provide the usual personal information along with your Social Security number and a bank or financial reference.

FULL-SERVICE VERSUS DISCOUNT BROKERS

Every time you buy or sell a stock, bond, or mutual fund, you pay a sales commission based on the number of shares traded or the value of the transaction. If you're trading high-priced stocks, there will be probably be fewer of them, so you're better off being charged by share. Alternatively, you may pay a *wrap fee*, an annual charge of 2 percent or less based on the total amount in your account that may cover as many as forty trades.

The alternative to a full-service broker is a discount brokerage firm, which may save you 20 to 70 percent on your trades. But you should be aware that some of the big-name "discount" companies that advertise nationally charge commissions two or three times as high as those of a true no-frills, deep-discount operation.

Despite the higher costs, and particularly if you're a novice, there are some definite advantages to dealing with a full-service broker rather than a discount broker:

• ***Selling some items may be easier.*** Though it may cost you $40 to $60 to buy Treasury bonds through a broker rather than directly from a Federal Reserve Bank, a full-service broker can help you find a buyer for a Treasury bond—and for a CD, too, perhaps even at a profit. You couldn't do this on your own or with a discount broker.

• ***You can earn extra income.*** If you have an asset management account (fees range from zero to $150) at a brokerage house, whenever you sell a security, the money is automatically transferred into an interest-bearing money market account.

• ***You have a better paper trail.*** With an asset management account, your monthly statement reports what you bought and sold, dividends earned, income from bond interest, and possibly even an asset allocation breakdown. You'll know the current total value of your account. You'll also get a year-end report, summarizing all of the activity in your account for that year, which is extremely useful when you're preparing your taxes.

• ***You may be offered other services*** such as checking accounts and bank credit lines.

• ***You may get better deals.*** If a large firm has an inventory of bonds and stocks, you may pay a lower price than with a discount broker. The firm may also be able to time a sale of your stock to get the best price in a particular time frame.

• ***Most important, a full-service broker offers the service you need most: advice.*** At a big firm, every recommendation is backed by substantial research produced by teams of economists and staff analysts. The brokers have access to this information and to many other kinds of informational tools.

For bond trades, discount brokers charge the same commission as a full-service broker, just as you pay the same for airline tickets bought direct from the airline or from a travel agency. But, as noted, a full-service house may provide better service, have a bigger inventory of bonds, and do a better job finding a buyer.

Bond prices vary among brokerage firms and banks, depending on the size of the built-in commission. When you're buying, shop around. Make sure you're comparing bonds that have the same maturity date and are paying the same interest rate. Even so, the differences in purchase price can be significant.

GETTING THE BEST FROM YOUR BROKER

Go in with the whole story. Be truthful when you report your financial information and other holdings. With the whole picture, the broker can better determine what kind of risks you should be taking, what kind of investments you're comfortable with, and where your portfolio should be expanded or reduced.

Learn how to read your statement. For example: a good broker usually moves excess cash in a client's account into a money market fund so it can earn interest at no cost to her. But a new client may see a money market mutual fund on her statement and think she's been put into a mutual fund by a broker who is trying to earn a commission. If necessary, have your broker, or an assistant, walk you through the statement.

Prioritize your needs. Must you speak with the broker, or can the administrative assistant handle your call? Or can you communicate your message by fax or voice mail? If you're calling to inquire about a particular stock, leave a message regarding the purpose of your call. The broker can gather the information before getting back to you.

Put it in writing. Follow up faxed instructions with a phone call to make sure your instructions have been received.

Take responsibility. Don't stay by the phone waiting for the broker to call. This isn't a date. If you have a question or you hear about a particular stock of interest, initiate the call yourself. You have an equal if not greater obligation than the broker to monitor your own account. The best broker in the world will not be as concerned about your money as you are.

Don't churn your own account. "Churning" is making a lot of trades, which jacks up the commission costs. If you rush to sell a stock after you've made a small gain, the commission on the trade may wipe out your whole profit.

Be patient. One or two bad months doesn't mean a bad year. Some investments take time. You don't pull up a plant every day to see if the roots have grown. If an investment is disappointing you, call your broker to discuss it and review your original expectations and time commitment. Don't change brokers with the seasons. One of our club members who is very risk-averse has considered the idea of opening two accounts, one with trading money and one with "safe" money.

Avoid Monday madness. If you've spent the weekend stewing over a bad investment, wait twenty-four hours before you sound off.

Have realistic expectations. If you have been a frequent trader, your broker may call you regularly with new opportunities. But if you are a conservative investor and infrequent trader, it's unrealistic for the broker to call often, or for you to expect the call. However, it is reasonable for you to ask for a semi-annual review of your portfolio.

Give your broker a referral. If you want your modest account to get as much attention as a huge one, give the broker more business. Your call will be one of the first he or she returns. (It also helps to be nice to the administrative assistant.)

KEEPING YOUR RECORDS

For information about what paperwork to keep, see "What Belongs in Your Home Financial Files" in the Resources section at the end of this book. It's essential to keep complete records of all the activity in your investment account for tax purposes.

Complete records can also help you strategize. If, for example, you buy different amounts of the same security at different times and then sell off chunks, the IRS assumes that the first lot you bought is the first lot you've sold, under a policy call FIFO—"first in, first out"—unless you state otherwise. Suppose you bought some shares at $5 and some at $10 of a stock now selling at $15, and now you want to sell. If you're trying to reduce the capital gains taxes, you can claim that you're selling the shares you bought at $10, so your profit is only $5. Have your broker fill out the order ticket accordingly—"versus purchase dated [date]." If you don't know how many shares you bought at what price, you can't do this kind of planning.

My grandparents gave me some AT&T stock that cost them very little. Years later, I bought some shares on my own. When I sold several shares to raise some cash, under the FIFO theory the IRS assumed I was selling my grandparents' gift shares, which had appreciated substantially. I wound up paying a big tax on the huge capital gain. I made the trade through a discount broker. I think a full-service broker would have asked the right questions to avoid this situation.—"Adrienne McKay," 29, city planner, married

MAKING YOUR NEST EGG GROW

Use dollar cost averaging to invest regularly. If you're not making monthly payments to an investment club, then arrange for an automatic electronic monthly transfer from your bank to a mutual fund or brokerage account. Start with as little as $100 or $250 every month or two and increase the investment over time. The point is to make investing into a habit that you continue every month, even when the market is down. That is when you might not be inclined to buy, though that is when the stock is a bargain. You'll buy more shares in a depressed market, and fewer when it goes back up, which enables you to average the cost and continuously increase your holdings.

HOW DOLLAR COST AVERAGING WORKS

Suppose you put in $100 a month over six months in AAA Company.

Month	*Amount You Invest*	*Price per Share*	*Number of Shares You Buy*
1	$100.00	$10.0	10.0
2	100.00	8.0	12.5
3	100.00	6.0	16.7
4	100.00	7.0	14.2
5	100.00	9.0	11.1
6	100.00	12.0	8.3
Total	$600.00	$52.00	72.8

Average Market Price per Share
$52 ÷ 6 = $8.6

Your Average Cost per Share
$600 ÷ 72.8 = $8.2

In a falling market you come out ahead by accumulating more shares. In a rising market, you also come out ahead, though not as far. In either case, you increase your net worth.

Take advantage of dividend reinvestment. If your company is doing well, the board of directors might declare a dividend for each share, so shareholders can participate in the profits. You can choose to take money or the equivalent amount in shares (or fractions of shares). This is a way to invest without putting in additional cash. In other words, if you're entitled to a dividend of $200 and the stock is selling at $20, you can have ten shares instead; if the dividend is $20 and a share costs $40, you can have half a share. As a plus, many brokerage houses won't charge you a commission or any other fee on a dividend reinvestment. However, you will be taxed on the dividend by the federal government, unless the investment is in a tax-sheltered situation.

Sock every penny you can into a retirement fund. If you work for a company or have your own business, put the maximum the law allows into a tax-sheltered retirement account.

Keep working. When one of the club members was offered an early retirement package, we all told her to pass on it. An early retirement package is always smaller than the package you'll get later on. And though her plan was to take the money and find another job, that was an iffy proposition. If she couldn't find another good job, she'd miss out on income from what would be her peak earning years. If you have a current husband or an ex-husband paying alimony or child support, encourage him to keep working, too.

Make yourself marketable. If you hate your job, look around for a new one or train yourself for a different, better one. If your specialty is too narrow, get more education. If you don't have a job, apprentice somewhere to learn a skill. Figure out where the opportunities are and prepare for them. Explore the possibilities of working from home. Lots of people start a new career in their forties; many don't start until even later. There are countless stories of people who have started over and been hugely successful. We know many of them personally:

- At fifty, our friend Sylvia Weinstock was diagnosed with breast cancer and her husband had wearied of practicing law. The children were grown, so they sold their house and moved to Manhattan, where Sylvia decided to turn her interest in baking into a career. She began by showing her cakes to hotel banquet managers. Eighteen years later, Sylvia and her husband run a unique and enormously successful designer cake business. A Sylvia Weinstock design is the Tiffany's of wedding cakes.
- Club member Diane Steiner, who had several careers—speech pathologist, audiologist, entrepreneur running a cottage industry from her home—determined after her own divorce to find a career with more opportunity. Despite her fear of being a student after so many years, she applied to law school and was accepted. She and her son received their law degrees in the same year and were the first mother-son team to be admitted to the New York State bar on the same day. (Diane's grown daughter, to her mother's satisfaction, has continued to pursue a

career along with motherhood.) The lawyer who represented Diane in her divorce gave Diane her first job.

- Club member Carol Safir started out as a teacher, took a few years off to raise her children, then became a real estate broker because the flexible schedule accommodated child-rearing. Since her husband was devoted to a career in public service, she made it her goal to supplement the family income. In addition to selling real estate, she began to buy some as investments. When her husband retired from his government job, she switched gears again to help him establish an international consulting business. When he became Fire Commissioner and subsequently Police Commissioner of New York City, she took over the reins of the business herself.
- Another friend's second husband told his mother that our friend could take care of herself. When the marriage fell apart, she had to prove it:

I was in midlife, looking for a job. My self-esteem was zero. I thought, "Who will take me? I don't know how to type. I don't have any real skills." But I resolved that nothing was impossible and no one would get me down. I'd cry in the privacy of my home, keep my troubles to myself, work, and persevere. I was determined to accomplish something. I got a job in Patient Relations for Lenox Hill Hospital and over the years achieved an excellent salary and a great reputation. Recently I looked around my vacation apartment in Florida and I thought, "Imagine. In 1974, I didn't have two pennies." Work hard. Don't ever give up. Things may not turn out exactly as you had wanted, but if you hold on, something good is going to happen for you.
—Harriet Blum, 65 plus, retired, three sons, three daughters-in-law, and five grandchildren

If those options are totally unavailable to you, maximize what you're doing and turn yourself from a wife into a Wife (see pages 239–241).

Actively manage your investments. At first, this seemed like an overwhelming, impossible job. Some of the club members would look at the financial pages and think, "I can't do this." Do not underestimate yourself. There are, trust us, a lot of people no smarter than you who are managing their investments. Haven't you handled many equally complicated things in your life already? For example, didn't you furnish your home? You picked a color scheme, selected the paint and wallpaper, chose the furniture and rugs, bought the fixtures and appliances, decided on the hardware, shopped for the accessories. Did you raise a child? You learned the skills of a doctor, teacher, negotiator, lanyard maker, and then some. In your life, you have made dozens of choices that required a lot of specialized knowledge. Making decisions about money is no different. Yes, there's a lot to know, but you can learn it a day at a time. And as you do, you will gain a sense of control that will make you feel much more secure about your future.

> *I've done extraordinarily well in the market these last couple of years because I finally started paying attention to my account. I won't even buy a pair of panty hose without knowing what outfit I'll wear them with, yet I used to hand over money to brokers without ever articulating a long-term goal or engaging in a conversation about strategy. That's changed. I've learned enough to ask some of the right questions and get out if I've made a mistake. I'm in this for the long haul. Of course, I'm not giving up all my luxuries for a retirement fund! I still have a present. But I'm making my money work for me.*—Karen Fisher, 47, interior design referral consultant, single

TRACKING YOUR SUCCESS

When you're on a diet, you look forward to getting up in the morning and weighing in to track your success. Managing your money can give you that same daily thrill.

> *Now all of us [in the club] are constantly figuring our net worth. I look at my statement and I question it and I total it. I used to do that once a year. Now I do it all the time.*—Margot Green

In judging how well you've done, don't just total up your assets or look at the bottom line on your asset management account. To track your progress accurately, the most important measure is percentage of growth.

A $15 profit on a $100 investment is, well, only $15. But it's 15 percent, which is an excellent return. However, if the market overall has gone up just 3 percent, don't expect a 15 percent return in your own account.

To calculate your percentage of return, (1) subtract the amount of your original investment from the current total; (2) divide the result by the amount of the original investment. Example: You started with $1,000 and now have $1,500. $1,500 minus $1,000 equals $500. $500 divided by $1,000 equals 50 percent.

To see how fast your money is growing, apply the Rule of 72. Divide whatever rate of return you're getting into the number 72 and you'll see how long it will take to double your money. For example, say you're making 7 percent. When you divide 72 by 7, the result is 10 plus a remainder. That means it will take you a little over ten years to double your money. If you're getting 3 percent in a money market checking account, divide 72 by 3. It would take you 24 years to double your money. If you're getting 25 percent, as some people were doing in the recent excellent markets, divide 72 by 25. You could double your money in less than three years.

The members of the club have learned to think of investing as a big treasure hunt. We have a map and a guide and the workmen to help us dig. The treasure is guaranteed to exist. Perhaps the first hole doesn't hit the mark, or it's too deep; perhaps the shovel breaks. Do we give up or do we carry on? Naturally, we keep on digging. And so should you.

CHAPTER 4

GROWING YOUR MONEY

Where to Put It, and Why

I used to think that making investments was like going into Baskin-Robbins. There were thirty-two different flavors and every once in a while they'd come up with a new one. It was a pleasant dilemma, trying to decide among ice creams. But when I thought of having to choose among investments, I *was frozen. Then through the club, I realized that there was just one big distinction—between stocks and bonds. Mutual funds are just a mix of different stocks or bonds, or a combination of both. And everything else is cash. Once I understood that, it all seemed less mystical and much clearer.*
—Vivian Serota

Although as a club we invest primarily in stocks, we are very aware that as individuals we have to balance our holdings among stocks, bonds, and cash. This is true for every investor.

CASH: THE PARKING LOT

Because they pay little or no interest, checking accounts, savings accounts, and money market accounts are all considered a form of cash rather than an investment. The point of putting money into any of these places is to keep it very accessible, not to make it grow.

CHECKING AND SAVINGS ACCOUNTS

Up to $100,000 of your money is guaranteed safe by the U.S. government if it's in a bank insured by the Federal Deposit Insurance Corporation (FDIC). (If you have more than $100,000, put the overage in another bank.) But in a checking account, it earns no interest, or just a little. In a savings account, it earns only a bit more. Your principal is secure, but since you're usually not earning more than inflation, you're losing purchasing power. This can have a devastating effect on your savings.

MONEY MARKET ACCOUNTS

Don't think of a money market account at a bank, mutual fund, or brokerage house as an investment. Though it usually pays slightly more interest than a checking and/or savings account, the rate is still always very low because your risk is small or nonexistent. Up to $100,000 of your money is insured by the FDIC in bank money market accounts, so they usually pay even less than mutual fund and brokerage firm money market accounts. But many of the latter cover up to $100,000 of your cash with supplemental insurance from the SIPC (Securities Investor Protection Corporation).

Like savings and checking accounts, money market accounts are *demand accounts:* you can get your money as quickly as your check clears. But this type of account isn't useful for paying day-to-day bills. There may be restrictions on the number of checks you can draw and a minimum amount per check. You may have to maintain a minimum balance (usually $500 or $1,000). And you may be charged service fees.

You receive one *share* for each dollar you put into a money market account and earn interest in the form of additional shares. The bank, mutual fund, or brokerage house earns the interest by investing your money in high-quality, interest-paying investments—usually half in government-backed investments like Treasury bills and certificates of deposit, half in short-term corporate investments—and sharing the profit with you. Generally, money market funds make investments that pay off in ninety days or less. Short-term investments are always the safest. If you lend someone $10 for a week, you'll have a better chance of collecting it than if you lend it to him for ten years.

BONDS: THE LITTLE BLACK DRESS OF INVESTMENTS

When you buy a bond, you are lending your money to a company or government entity for a certain period of time. In return, you get a certain amount of interest twice a year. At the end of the period of time, the loan is repaid to you.

If you buy a bond that has just been issued, you pay face value, or *par:* a $1,000 bond costs exactly $1,000. Sometimes you must buy a minimum number of bonds—$5,000 worth when you're buying municipals, $10,000 or $25,000 worth of Treasuries.

The interest, or *coupon rate,* is what you are paid for the use of your money. A bond with a 7 percent coupon returns $70 a year for each $1,000 you invest. Payments come twice a year. When a bond matures, it pays you back every penny you've put into it. (This is how a bond and a child are different.) But it doesn't grow in value.

However, almost all bonds can be bought and sold through stockbrokers. When you buy or sell bonds through brokers, they may cost more or less than face value. You may pay a premium or get a discount, depending on the amount of interest the bonds are paying and how that compares to current rates.

Say your periodontist announces there is gum surgery in your future. You're short of cash, but you do have some $1,000 bonds yielding 7 percent. Checking the financial pages, you see that your bonds are selling for 97. (Bond prices are quoted in percentages. To get the actual dollar figure, just add a zero.) In other words, you're being offered just $970 for bonds that cost you $1,000. That's because newer bonds are paying 8 percent—1 percent more than yours. If you held your bond to maturity, you would get your entire $1,000 back. And you would continue to collect your 7 percent yield. But you have to sell now, at a loss.

If, however, current bonds are paying only 6 percent, your 7 percent return looks good. Instead of offering you 97 ($970) or even 100 ($1,000), buyers are willing to pay a premium and offering 110 ($1,100). You'll have to pay capital gains tax on the profit.

However, though professional money managers trade bonds like stock, the typical investor usually buys them to hold—for income.

With bonds, you know just what return you will get on your money and at what intervals. Being a creditor also puts you in a secure position. If the company or municipality you backed goes under, you get paid off first, though perhaps not your total investment. Bonds are as unexciting yet dependable as a basic black dress. We asked bond experts to speak to our club since we knew it was important to balance our more volatile stock holdings with bonds.

On the financial pages, alongside the bond price is the *yield to maturity.* This includes the rate of interest, the cost of the bond after the premium or discount, and the number of years your money will be tied up if you hold the bond to the date it pays off. People who buy discounted bonds (like that fellow who paid $970 for your $1,000 bond) are more interested in a larger rate of return and future, rather than current, income. On the other hand, some people will pay extra to get more income now, even if in the long run they'll come out with less income. A booklet, "The Arithmetic of Interest Rates," can be requested from the Federal Reserve Bank of New York, 33 Liberty Street, New York, NY 10045.

BOND RATINGS

Financial rating services rate the institutions that issue bonds to indicate how creditworthy they are. Standard & Poor's and Moody's are two of the principal rating services. Their reports are available from the library or your stockbroker. In order of excellence, Standard & Poor's four top ratings are AAA, AA, A, and BBB. Moody's top four are Aaa, Aa, A, and Baa. (The people who designed these ratings subsequently helped pantyhose manufacturers develop their sizing system.) Although we might consider buying bonds with lower ratings—respectively BB and B, or BA and B—anything below that is extremely high-risk. If thirty-year corporate AA-rated bonds are paying 10 percent and you find a CCC-rated bond paying 18 percent, you haven't found a great deal. You've stumbled across a bond with an uncertain future. Check ratings before you buy, and always compare the ratings of the two companies on a particular bond. If they don't agree, find out why.

"Under review" by Moody's or on the "Credit watch" list in *Standard &*

Poor's Bond Guide can be a signal that a rating is about to go up or down. A rating of D means "default."

> *In the early 1980s, a friend advised buying municipal bonds paying 16 percent. My broker said the ratings were low, but I thought he was being an old fogey. End of story? I lost the 16 percent return along with much of the principal when the bond defaulted.*—"Abby Thompson," 50, office manager, unmarried

RISKS OF BUYING BONDS

The previous chapter covered *inflation risk, market risk, opportunity risk,* and *reinvestment risk.* Other risks include:

Income risk. A bondholder's biggest concern is that her investment will stop producing a level of income that she had been counting on. You have some warning this may happen if the bond issuer reserves the right to *call*—prepay—the bond. If rates decline significantly, the bond issuer may pay off the existing bondholders and issue new bonds at lower rates. (To find out whether a bond may be called, ask your broker. Or look at the back of the bond certificate or in the prospectus. Or consult *Standard & Poor's Bond Guide.*)

Ratings risk. A city or a corporation that issues a bond may be financially shaky. If its rating declines, your investment may lose value or even be wiped out. Though Abby was willing to overlook the fact that the bonds she bought were low-rated, if she had watched them over time and noted a further decline, she might have gotten out in time to cut her losses.

Default risk. When you buy a thirty-year bond, you're taking a gamble on whether the bond issuer will be in existence in three decades. Thirty years ago, Pan American, Eastern Airlines, and B. Altman & Co. looked pretty solid. Today, they're just a memory. Because of that risk, long-term bonds usually pay higher rates. Long-term U.S. government-backed bonds are an exception. Thirty years from now, it's unlikely mail you send to the government will come back "addressee unknown."

Ups and downs in the bond market

Check the *yield curve* in the financial pages. This is a graph that plots the interest rates of short-term and long-term Treasury securities. The curve usually goes up, as long-term bonds usually pay more. The institution that issues the bond knows that investors are less willing to tie up money for a long period and therefore are willing to pay higher rates to attract their money.

In a market when interest rates are expected to fall, investors want to lock in high long-term rates and borrowers want to make only short-term commitments. When short-term rates are higher than long-term ones, the yield curve slopes down instead of up and is said to be inverted.

The Federal Reserve Bank sometimes raises interest rates to slow down economic growth and thus slow inflation. Bonds start looking good, so people put their money into bonds rather than stocks. When investment money is drained away from the market, the market cools down.

Different types of bonds

The variety of bonds is described below. As beginners, we wanted to know what they were, but we are willing to invest in certain categories of bonds only through mutual funds. (See pages 131–139.)

Certificates of Deposit
Risk: Lowest possible
Resale possibility: Yes
Return: Historically low
Usual minimum investment: $500

Certificates of deposit come in denominations from $500 to $100,000 and require investment commitments that range from three months to a few years. The longer your money is tied up, the higher the rate. Banks compete to offer the best interest rates. CD rates quoted in the newspaper or displayed in the bank give two figures, the stated (or nominal) interest rate and the yield. The yield is a bit higher thanks to compounding.

You can buy a CD directly from a bank or a savings and loan association or through a brokerage firm. Buying through a firm has several advantages: The firm will shop the entire country for the best rate. And though a bank will automatically *roll over* a CD—reinvest the money—at the end of a term, a brokerage house needs your permission. If rates are higher elsewhere, you may want to make a move. Finally, if you want to take the cash out without paying a penalty, a brokerage firm may find a buyer who may even be willing to pay a premium. Though you'll pay a capital gain on the premium, if you sell a CD before the end of the term you pay a penalty only on the interest you've earned.

Since the FDIC insures CD accounts in banks up to $100,000, your investment is very safe. As a result, it doesn't produce high returns. You can't plant lemons and expect oranges.

Treasury Bills, Notes, and Bonds
Risk: Extremely low
Resale possibility: Yes
Return: Variable, depending on maturity dates and interest rates
Minimum investment: $1,000 to $10,000, less in a mutual fund

The U.S. government issues these securities to raise money for federal expenses and deficits. Because the United States is regarded as such a strong credit risk, these are the most popular investments in the world. And while rates on these securities don't often seem stupendous to Americans, they are whopping compared to what foreign investors may be getting for their government bonds. Some Japanese bonds pay such small returns that it would take 174 years to double your investment. Another bonus is that there are no state and local taxes on the interest from U.S. Treasury securities.

The difference between Treasury bills, notes, and bonds is just the length of the term of your investment. *T-bills*, which are the shortest-term, are the most common Treasury security. The T-bills that mature in three months or six months are auctioned weekly. Those that mature in a year are auctioned every month. There is a minimum purchase of $10,000 for a T-bill, with incremental purchases of $5,000. When you buy one, you immediately get a check for the interest, also called the *discount*. This is a great advantage: you don't tie up the entire face amount of the bill, and you have the interest available for immediate reinvestment.

Treasury notes have terms up to ten years, pay a higher rate of interest than T-bills, and come in denominations of $1,000, $5,000, $10,000, $50,000, $100,000, and $1 million. You pay the full face amount, get back a portion of the discount right away, and receive interest twice a year.

Treasury bonds mature in ten to thirty years and come in the same denominations as notes. You pay full face value and get interest twice a year. These bonds are most desirable when people feel interest rates are going down and they want to lock in a rate that exceeds inflation.

You can buy T-bills directly from a dozen regional Federal Reserve Banks (call 800-234-2931). But there are several advantages to buying them from a stockbroker. When they're in a brokerage account, you can borrow up to 90 percent of the face value of Treasury securities—and also CDs—at much lower rates than from a credit card or home equity loan. (You can also borrow against stocks, but not as much, because they are more volatile.) The interest on a loan against your securities is usually tax-deductible. And a broker can help you sell a bond if you need cash.

Price quotations for U.S. Treasury bills, bonds, and notes are listed in *The Wall Street Journal.*

Inflation-indexed bonds paying a low interest rate were introduced in late 1996. Normally, if investors feel rates are going up, they are unwilling to purchase bonds at present rates. These bonds are different because their value goes up as interest rates rise. The increase will be taxed as a capital gain when the bond is sold. It remains to be seen how popular such bonds will become.

Government Savings Bonds

Risk: Extremely low
Resale possibility: No
Return: Low
Minimum investment: $25

Not long ago, the only form of investment with which many of our club members had personal experience was U.S. government bonds. Guaranteed by the government and available in small denominations, they are often given as wedding and birthday gifts. The gift of a Series EE bond makes you look very generous. You pay no fee or commission and just half the face value: $25 for a $50 bond, $37.50 for a $75 bond, and so on. The bondholder can cash in the bond in just six months, but at that point the return will be tiny. How long you have to hold a bond to get the face value depends on when it was purchased. A bond purchased in 1987 matures in 1999. But for a bond purchased in 1997, the bondholder will have to wait eighteen years to get the full return. Personally, we think stocks are a better investment. But having an employer deduct the money from a paycheck is appealing to many people as a form of forced savings. So is the fact that the money is relatively hard to get at.

There are no city or state taxes on U.S. bonds. They're also free of federal taxes to people under a (relatively high) income limit if they are used to pay for college tuition. Otherwise, you must pay deferred federal tax when you cash them in. If you've held them a long time, you might be surprised by a big tax bite, as some of us were. (The exact amount will depend on your current income bracket.) When Series EE bonds mature, you can continue to defer taxes if you exchange them for HH bonds. After six months you can sell these back to the bank or the Federal Reserve, or you can hold on. HH bonds pay interest every six months.

For complete information about these bonds, call the Federal Reserve Bank in Buffalo, New York, at 800-234-2931.

Zero Coupon Bonds

Risk: Low
Resale possibility: Yes
Return: Variable, depending on maturity dates and interest rates
Minimum investment: $150

Zero coupon bonds, sold through brokers, have been around only since the early 1980s. They are really repackaged Treasury bonds that pay slightly more than regular Treasuries. Zeros named LIONs, TIGRs, CATs, and REVCORPS have been assembled by brokerage houses; STRIPS are Treasury zeros.

Zero coupons are so named because like EE bonds they pay no interest during the life of the bond, but all the while the return is reinvested at a constant rate. You can buy a zero coupon bond for $150, get no income while you're holding it, and then receive $1,000 when it matures. The

$1,000 represents your original purchase price plus the accumulated interest. How fast the bond matures—it may take twenty or thirty years—depends on the interest rate being offered when you buy it.

Zero coupon bonds are often used for a specific future expenditure of a specific amount—for example, to pay off a mortgage at retirement. After we had a bond expert speak to us, several of us in the club worked out plans using zero coupon bonds to pay college tuition. At least one of us is planning to buy one zero coupon for four years in a row, timed to mature in the year and perhaps even the month that each tuition payment is due. (Zeros mature in February, May, August, or November.) If your child or grandchild is now a teenager, you can predict your needs quite accurately.

There is a sort of catch with zero coupon bonds. Unless they're in a tax-deferred plan, as the income is earned you have to pay federal taxes (though they're free of city or state taxes). Yet you may not actually receive the money for years. You can avoid this problem by buying zero coupon municipal bonds, which are tax-free. But they pay lower interest rates. See the table "What Tax-Free Means to You" on page 108.

You can find a table listing the bid and asked prices for zero coupons in the financial pages. To see the true return, check the net yield to maturity after sales charges have been deducted.

Government Agency Bonds

Risk: Low to medium
Resale possibility: Yes
Return: Variable, depending on maturity dates and interest rates
Minimum investment: $1,000 in a mutual fund; otherwise $5,000

Like Treasury bonds, these are (generally) free of state and local taxes and low-risk. Though no federal agency has ever defaulted on a bond, these are backed by a "moral obligation" only, not the absolute guarantee that comes with Treasury bills, notes, and bonds. Because your risk is slightly higher, they pay slightly higher yields.

Many government agencies issue bonds, but the best known are issued by the Government National Mortgage Association (GNMA), the Federal National Mortgage Association (FNMA), and the Federal Home Loan Mortgage Corporation (FHLMC). These have become known respectively as Ginnie Mae, Fanny Mae, and Freddie Mac.

These bonds are mortgage-backed. Like mortgages, they are paid off partly as interest and partly as principal, which creates a reinvestment problem. As your principal comes back, you have to find a new place to put it to earn interest.

In the club, we agreed that agency bonds are too costly and complex for beginners to buy except through a mutual fund. Buying through a fund gives you an additional advantage: your money is automatically reinvested. Ask the broker or check the prospectus to make sure any fund you're considering consists of GNMAs that pay off in seven to ten years. Longer payoffs are too risky, and shorter ones pay only small returns.

Municipal Bonds

Risk: Low to very high, depending on the rating
Resale possibility: Yes
Return: Variable, depending on maturity dates and interest rates.
Minimum investment: $250 in a mutual fund; otherwise $1,000

Cities, states, utilities, and airport authorities get the money to build, rebuild, and expand airports, state college dormitories, toll roads, and other big public projects by selling municipal bonds. For supporting these efforts by buying the bonds, you pay no federal taxes on the interest you earn. Though some states impose state and city income tax on bonds issued by other states, you also pay no state or city taxes on bonds issued by your home state, Puerto Rico, Guam, and the Virgin Islands. However, if you sell the bonds for a premium to other investors, you owe federal, state, and city taxes on your capital gain. Of course, if you lose money on the sale, that's a capital loss.

There are some $1,000 "baby bonds," but most municipals are sold at face value in minimum units of $5,000. All pay interest twice a year, and come in a variety of maturities up to forty years.

Money to pay off a *revenue bond* comes from tolls and fees generated by a sewer, gas, or electric system, airport, or toll road. Money to pay a *general obligation (GO) bond* comes from taxes. GOs were always considered the more solid investment of the two, but in the 1980s some municipalities passed legislation that prohibited raising property taxes. Until then, raising property taxes had always been a surefire means of financing general obligation bonds; no one ever expected the public to refuse to allow such taxes to be hiked. Even so, revenue bonds are still considered riskier, particularly those that back hospitals, low-income housing, nursing homes, and retirement developments. As a result, they pay a higher yield. Many municipal issues now offer insurance to reimburse the principal in case of default. When its cost is factored in, the yield of lower-rated bonds is reduced.

Similar to these bonds are taxable municipals, industrial development and pollution control bonds, and a couple of other varieties, including zero coupon municipals.

Trading of municipal bonds isn't very active, and the spread between bid and asked prices (what the buyer wants to pay and the seller wants to get) is fairly wide. The amount of commission you pay on a municipal bond trade can vary widely among brokers who may not be familiar with a particular issue or know where to find a buyer.

The Wall Street Journal lists some of the newer issues along with information including the coupon rate, maturity date, and yield to maturity (which is the true return). In buying municipals, we in the club look for bonds that mature within ten to fifteen years and avoid any with an early call—prepayment—date. Otherwise, your money will come back to you and you will have to find another investment.

WHAT TAX-FREE MEANS TO YOU

First, identify your tax bracket.

If your adjusted gross income is at least	but not more than	your tax rate is
For single taxpayers:		
$0	$20,350	15%
$20,351	$49,300	28%
$49,301	no limit	31%
For married taxpayers:		
$0	$34,000	15%
$34,001	$82,150	28%
$82,151	no limit	31%

What would you have to earn on a taxable investment to equal the earnings of a tax-free investment? To find out, divide the tax-free coupon rate by 100 minus your tax bracket.

Let's say the tax-free coupon rate is 6 percent and your tax bracket is 28 percent. Divide 6 by 72 (100 minus 28), and you get 8.3. You'd have to earn 8.3 percent taxable income to net the same as you would getting 6 percent tax-free. Your accountant can help you make these calculations.

One of our speakers, Patty Hoecten, introduced us to a wonderful concept known as "swapping" to help reduce your taxes if municipals are down at the end of the year. You sell what you're holding and immediately reinvest the money from the sale in bonds of a similar term that pay similar interest, which are generally easy enough to find. With this technique, you can deduct the amount of the loss from your income tax, but you're holding bargain-priced, similar bonds. Caution: you can't take a loss if you replace the original bonds with identical bonds within thirty days.

Corporate Bonds

Risk: Medium to very high, depending on the rating
Resale possibility: Yes
Return: Variable, depending on maturity dates and interest rates
Minimum investment: $250 in a mutual fund; otherwise $1,000 and up

To raise money, corporations may be better off issuing bonds than selling stock. Besides, the interest payments on bonds cost them less than borrowing from a bank. Public announcements of new corporate bonds are published in the financial press, but many are presold and not truly available. When they are, corporate bonds generally sell in $1,000 denominations and pay interest semi-annually.

After the initial distribution, bonds can be traded through a broker. Investors can shop for a particular type of bond: you could, for example, ask the broker to find you an investment-grade utility with a yield to maturity of 8 to 9 percent. When you buy, you owe the seller the price of the bond plus whatever interest is due from the last interest payment right through the day before the delivery date.

Corporate bonds pay a higher rate than Treasury bonds and municipals because they don't have the U.S. government backing of the former or the tax advantages of the latter. However, if you're in a low tax bracket, you can make more money from corporate bonds than from tax-exempt municipals.

In a recession economy, highly rated corporate bonds don't pay much more than Treasury bonds, but in boom times, when companies need a lot of credit, corporate bond yields can skyrocket. But we have been told many times that these can be a very risky investment for a beginner. Some corporate bonds may be called after five years. Also, a company may go into default and/or the economy as a whole may go downhill, dragging the company with it. If you want to buy corporate bonds, try a well-managed, diversified mutual fund that spreads its risk by investing both in bonds—make sure they are highly rated—and in government-backed securities like Ginnie Maes.

Convertible Bonds
Risk: Medium to low
Resale possibility: Variable, depending on maturity dates and interest rates
Return: Medium to high
Minimum investment: $250 in a mutual fund; otherwise $1,000 and up

Convertible bonds usually can be turned into stock. They have a maturity date and stated interest rate, which is paid semi-annually. Not all are rated, but you should stick with those that are investment grade or above—no lower than Baa or BBB.

A convertible bond gives you the right to buy a particular number of shares at a specific price, usually well above what the stock is selling for when the convertible is issued. The purchase date may be stipulated as well. Not all convertible bonds keep the conversion privilege to maturity. Some have a call provision with a date by which the conversion must be made.

Convertible bonds usually pay a higher yield than dividends on common stock and a lower rate than interest on corporate bonds. They combine the relative stability of bonds with a chance to take advantage of rising stock prices. If the stock market falls, convertibles will fall only about 40 percent as far as stocks; if the market rises, convertibles will rise only about 70 percent as high. With a growing company, you get interest payments while waiting for the stock to rise. If the stock grows substantially, the convertible can be worth a lot. If not, the bond is worth only its original investment value. The time to buy convertibles is when stock prices and bond yields are both low. A beginning investor should invest in convertibles only through a mutual fund.

High-Yield Bonds
Risk: Very high
Resale possibility: Yes
Return: Low to high; potential is commensurate with risk
Minimum investment: $250 in a mutual fund; otherwise $1,000 and up

High-yield bonds are issued by new companies with no credit histories or old companies with bad ones. They are very risky, but they may appeal to an older investor who wants current income and can afford to take a risk or a young investor who has a long time to recoup in the event of a loss. They're not for everyone.

> *I consider myself very conservative and was advised to invest in bonds. Someone sold me a "high-yield" bond fund that was producing terrific returns. When I mentioned this to a club member, I discovered that "high-yield" is another name for junk bonds! I was reluctant to leave the fund, which had been performing so well, but I just didn't have that kind of risk tolerance.*—"Jackie Miller," 30, department store buyer, married, two children

Some of the more adventurous club members decided to go out on a limb and invest a small portion of their funds in junk bonds. They were advised to ask the help of a broker or fee-based planner in locating a fund managed by someone with a great track record.

BOND BUYING FOR CONSERVATIVE INVESTORS

Most of us in the club are generally conservative investors. We buy only Treasuries and top-rated municipal bonds, and we stick with medium- or short-term bonds. The former mature in seven to twelve years and the latter in three to five years. At this point in our lives most of us are investing for growth more than income, so we have our brokers move any bond interest (or stock dividends) into a money market account and leave it until we have enough to purchase more bonds (or stocks). You could do the same. Or you could put it into a corporate or municipal bond fund, depending on your tax bracket, if you're willing to take a slightly higher risk.

We were also introduced to a bond-buying strategy called "laddering," which combines a good return with low risk. Buy ten bonds (or, if you have less money, ten CDs), one maturing a year from now, one maturing two years from now, and so on, all the way to ten years. At the end of a year, when the first bond comes due, you can reinvest in a ten-year bond, depending on how you're building your ladder. At the end of the second year, do the same with the next bond that is due. The idea is to build a "ladder" of bonds maturing one year at a time. Some people build fifteen- or twenty-year ladders. If interest rates decline, your reinvestments are paying lower interest, but in any other situation, you're ahead.

STOCKS: WHERE THE MONEY GIRLS ARE

The reason our club began investing in stocks rather than bonds is not because stocks are easier to understand but because they're where the action and potential are.

How is stock like a sexy man? It's risky. How is stock not like a sexy man? If you're loyal to it, it usually comes through for you.

Since the 1920s, stock growth has outpaced other investments by three to one. Real estate may be hot one year, everyone's talking about gold the year after that, and the next year the money is in Remington sculptures. But over time, stocks are as close as you can get to a sure thing in the investment world.

True, they have plummeted from time to time in the past. After the recessions of 1929–32 and 1973–74, it took years for investors to break even. But eventually stocks yo-yoed back up, even higher than before. Only stocks have consistently kept investors ahead of inflation and earned 10 to 11 percent *provided the investor got in and stayed there.* Whoever jumped in and out whenever there was a blip didn't do as well.

How stocks work

If a company needs money to purchase equipment, build plants, or cover other expenses to help it grow, it raises the money by selling shares of stock. Anyone who buys one or more shares becomes a part owner in the company and shares the risk of the company's operations. As a part owner, you have the right to vote on certain issues such as whom to appoint to the board and whether to merge with another company. You can vote in person at the annual stockholders' meeting or by mail.

The primary way to make money from stocks is through *capital appreciation:* you buy shares of stock, they rise in value, and you sell them for more than you paid. Many stocks also share the profits with stockholders in the form of *dividend* income. If the board of directors votes to declare a dividend, the money is distributed monthly or quarterly. Dividends are taxable both to the company and to you. Naturally, whatever the company pays in dividends and taxes reduces what it can invest in itself. Smaller, fast-growing companies pay little or nothing in dividends because they need cash to grow on.

Stockholders buy and sell shares through various stock exchanges, called secondary markets. Many foreign countries and regions in the United States (such as the Midwest and Pacific) have their own exchanges. Two U.S. national exchanges, both located in New York City, are the New York Stock Exchange (NYSE) and the American Stock Exchange (AMEX). The NYSE, the biggest in the country, lists stocks of most of the older, more established companies. To qualify for listing, a company must have a solid financial background including a net worth of at least $18 million and have issued at least 1 million shares of stock. To be listed on the AMEX, a net worth of $4 million is required. Trading on the American Stock Exchange amounts to just 5 to 10 percent of what is traded on the NYSE.

The over-the-counter market (OTC), unlike the exchanges, isn't a physical location. It is the largest segment of the secondary market, listing thousands of companies, many of which are small and new. The National Association of Securities Dealers (NASDAQ) is an electronic trading network that provides current prices on about one fifth of the most widely traded OTC securities. At one time, NASDAQ companies were mostly aggressive young upstarts that couldn't meet the financial requirements to be listed on the big exchanges. Today, many big companies are listed on NASDAQ, including former upstarts such as Apple Computer, MCI Communications, Microsoft, and Intel. Through the network of NASDAQ members, you can also get quotes for 20,000 additional small and unlisted companies. Savvy investors follow NASDAQ companies in hopes of finding a little engine that could make it big tomorrow.

DOING YOUR RESEARCH

There are several ways to decide whether to buy a particular stock. When our club members are serving on the stock selection committee, they use them all.

Work the phones. You can get the toll-free number of most large companies from directory assistance (800-555-1212) or the reference desk at your local library. When you call, ask for investor relations and request an annual report, quarterly reports, and any other information. For example, a research firm in the company's region (or a regional broker) may follow the company's progress. You can get their material from the investor relations officer or, better still, ask for the name of a person you can contact directly. Getting one-on-one information will give you insights about making an investment decision.

Read the reports. Look up information about the company in the *Value Line Investment Survey,* which is updated every three months. Call 800-634-3583 to ask for the form "How to Read a *Value Line.*" Also check out *Standard & Poor's Stock Report* at the library or through your broker.

Use the library. Check the reference materials. You may find articles about the company you're researching in back issues of business magazines such as *Business Week* and *Forbes* or other financial publications such as *The Wall Street Journal* and *Barron's.* The librarian can help point you to additional sources.

Read the annual report.

TRICKS OF READING AN ANNUAL REPORT

The annual report generally is the primary and only communication the management of a company has with its shareholders. The purpose of the annual report is to make the company look good. As a potential investor, you should be looking for clues to any potential problems. Three important places to look:

• The *balance sheet* lists what the company owns—its current assets (cash and accounts receivable, which is money due the company); its inventory (finished goods, raw materials, and work in progress); its fixed assets (plant, equipment, and real estate) and intangible assets (trademarks, copyrights, and goodwill). It also lists what the company owes: current debts (outstanding bills, taxes, and so forth due in the current year); long-term liabilities (such as bonds and debts due in the future); and the holdings of the stockholders (including the value of all shares issued).

• The income or *profit-and-loss statement* summarizes how much the company has made (revenues), subtracts various expenses, and comes up with a bottom line—net income and earnings per share. Where the income is generated depends on the nature of the business: for manufacturers, it comes from sales. Banks get dividend or investment income. You may not be able to interpret all the information, but you can check out the auditor's statements at the bottom of the page.

Two standard paragraphs normally state that the information has been prepared to conform with generally accepted accounting principles. Additional paragraphs that contain a phrase such as "Figures are dependent upon [uncertain] future events" or "Figures are dependent on obtaining adequate financing" may be a warning that the company is having financial problems.

• Troublesome news can also be buried in the notes to the consolidated financial statement. Take the time to read them. You may learn that the company is facing litigation or increased costs for warehouse leasing. If anything seems unusual, check with your financial advisor before you buy.

In investigating one company, our club noticed that the notes section took up about a quarter of the annual report and was devoted entirely to special employee benefits. We would have like to work for the company but decided it wouldn't work for us! We didn't buy.

Ask a broker. The research department of a brokerage firm will probably have all the information you need.

EVALUATING THE STOCK

I decided to buy Kmart based on woman's intuition. The stores were in convenient locations. And the company was bringing in a new executive, a hardworking guy with a lot of experience and Midwestern ethics. I had heard he was very nice, and he lived in a house that was a twin to mine. That was the capper, of course. I bought the stock at 14. It dropped to 6. When it went to 8, my husband said the gutsy thing would have been to buy more. But I don't have any guts. I've learned that woman's intuition isn't such a hot way to buy stock. I think what counts is studying and learning (though getting lucky doesn't hurt). Also, you need expert help. I rely on professionals in every other area. Why should I choose my own stocks without some guidance?—Carol Levin

You don't always have to buy what you know, but you do have to know what you buy. Based on our club's risk tolerance (low) and desire for growth (high), Marilyn developed these guidelines to help us figure out if the stocks we were considering were right for us:

1. ***The company's business focus***
   - What industry is it in? What products or services does it offer?
   - Is it a leader in its industry group? What's the competition like?
   - Is it a niche business? Does this give it a monopoly, or does it keep its prospects too narrow?

2. ***The general state and outlook of the industry***
   - How's business?
   - Is it independent of the economy (like foods and beverages) or tied to it (auto manufacturers)?

3. ***Major factors likely to affect the company***
   - What are the prices of goods that it uses? Are the goods from unstable areas?

- Is it vulnerable to currency fluctuations? Does it operate in countries where the dollar is weak?
- What's the mood of the economy and the inflation rate?
- Are there takeovers or mergers pending?

4. ***The company's long-term earnings history and earnings outlook***
   - Has it had at least three quarters of earning improvements?
   - How fast per year does it expect to grow?

5. ***The company's dividend record***
   - What is its payment history for the past three years? (Note, however, that growth companies don't usually pay dividends, because they reinvest profits in the business.)
   - Has the company done well for a while? If not, is there an indication that things are changing?

6. ***Stock highs and lows for the past year and the past three years***

7. ***Price-earnings ratio***
   - Is the ratio (the price per share divided by the company's earnings per share for the past year) in line with industry groups? (This term is explained on page 126.)

8. ***Management***
   - Assess caliber and reputation from annual reports and news stories.

9. ***Price objective***
   - What is your target price for the stock?

10. ***Time objective***
    - How long do you think the stock will take to show results?

11. ***Other opinions:***
    - *The Wall Street Journal,* Value Line, Standard & Poor's; magazines; other stockbrokers.

You have to buy according to the fundamentals. If you like a company, and it meets the above criteria, then you buy. If you like it and it doesn't, then you make a decision about whether to take a risk. Maybe you keep 10 percent of your portfolio in high-fliers.—Carol S. Kogan

MAKING YOUR PURCHASE

On the cable TV network CNBC, the NYSE ticker and NASDAQ ticker appear simultaneously at the bottom of the screen. NYSE is on the top. These list stock prices electronically and continuously. Your local paper may list prices only of the more active stocks on its financial pages but *The Wall Street Journal* has a comprehensive daily listing. All listings are organized the same way.

- The two columns to the extreme left are headed "Hi" and "Lo." They report the stock's highest and lowest prices over the past fifty-two weeks. An upward arrow (or the letters "U" or "H") to the extreme left indicates that yesterday's price was the highest for the preceding fifty-two weeks. A downward arrow (or the letters "d" or "b") indicates the stock has hit a new low.
- The name of the company is in the third column (in abbreviated form). Usually its name is followed by its symbol—one, two or three letters if it's on the American or New York Exchanges, four or five if listed by NASDAQ. General Motors, for example, is listed as GM, Ford is F, Philip Morris is MO, and Coca-Cola is KO. When the markets are open, current price quotes are reported electronically by symbol over computer screens.

  Be careful about tossing around an alphabet soup of symbols.

Once I knew a little bit, I thought I was an in-the-know trader. So I faxed my broker an order for 100 shares of GAP—thinking I was buying shares of the clothing chain. Instead, I became the owner of 100 shares of Great Atlantic & Pacific [*A&P stores*].—"Patricia Linder," 39, insurance adjuster, married, two children

- Explanatory notes on the financial page interpret a variety of code letters used in the listings. An "s," for example, indicates the stock has split within the last year. (Often a split is two for one—you get two shares for each share you once held. Thus if the price goes up a dollar in the future, you get twice the profit you had before. There can be other kinds of splits—a three-for-two, or even a reverse split, where two shares become one.) The letters "pf" next to a company name mean preferred stock.

- The columns headed "Hi" and "Lo" refer to the stock's latest price. The high lists the asked price (what the seller would like to get) and the low is the bid (what buyers are offering).
- The following columns list the "close"—the final price of the stock at the end of the previous day—and the "net change" from the day before that. The closing price may vary slightly from what you may have to pay when the market opens the next morning or greatly if news develops that changes the value.
- The amount of any dividend, the yield, and the P/E ratio are also listed, along with the number of shares traded that day. Shares are usually sold in groups of 100, known as a "round lot." An "odd lot" is any number of shares less than 100. The number 45 in the "volume" column indicates that 4,500 shares were traded. If, in fact, just 45 shares were sold, the number would be preceded by a tiny "z."

In addition to the main exchange listings, you may find a separate listing for the NASDAQ.

When you're ready to buy, ask your broker for the bid and asked prices. Then you can place either a *market order* or a *buy limit order*. A market order means you'll pay the best price available. A buy limit order means you'll buy only if the price drops to a certain level. Even when we're buying for the club, we place a market order rather than a buy limit. The difference in price comes to just a few cents a share, and is insignificant unless you're a professional trading thousands of shares at once.

Selling works the same way. You can place a market order (for the best price you can get) or a *sell limit order*. The sell limit order means you'll sell only if the stock rises to the price you have stipulated.

Our club members thought we knew all about speed spending, but buying stocks is a category of its own. An order for thousands of dollars can be processed on the NYSE in an average of twenty-two seconds. Because the transaction goes so quickly, it's critical to make your intentions very clear.

> *I got the confirmation of my order and nearly fainted when I saw a $12,000 charge to my account. I'd placed an order for "a thousand"—meaning dollars, not shares! Fortunately, I had an emergency fund to cover the difference. I sold the stock as soon as I could and luckily came out even. But believe me, I'll never make that mistake again.*— "Leslie Michaels," 39, textile designer, unmarried

You usually get written confirmation of the trade the next day. The *settlement date,* when payment is due, is always three days later. Pay as soon as you have a faxed confirmation, or if you are willing to take the quote over the phone from your broker; otherwise you run the risk of paying late-payment interest charges.

Ask the broker to hold the stock certificate *in street name,* i.e., at the brokerage house. If you receive it personally, you'll have to put it in a safe deposit box for safekeeping and deliver it physically to the firm within three days if it's sold. Keeping it in street name helps the broker stay on top of it. Also, if a stockholder dies, a broker can handle everything with one death certificate and one set of beneficiary instructions. If stocks aren't held in street name, each stock must be dealt with separately, and heirs will face a sea of paperwork.

What makes a stock rise	***What makes a stock fall***
Being in a "hot" industry	Being in an industry that's not currently in favor
Hiring respected new executives	Losing high-profile executives
Increasing the dividend	Decreasing or omitting the dividend
Exceeding earnings projections	Missing earnings projections by even a penny
An important new product or breakthrough that shows potential for increased earnings	Product failing or being recalled, product denied FDA approval, and/or litigation against company

Increasing demand for product	Decreasing demand for product
Good economic news	Bad economic news
Good employment reports	Bad employment reports
Inflation under control	Inflation running rampant
Decreasing interest rates (since money can be borrowed more cheaply)	Increasing interest rates (expanding the company will cost more)

Some studies indicate that 85 percent of the gain or loss in a stock is due to the overall movement of the market rather than to any especially good or weak point of the company itself.

U.S. politics, economic change, foreign affairs, even the state of the President's health—whatever happens in any corner of the world and affects of the country as a whole affects the movement of the market.

Not only have the club members become avid readers of the financial pages, but we also read the entire newspaper from back to front. You can't consider a stock purchase without being aware of what's going on nationally and internationally.

MARKET TIMING: WHAT'S HOT WHEN

Economic cycles may even predate the seven years of feast and famine reported in the Bible, and there have been up periods and down periods ever since. While it's impossible to predict market movements consistently, understanding the concept of cycles can be helpful. There are five stages to a cycle: revival, expansion, maturation, retraction, and recession.

During *revival,* employment goes up. The number of hours worked increases. The Federal Reserve Board may cut the discount rates (rates at which banks borrow from one another) because making loans easier to get pumps up the economy. This stage provides an excellent investment opportunity. So is *expansion,* when manufacturers start receiving big orders of expensive items such as automobiles and homes.

At the *maturation* stage, consumer spending declines and new construction drops off. Interest rates may go up. Cyclical stocks such as automobiles, housing, chemicals, iron and steel, and capital equipment continue to do well because their earnings were boosted by activity during expansion. The best buys at this point are "defensive" stocks—those that are resistant to economic cycles, like companies that manufacture food and drink, soap, and toilet paper (also known as consumer nondurables or "products that go down the drain"). They won't be much affected during *retraction*, the fourth stage, when orders of items like automobiles and homes are down significantly, there is less spending, and interest rates are higher.

Retraction is followed by *recession*, the best time to buy. While it takes guts to plunk down your money when experts are predicting that the economy won't recover, at least you know your risk is reduced. Airplanes don't crash when they are on the ground. However, timing the bottom is difficult, and you may wait a long time for recovery.

Stock prices tend to be ahead of business cycle changes by about four months. Experienced investors seem to sense when the economy is about to move into a revival mode and take advantage of the chance to buy stocks relatively cheap. The experts talked about the advantages of buying in a down market in terms that were easy for our club to understand: if your favorite brand of tuna is 89 cents a can and goes on sale at 69 cents, do you load up, or do you wait until it goes back to 89 cents to buy more?

In modern times a complete economic cycle, from a bear market (low) to a bull market (high), lasts between three and five years. We were surprised to learn that since 1929, with the exceptions of the crash of 1929–32 and recession of 1973–74, from which recovery took years, recessions have lasted an average of only eleven months. Bull markets last an average of 3.75 years and gain an average of 177 percent from bottom to top, though in the past few years the market has had an unprecedented steady upward climb.

TAKING THE TEMPERATURE OF THE MARKET

Anyone who has ever listened to the nightly news has heard the announcer report, "Today, the Dow was up (or down)." The Dow Jones Industrial Average (DJIA) has been the traditional indicator of stock movement. It is based on the stock activity of thirty major U.S. companies, all of which are traded on the New York Stock Exchange. The list changes infrequently. Old-timers include General Electric and General Motors. McDonald's and Disney are relative newcomers.

The companies on the DJIA are considered blue chip stocks, though not every blue chip is included in the DJIA. The reference comes from gambling, where chips are used in place of money and blue ones are the most expensive. Blue chip companies generally have enormous revenues, a history of steady growth and top management, and a highly recognizable name.

Now that the NASDAQ has grown so important and there are so many stocks on the NYSE itself, some people feel the DJIA is not the best indicator of what's really going on. Others don't like the fact that the DJIA is calculated on actual price changes rather than percentage changes. Since a high-priced stock goes up and down in bigger dollar amounts than lower-priced stock, it has a disproportionate impact on the average.

The Standard & Poor's 500-stock index reflects the performance of 400 industrial companies, 20 transportation stocks, 40 utilities, and 40 financial companies. Since it is calculated to show whether the aggregate value of all the stocks is rising or falling, it is more representative of both the economy and market than the DJIA.

There are several other indices of the market, some calculated by major publications like *Value Line* and others based on a particular sector such as transportation or utilities.

THE RISKS OF BUYING STOCKS

If there are so many ways to see that a disaster is coming, why is investing in stocks considered so risky? For one thing, if a company does go under, the stockholders lose everything. Unlike the bondholders, they can't share in the spoils. For another, things can move very fast. Ask the investors who were in the market in October 1987. Many panicked and sold at a loss. Some who wanted to stay were forced to sell because they needed cash. The people who were able to hold on recouped their losses fairly quickly and saw their investments grow substantially.

A crash is the most dramatic risk for a stock investor but not the only risk. You are also susceptible to *economic risk,* slow growth that causes a gradual decline in stock prices; *interest rate risk,* when higher rates draw money out of the market and into bonds, so the market declines; *business risk,* if a company has bad management or a flawed product; *financial risk,* if the company has taken on too much debt; *information risk,* if a company has concealed bad news about its finances, its services, or its goods; and *competitive risk,* if rival companies do a superior job.

Investors may also subject themselves to *firm-specific risk* or *unsystematic risk*—risking everything on a single company or too few of them. Some experts calculate that you can eliminate about 91 percent of firm-specific risk if your portfolio contains twelve to fifteen different stocks.

Most commonly, people lose money in stocks because they follow the trend instead of anticipating it. They watch as prices rise, then buy at top dollar, or they sell after the market has begun its fall. And they aren't sufficiently diversified. Some people buy only stocks of products they use. But household equipment isn't always where the market is doing best.

WAYS TO DIVERSIFY

Our club members are very careful to diversify with a combination of growth stocks and value stocks.

- *Growth companies* usually have a track record of steady growth and offer a product or service for which there's a steady market, no matter what's going on with the economy. You can find growth stocks in every industry—for example, a company involved in waste disposal that has a unique and environmentally safe procedure or a company involved in agriculture that has genetically engineered a crop that resists a certain kind of pest.
- *Value stocks* parallel the general movement of the economy and do well only when everything else is rolling along. They include industries such as steel, aluminum, paper, automobiles, and airlines, and they depend on big-volume sales. Making money on these stocks is a matter of good timing more than anything else, and good timing is a combination of skill and luck. Value stocks are also defined as stocks that have a lower P/E ratio than other stocks in their industry and pay higher dividends. Sometimes growth stocks become value stocks when they fall out of favor. This is where the bargains are. In some markets, growth stocks are the best-value stocks, so the terms are not mutually exclusive.

A diversified portfolio could contain a combination of the following:

Stocks chosen by industry, such as finance (banks, brokerage firms, insurance companies, credit card companies), manufacturing and distribution (chemicals, food, clothing, paper, pharmaceuticals, oil, steel), transportation (airlines, truckers, railroads), and utilities (electric, gas, and telephone service providers).

Stocks chosen by sector, such as consumer staples (everyday products and services from health care to hot dogs), capital goods (products for industrial production and service), and basic industries (material for industrial production and consumption, such as paper, steel, chemicals, and lumber).

Stocks chosen by sensitivity to interest rates: banks, utilities, and financial service companies are sensitive to rates, while other types of service companies (such as health care) are not.

Stocks chosen by size: large, blue chip companies, mid-cap companies, or small-cap companies. ("Cap" means capitalization; "small-cap" companies are just small companies.) Small caps are riskier: they're newer, and they're less liquid. Trying to unload a block of little-known stock can take days. Selling a big-name stock can be done in seconds. Among the small caps, you may find the very company that zooms to the top—or the one where you can lose your shirt.

If you don't have enough money to diversify your stock holdings adequately, or you don't feel secure about checking out stocks on your own, a mutual fund, which diversifies for you, is an ideal solution. (See pages 131–139.)

IT'S TIME, NOT TIMING, THAT COUNTS

It's not when you get in that matters, it's how long you stay. We were surprised to learn that getting in at the "right time" is relatively unimportant. Suppose Wilma and Louise began to put money into the market on January 1, 1964, and continued to invest for the following thirty years.

Wilma always managed to put her money into the market at the bottom and got the lowest prices. But Louise had terrible instincts and always bought at the highest price. Over the years, Wilma would have averaged a 12.04 percent return on her money. And Louise would have made 10.98 percent—a little more than 1 percent less. The important thing is to keep adding to your investment, most efficiently with dollar cost averaging (see pages 90–91).

WHEN STOCK IS OVERPRICED

You could have bought a magnificent home in Los Angeles several years ago for $5 million and been forced to sell for half that price only a couple of years later. It was still the same beautiful house, in the same excellent location, but you may simply have overpaid at the time that you bought. You can do the same with stock.

A company's annual EPS (earnings per share) will tell you if it is making money, and a company with an increasing EPS quarter after quarter and year after year is a healthy company; but the EPS is only one gauge of its worth.

More important is the *price-earnings ratio (P/E),* which you get by dividing last year's EPS into the stock's current price. Club members struggled to comprehend the significance of the P/E ratio until we realized that it is, above all, a measure of how much faith investors have in a company or how highly they value its earnings. Though a company with a low P/E may be performing well because it is earning a lot compared to its price, investors are staying away. A high P/E means that investors are betting on this stock. A company with an extremely high P/E may not have been around long enough to produce a lot of earnings, but investors may be snapping it up because they think it's got promise.

Barron's publishes P/Es weekly for individual stocks as well as the Dow Jones Industrial Average and the S&P 500 as a whole. Historically, the price-earnings ratio of the market as a whole has averaged about 15 to 17. When the entire market is on a roll, the P/E average rises. Stock prices are rising faster than earnings. Usually a correction follows: either earnings rise or the market falls, and the P/E will be back to average.

Use the P/E to compare a company:

- **to itself.** If for five years the P/E has been between 5 and 10 and is now just 4, ask why.
- **to others in the same industry.** If a P/E of 28 is typical and this company has a 12, investors are staying away. If the reverse is true, the company is hot.
- **to the market as a whole.** If the P/E is low in a boom time, the company may be a dog—or an undervalued treasure. Investors sometimes specifically seek out companies with P/Es that are low compared to others in the industry, hoping to find a bargain that will ultimately pay off.

You can also use the P/E to estimate what people might be paying for the stock next year. Multiply the current P/E by next year's projected earnings per share. (Your broker can get that projection for you.)

A company with a high P/E may indeed be overpriced. But in response to low earnings, the management may have trimmed costs and now the company is a good buy.

The *dividend yield* is another gauge of the market. Add together annual dividend payments of all the stocks on the DJIA and divide that by the number the Dow closed at. Say the total annual dividends are $300 and the Dow closed at 6,000. The result of $300 divided by 6,000 is 5 percent. You can find the dividend yield in *Barron's*. The number was something over 5 percent through the 1950s, and over 3 percent for a long time after that. Often people believe anything below 3 percent is dangerously low.

The P/E and the dividend yield tell you what happened in the past. Can they predict future prospects? Consider the "roach theory:" if you see one roach in the kitchen, there are probably more where it came from. If a company has a good quarter, there's probably another one coming. And once there's a bad quarter, start looking for more just like it.

TOO RISKY FOR BEGINNERS

There are certain investment strategies that novices should avoid.:

Buying on margin. If you meet the financial requirements, you can set up a margin account with your brokerage house. It is like a line of credit.

You can borrow up to 50 percent of the cost of stock you buy and pay interest on the loan with the securities you already own as collateral. When the stock goes up, you sell it, repay the loan, and keep the profit. Catch: the stock may go down. In that case, you will receive a margin call and must repay the loan plus the commission and the interest you paid on the loan. If you don't have the cash, your securities will be sold. Margin calls were one of the reasons for the crash of 1929. Since then, there have been stricter limits on the amount you can borrow.

> *I lost my entire portfolio in October of 1987 because I was heavily margined. I thought I was so savvy and was certainly making a lot of money on paper. No one had bothered to tell me that all my investments could be lost in twenty-four hours. If I'd handled my business affairs the way my investments were handled, I wouldn't have a career today.*—Carol S. Kogan

Selling short. This is a way of gambling that a stock will go down. If you have a certain amount in your account, the brokerage firm will let you "borrow" stock from another investor and then sell it. When the stock drops in price, you buy it back and return it to the other investor. You make the difference between the amount you borrowed and the amount it cost you to replace it. Catch: if the stock goes up instead of down, you could be out a bundle. This is one form of investment where losses are theoretically unlimited.

Penny stocks. Penny stocks (so called because they sell for under $1) are like—well, penny candy. You can buy a lot with a small amount of money, and they're not good for you. The big action in penny stocks usually takes place just as they're introduced to the market. The stock may zoom up immediately. Catch: those in the know manage to bail out quickly before the stock sinks (as it does most of the time). That ship you hoped would come in is leaking in the harbor.

IPOs (initial public offerings). Fannie's Fabulous Frocks needs money for expansion and calls in an investment banking firm. It works with lawyers to help prepare the prospectus, the document that describes the company's benefits and risk. The team goes on the road to meet with big potential buyers: institutional investors (people who manage pension plans and other large purchasers of stock) and analysts from brokerage firms. Investment bankers set the price of the stock, buy it from the company, and resell the new shares to investors. If the bankers think a stock will be a winner, their preferred clients get first dibs. Catch: by the time the public can buy in on the first day of trading, the price may have soared. It will probably go down pretty fast, too, and you won't get any warning.

Options and futures. How can you play in the market without even owning stock? You can make bets by buying and selling stock options and futures, which are speculations on whether the market will rise or fall a specific amount. You can speculate on the movement of the market as a whole or with individual stocks. Catch: unless you're a very experienced money person—or you have a crystal ball—this isn't for you.

Commodity futures. Futures fall into group categories: grains, foods, meats, oils, precious metals, industrial metals, woods and fibers, financial issues, and stock indexes. The rules and terminology differ from those for trading in stocks. Catch: extremely high risk. Most trades result in losses.

GETTING OUT

When is it time to sell? If we knew the answer to this, we wouldn't be writing books and advising clients in public relations and investments, we'd be sitting on a beach and sipping colorful rum drinks. If you want a warranty with your purchase, buy a refrigerator, not a stock.

The most sophisticated financial analysts spend a great deal of their time trying to figure out market timing: when to get in and—probably more important—when to get out. We founded our investment club when the market was soaring. For months, everything we bought went up. When the inevitable reversal came and the market was down for a while, all we could think about was how many months it had taken to build our profit, and now we were losing it! Marilyn reminded us we were in for the long run. We had to look at the whole picture before panicking. If the market or economy is down as a whole, the problem isn't the stock.

If there is a problem you believe is correctable, hang in. If the stock drops more than 15 to 20 percent of its purchase price and you believe in the company, review the stock-purchasing guidelines. If the company still qualifies, don't sell. If the price has gone down, it might be time to buy more.

If you love a stock that's gone down, ask your accountant whether you can use a tax loss. You can deduct a loss against your income up to $3,000 a year (and losses in excess of $3,000 can be "carried forward" to use in a future year). Sell whatever stock you can in order to realize just that amount of loss—and then buy it back. You can't take the loss unless you wait thirty-one days to repurchase the stock. You can make a similar move with a mutual fund and (as we've mentioned before) with a municipal bond.

On the other hand, if waves of people are selling off, you can't just assume you're right and they're wrong. Investigate. Has management changed? Is there a fundamental problem, like a bad earnings report or a product recall? Then don't wait for more bad news. Sell. Marry a person, not a stock.

Two myths keep people hanging on in the market:

Myth No. 1: "The stock will come back soon, and the only way to get it back is to hold on."

Myth No. 2: "Until I sell, I haven't taken the loss." By holding on, you may be in for an even bigger loss. Besides, remember that when your stock drops from, say, $100 to $50, it has to go up more than 100 percent just to get back to your starting point. That's a big challenge.

Some money market managers discipline themselves to sell any stock—no matter how much they believe in it—when it goes down a certain percentage of the purchase price. In a month, they either buy it back or go on to something else.

If a stock looks shaky, consider placing a *stop-loss order*. Don't confuse this with a sell-limit order, which is meant to maximize your gains. A stop-loss order is a technique used in a declining market to protect your profit and limit your losses. Ask your broker to tell you at what level the stock has price support and set your stop-loss order accordingly. It's usually 10 to 15 percent below whatever the stock is now selling for—so for a $45 stock, the stop-loss might be set at $40. If the stock falls, your order is activated.

Normally, your order is considered a market sell order: in other words, you are willing to take the best price available. However, if there is a stampede to sell the stock, your shares may not come up for sale until the price has dropped to $38. If you want to prevent a bargain basement sale, you can set a *stop-limit order* of a certain minimum below which you refuse to sell. Yes, you're still holding the stock, but you may plan to hold until the market corrects itself.

Adjust the level of your stop-loss periodically, and take care not to set it too close to a stock price. Our club made this mistake. There was a small setback, the market declined for a day or two, and then it went back up. By that time we were already out of our stock. We tried to learn from that experience, as from all others, without dwelling on it.

I have an expression that I live by: You can look back, but don't stare.—Judith Ripka

MUTUAL FUNDS: LET THE PROS DO IT

You shouldn't be in individual stocks unless you have the money to diversify. People who bet the farm on one stock often lose their principal, take it personally, and never go back. If you can't afford 100 shares apiece of eight to ten different issues, and/or you're a beginner at investing, go with the mutual funds. A mutual fund is simply a group of stocks and/or bonds or a combination of the two, chosen by a professional manager with a particular investment goal—growth, income, or a combination of the two. There are many advantages to investing in a fund:

You have an expert working for you. Mutual fund managers who run funds spend their days staying on top of the financial news and networking with other professionals. They are courted by investment bankers who pitch them new offerings that an individual investor wouldn't hear about. They're not right all the time, but they usually do better than a nonexpert.

You can diversify with limited capital. If there's trouble with a particular issue, a good manager not only knows when and how to head for the exit, she also knows the best place to relocate. While an individual is told to divide her portfolio among eight to ten or, better yet, fifteen to twenty individual stocks, a mutual fund may own from fifty to a hundred. That kind of diversity minimizes risk.

You can invest relatively small amounts. To purchase certain bonds, you might need a $25,000 minimum. Though there are some mutual funds that require a $25,000 investment, there are thousands that will let you get in for $1,000 and hundreds that ask only for $250 or less. Some let you get in for as little as $50 if you agree to make automatic ongoing investments.

Unlike bonds, bond funds provide an income flow monthly, not just twice a year. Because the manager is buying in quantity, he or she may also get a better discount—which translates into a better yield.

How mutual funds work

A mutual fund is created by a sponsor—a bank, an insurance company, or a brokerage firm. It hires a manager, deals with the legal work, gets clearance from the Securities and Exchange Commission, and advertises the fund.

The manager has considerable discretion, within the guidelines of the fund's objective. Even if the goal is growth, a manager doesn't have to be fully invested in the stock market at every moment; he might decide to hold a certain amount of cash in reserve until the timing is right.

There are two types of mutual funds. In an *open-end fund* you can put in money and take it out at any time. (Usually you must make a minimum investment of $500 or $1,000 that buys you a certain number of shares.) The price per share is determined by the net asset value (NAV): the total value of all the securities the fund holds, minus their costs, divided by the number of shares that have been issued. *Closed-end funds* are traded like stock, so a share may cost you a premium or be available at a discount.

Once you're in the fund, when any stocks pay dividends or are sold at a profit, you are paid your share on a monthly, quarterly, or yearly basis. Bond funds pay monthly. You may spend or reinvest your earnings.

CHOOSING THE TYPE OF FUND

A fund may hold stocks, bonds, or both. A bond fund may hold government securities, corporate bonds, or Ginnie Maes. Some hold only AAA-rated securities of a particular type (such as corporate or municipal). Some invest in overseas companies; some invest in stock in a particular sector (such as utilities). The funds range from high-risk to low-risk.

The basic rules of asset allocation apply in picking a fund. Choose according to your investment objective and risk tolerance. Although there are thousands of funds, all of them generally have one of the following four objectives:

Long-term growth. Aggressive growth funds, made up of stocks of companies that pay low dividends (because they plow money back into their own growth) can do very well in a terrific market and lose big in a downturn. From 1983 to 1993 the average stock fund gained 223 percent. The top performer gained 637 percent and the worst lost 63 percent. However, if you can leave your money alone for five or ten years, this is probably your best bet.

Growth with some income. If you've got children approaching college age but a number of years until you retire, you'll want some money invested conservatively and some invested for growth. You should chose a combination of bond and stock funds, "balanced" or growth and income funds that invest in both, or funds that invest in stocks with relatively high dividends.

Income with some growth. The closer you are to retirement, the more conservative you will probably become. You may lean toward funds that are made up entirely of bonds, or have a few stocks, or have the kinds of stocks that pay relatively high dividends, such as utilities.

Income and capital preservation. Money market or short-term bond funds are for holding your money for a brief period, say under three years.

The New York Times regularly tracks the performances of mutual funds and divides them into the following categories. Other publications use similar though not identical categories.

Domestic general stock funds. Ten categories include funds grouped by size (small, medium, and large) and by type (growth stocks, value stocks, or a blend of growth and value).

Domestic specialized stock funds. Nine categories grouped by type of industry: communications, financial, health, natural resources, precious metals, real estate, technology, utilities, and others.

International stock funds. Nine categories grouped by geographical location such as foreign (includes no U.S. stocks), world (includes some U.S. stocks), Europe, Pacific (including or excluding Japan), Japan, diverse emerging markets, and Latin America.

General corporate funds. Three categories grouped by maturity: long-term, short-term, and intermediate-term.

Government bond funds. Funds issued by the federal government: three categories grouped by maturity (long-, short-, and intermediate-term).

Specialized bond funds. Five categories grouped by specialty: convertibles (bonds of corporations that convert to stock); ultrashort-term (bonds that pay off very quickly); high-yield (otherwise known as "junk") bonds; multisector (varied industries); international.

Municipal bond funds. Five categories grouped by maturity: long-, short-, and intermediate-term.

RESEARCHING THE FUNDS

Forbes and *Business Week* do comprehensive annual reports in September and February, respectively. *Money* reports on funds (usually no-load) periodically, and *The Wall Street Journal* does a weekly review. *Barron's*, the financial publication, prints Lipper Analytical Services' mutual fund performance data every quarter. The library may have back issues of these publications.

Morningstar Mutual Funds, a bible of the industry, tracks more than 1,000 funds, rates them against others, tells what the fund holds, advises of any recent changes, and tracks the fund's performance versus the S&P 500 and other benchmarks in very clear language. It comes in notebook form with insertable pages and is updated regularly. You can subscribe (800-876-5005) or use a library copy. *Value Line's Mutual Fund* survey is a similar reference.

Get the prospectus of any fund that interests you (often you can get a number from the toll-free information line 800-555-1212) and/or discuss the fund with your broker.

Criteria for a fund

- Long-term performance. Don't look at a single quarter, because that can be misleading. What's important is performance over the past one, five, and ten years. Find this under "Financial Highlights" in the front of the prospectus or "Performance" in the fund's annual report. The fund's performance may be compared to measures such as the Standard & Poor's 500-stock index and to similar funds in the category—"small cap," "growth," or "sector." Look for consistency: How many years has the fund finished with a loss? How it has performed in up markets and down markets? How does that compare to other, similar funds?

  Funds without a track record may not be a good bet because you cannot judge how a manager has performed in both up and down markets.
- Manager. Avoid a fund whose manager has been in place less than three years or is leaving. When you buy a fund, what you're really buying is the fund manager's expertise.
- Holdings. If they are in value stocks, the fund should be buying stocks that are paying dividends and that have a low P/E ratio. A growth fund should be full of stocks that are producing terrific earnings. Some funds that sound relatively low-risk—"income" or "balanced" funds—may in fact invest in high-risk securities such as high-yield bonds.

- Fees or load and operating expenses. You will often hear funds referred to as *load* or *no-load,* which refers to whether or not you pay a sales charge on a purchase. A *low-load* (under 3 percent) fund may call itself either a low- or no-load fund. The first section of the prospectus tells whether or not you pay this charge at first and/or on reinvested dividends, whether you pay exchange fees if you switch from one fund to another in a family of funds, and whether you pay redemption fees, also called back-end loads, when you leave. Sometimes these slide downward from, say, 5 percent to nothing at all in five years.

  Sometimes you have a choice of A, B, or C shares. On A shares, you pay the commission up front. On B and C shares, you pay only exit and other fees. B and C shares differ depending upon how you pay for them, but generally A shares cost more up front but are a better deal in the long run, B are next best, and C are third.

  Operating expenses, listed in the second section of the prospectus, include management fees, which can range from .25 to 1.0 percent, depending on the type of bond, and legal and accounting fees (1 percent). Some funds, even no-load funds, may include a 12b-1 fee, a marketing and advertising cost of up to 1 percent.

  You will find a determination of how the fees would affect a hypothetical $1,000 investment, assuming a 5 percent rate of return and dollar cost if you redeem at the end of one, five, and ten years.
- Total return. This reflects not only dividends but also changes in the fund's share price. Capital gains and dividend income are included in the NAV until they are paid out.
- Anything in capital letters. No kidding. This is a warning. If you don't understand what you're being warned about, ask the fund or your financial advisor to explain.

MAKING A MUTUAL FUND PORTFOLIO

Remember: diversifying reduces risk. If you own at least four different categories of mutual funds, your investment is 78 percent less risky than if you owned a single mutual fund. One possible combination:

Two or more stock funds. One growth, one value, and one aggressive growth, small company, total return, or emerging markets.

A global fund. A mix of U.S. and overseas investments or overseas only.

An intermediate-term bond fund. Government or high-rated bonds.

NO-BRAINER ALTERNATIVES

Index funds. Since some funds didn't do so well compared to the market's performance as a whole—measured by the Dow Jones Industrial Average or Standard & Poor's 500-stock index—investors were recently drawn to index funds, a group of stocks or bonds put together to mimic the behavior of either a broad index like the S&P 500 stock index or a specialty index (which concentrates on transportation stocks, small-company stocks, and so on). Managers don't have to supervise or trade the stocks in these funds: they buy them and leave them in place. Though as a result the transaction costs and management fees are relatively low compared to other funds, the existence of the costs means that index funds will always make slightly less money than the stocks they include.

Unit investment trusts (UITs). These are like samplers of different stocks or bonds (usually municipals or Ginnie Maes) or a combination of both, available in units of $1,000. There is also a fee, but it's lower than a mutual fund fee. All the securities bought by the trust are supposed to be held until the trust expires, a period that may range from six months to thirty years. The UIT pays a steady monthly, quarterly, or semi-annual income. Catch: if the trust paid a premium for high-yield bonds that are later called, there's a capital loss in the trust. To make up the difference, the trust managers may tie up the money in non-income-producing zero coupon bonds. If you need cash and have to sell, the resale market is limited and you may take a loss. However, if you hold these to maturity, you'll always get your money out.

A wrap account. For a fee based on your assets, your broker helps you determine your needs and desires regarding asset allocation and risk and, with money managers outside the firm and/or outside mutual funds, develops a plan that is monitored quarterly and reallocated as needed.

FINAL SUGGESTIONS REGARDING MUTUAL FUNDS

- Buy from a family of funds. Families are created when an investment company manages a group of diversified funds that includes at least one stock fund, a fixed-income fund, and a money market fund. Large families will probably offer many options. If you decide to move from, say, an aggressive growth fund to something more conservative, you can easily switch among "brothers and sisters" and often pay no fee. The better-known "families," which may offer dozens of funds, include AIM, Alliance, American, MFS, Oppenheimer, and Putnam, which are load funds, and T. Rowe Price, Scudder, Strong, and Vanguard, which are no-load. Fidelity has both load and no-load funds.
- Check on how your fund is doing periodically. Call, using the toll-free number that probably appears on all the literature. You can find out where the fund is (up or down, in percentage) for the year. Or check the financial pages. *The New York Times* and *The Wall Street Journal,* for example, track mutual fund performance in detail. Funds with fewer than 1,000 shareholders or less than $25 million in assets may not be listed, but most others will be.
- Stay with the fund for three to four years before considering a switch. The quarterly report on mutual funds from *Barron's* has a table called "Averages by Group." Compare your fund's performance to the performance of its competitors. If it's more than 20 percent behind its competitors, get out.
- Keep all the statements from your fund in a folder marked with the name of the fund. When you sell it, your tax accountant will have to figure out your average cost per share, including all the reinvestments.
- Invest regularly, and reinvest your dividends. You'll see your money grow faster than you can imagine.

I began investing in mutual funds because (a) a professional was in charge of my assets, (b) I could make small investments regularly, and (c) I didn't have to know very much, which suited me fine. Then, one day, someone asked me what stocks my mutual funds held. I couldn't name a single one. Investigating the portfolio of one of my mutual funds was a launch pad to my self-education. I read about each company, and I learned a great deal as I did. When I started the same process with another of my funds, I realized that the two of them held similar stock. I was less diversified than I had thought. As a result I began to search out more and different opportunities. I feel as if mutual fund investing helped me learn one baby step at a time—and my money was growing all the while.—"Nadine Carpenter," 45, social worker, married, two children

ONGOING STRATEGIES

If you're serious about investing, as we have become, you will continue to learn and grow. As you become more and more involved, these activities will seem less like obligations and more like pleasure.

Keep reading. Reading helps demystify the investing process.

- Read the financial page of at least one daily paper. If you're going to read only one, the most balanced is *The Wall Street Journal*, which we mentioned as a research source. It also gives you national and international stories, human interest, and tax and economic trends. *Investor's Business Daily* is excellent for straight financial news and graphics.
- Magazines that a beginner can start with are *Smart Money* and *Money*. Then move on to *Worth*. There's a lot of good reporting in *Business Week*, *Forbes*, *Financial World*, and *Fortune*.
- In addition to Standard & Poor's and Value Line, you can get nuts-and-bolts information from Moody's Investor Services and Morningstar. If you find a subscription too expensive, check these out at the library.
- There are dozens of financial newsletters. Test-read them and see which you prefer.
- If you have an account with a large brokerage firm, you may also receive its newsletter, which includes its analysts' recommendations for best buys.

- Also, keep your TV tuned to CNBC as often as possible. Watch the business news on any channel, especially CNN. *Wall Street Week,* hosted by Louis Rukeyser on PBS, consistently showcases Wall Street analysts and portfolio managers in their areas of expertise.

Get yourself a reputable stockbroker and/or fee-based financial advisor.

Go to seminars. Take adult education courses at the Y or a nearby school, and go to those offered free by brokerage houses.

Join an investment club. Or start one. You'll have the motivation and support to become a much more educated investor, make wonderful new friends, and make your future more secure—all at the same time.

CHAPTER 5

SAVING FOR THE FUTURE

Retirement Planning

My friend was talking about how much effort we put into taking care of ourselves at midlife. "We watch our weight, and we don't smoke, and we exercise regularly," she said. "And now I'm worried that I'm going to outlive my money."—Jane Bishop Shalam

In ads aimed at people of retirement age, a handsome, silver-haired couple strolls along a beach or golf course, seemingly without a care. But for those of us whose retirement is years away, the picture may not be as rosy:

- Only one third of today's workers are covered by a traditional defined-benefit pension plan, where the employer guarantees a certain, fixed monthly income during retirement. Most of us will depend on a plan primarily funded by ourselves with a payout that is uncertain.
- Social Security won't be the security blanket it once was. Today's benefits, which are already just one third an average worker's wages, are likely to decrease, and the qualifying age is increasing. Some experts speculate that the Social Security Administration will run out of

money entirely in 2030. Even if the situation isn't quite so gloomy, payments may be denied to those who are financially well off. While that may not be devastating, it does mean that people who retire in the future will have less of a financial cushion than today's affluent seniors.

- Your nest may not become a nest egg. When all the baby boomers decide to retire (at more or less the same time) and sell their homes to scale down or move elsewhere, who will the buyers be? With the aging of the population, there will be more would-be sellers than buyers, and the younger generation is finding it hard to put together a down payment. Instead of moving to a beach or golf course community, you might be forced to stay where you are.
- If you were among the many who deferred parenthood until your thirties and forties, you may still be writing college tuition checks and/or supporting adult children in your sixties. Many children are moving back home after college, unable to find work in a tight job market.
- You may be supporting elderly parents. The average married couple in the "sandwich generation" already has more living parents than children. Experts predict a big increase in the number of vertical families, with several generations sitting around the table. Your mother and father may need long-term financial support to sustain their extended life expectancy or cover special medical care.
- You will have to finance many years of your own old age. The average sixty-year-old woman can reasonably expect to live another twenty-five years. To be cautious, you should assume that you will live longer than 85 percent of the people your age, so a fifty-year-old man should be prepared to support himself to age ninety, and a fifty-year-old woman until age ninety-four. Yet in the year 2000, some 19 million women will lack adequate pension funds for retirement.

I saw the wisdom of thinking ahead when I needed some financial help. My parents were able to give me the support I needed precisely because they had planned for the future.— Audrey Landau

If you are just ten years or so from retirement, your best strategy is to put the maximum pretax money into your retirement fund or savings plan and as much as you can of after-tax money into a tax-deferred plan, such as an annuity, where it can grow and you can leave the principal intact. In some cases, you may be able to avoid paying the accumulated taxes until age eighty-five.

You should also be planning where you will live at retirement. Many women are trapped in a house that's too big and expensive to run because they didn't move when they were physically and psychologically more capable. Consider places where the cost of living is low and state taxes are low or nonexistent.

Many people plan to get by with pension funds and Social Security alone. Together, these typically replace only 40 to 60 percent of wages. Besides, if pensions don't have a built-in cost of living adjustment, they may be decimated by inflation. By one estimate, a thirty-five-year-old who manages on $40,000 today will need $109,000 to live the same way at age sixty-five. Yet the average person is putting aside as little as a tenth to one half of what is needed to build a retirement fund.

Starting early makes an astonishing difference. If one woman invests just $2,000 a year from age nineteen to twenty-six, a total of seven years, and if her money compounds at 10 percent a year, she'll have $1,035,160 at age sixty. If another puts the same $2,000 per year away at the same rate of return from age twenty-seven to sixty-five, a total of thirty-eight years, she'll have just $883,185.

Since we got this information, those club members with adult children have tried to drive this point home to them. But we have also learned that you don't have to start in your twenties to see your money grow significantly.

> *When I divorced my husband twelve years ago, I began to put $2,000 a year into an IRA. Now I've got $50,000. My nest egg gives me more security than any relationship ever did.*—"Francine Small," 45, administrative assistant, single

WHAT YOU'LL NEED FOR RETIREMENT

We were having a routine meeting with our accountant, and I asked what exactly had been put aside for our future. When I heard the answer, I nearly *fainted. My husband's entire "retirement planning" was a single IRA account with a total of $8,000 in it. Yet all along he'd been telling me, "It's all been taken care of." Every woman had better find out what exactly "it" is, and just how it has been taken care of.*—"Martha Sandberg," 40, housewife, married, two children

In Chapter 3 you were asked to calculate your current living expenses. If you were to retire within the next few years, your spending patterns might go up and/or down in the following ways:

HOUSE/UTILITIES

Up or down. Condominium fees, real estate taxes, and/or insurance rates may rise with inflation. Electricity and heating/air conditioning may rise if you spend more time at home. Telephone costs will all be at your expense. But you may pay off your mortgage or move to less expensive quarters.

TRANSPORTATION

Up or down. You may use your car more often, and/or both spouses may need cars. But commuting expenses will vanish.

PERSONAL EXPENSES

Up or down. You may spend more on vacations or travel. But business clothes expenses will go down.

MEDICAL EXPENSES

Up. The combination of aging and lack of employer-provided low-cost insurance may drive costs up. Also, some medications and procedures may not be covered.

MISCELLANEOUS HOUSEHOLD

Up. You may need help with maintenance, cleaning chores, possibly with personal tasks.

PET CARE

Up. Your pet is getting older, too.

INSURANCE

Up or down. You may need continuing coverage for income replacement and estate taxes. Term life insurance premiums may escalate; but at some point you may cut back the face amount, cancel the policy, or convert to whole life.

INCOME TAXES

Down. But if you continue to work and haven't yet turned seventy, some or all earnings will be taxed.

To calculate what it would cost to live on your own, use the numbers you gathered in Chapter 3 but omit expenses that relate directly to your husband, such as personal expenses plus medical bills, car payments, dues, and business-related expenses. With those exceptions, if you stayed in the same home, your living costs would remain much the same.

The usual assumption is that you will need 80 percent of your current after-tax income to support yourself after retirement. If you made an 8 percent return on your investments, you'd need $375,000 to earn $30,000 and $625,000 to generate $50,000. But that's not taking inflation into account. If you're making 8 percent, but inflation is growing at 4 percent, you're losing half your return. Your nest egg must be twice as big—$750,000 or $1.2 million for the $30,000 or $50,000 you're trying to earn. Since investment returns vary and tax laws change, the numbers need occasional recalculation. You'll need the help of an accountant to work out the numbers that apply in your case. Whatever they are, you'll probably find them surprisingly large. Where will you get that much?

Retirement income comes from four main sources:

- Your savings and investments
- Social Security
- Company-sponsored or self-employed retirement fund
- Annuities or nonqualified (tax-deferred) plans

RETIREMENT SOURCE NO. 1: PERSONAL SAVINGS AND INVESTMENTS

Total your current assets and liabilities, using the worksheet below.

CALCULATING YOUR WORTH

Item	*You*	*Spouse*	*Joint*	*Total*
		ASSETS		
Savings accounts	______	______	______	______
Checking accounts	______	______	______	______
CDs and savings bonds	______	______	______	______
Notes and accounts receivable (Personal loans)	______	______	______	______
Brokerage accounts (Use monthly statements.)	______	______	______	______
Other stocks/ mutual funds (Certificates not in street name)	______	______	______	______
Bonds (Municipal or other bonds not in street name, savings bonds)	______	______	______	______

Item	*You*	*Spouse*	*Joint*	*Total*
Retirement benefits (Statements from insurance company, mutual fund, or bank)				
Employee benefits Company stock options or deferred compensation (Get information from Human Resources.)				
Life insurance policies (Cash value of whole life, variable, and/or universal life insurance)				
House and other real estate (There is a charge for a broker appraisal, but you can ask for a "comp price" from any broker to see what other, similar houses are selling for. Also check the real estate listings				

Item	*You*	*Spouse*	*Joint*	*Total*
for prices of similar properties.)	______	______	______	______
Stock options (What do you hold, and when must they be exercised?)	______	______	______	______
Tangibles (Furniture, art, automobiles, jewelry, piano, sterling silver. Riders on property insurance may indicate appraised value; or pay for appraisal by a *licensed* appraiser.)	______	______	______	______
Business interests (What are assets of the partnership that you would get at retirement, proceeds from any business succession plans, and so forth?)	______	______	______	______
Total Assets	______	______	______	______

Item	*You*	*Spouse*	*Joint*	*Total*
DEBTS				
Real estate mortgages (What is the remaining principal? Should the mortgage be refinanced or paid off?)	______	______	______	______
Bank loans/notes (What percentage are you paying for the life of the loan?)	______	______	______	______
Loans on insurance policies	______	______	______	______
Unpaid income taxes	______	______	______	______
Unpaid credit card accounts (It might be cheaper to pay them all off with a home equity loan, which charges lower interest rates.)	______	______	______	______
Total Debts	______	______	______	______

Subtract the debts from the assets. That number is the beginning of your retirement nest egg.

RETIREMENT SOURCE NO. 2: SOCIAL SECURITY

If you work, you make a contribution to Social Security out of every paycheck. Once you've worked forty quarters (three-month periods), or a total of ten years—even if you've had periods of unemployment or taken time off to raise the kids—you're eligible for Social Security benefits when you reach the qualifying age.

Find out what you will be entitled to. Call 800-772-1213 and follow the instructions to get information regarding a personal statement of your earnings and future Social Security benefits, and you'll be sent a form. Once you complete and return it, you'll get a Personal Earnings and Benefit Estimate Statement. It will show what your monthly retirement Social Security check will be in today's dollars if you take early retirement, if you wait until you qualify for full retirement, or if you postpone retirement to age seventy. (The form also gives information about disability benefits and survivor's benefits your family will receive if you die.) The calculations assume your wages will rise at the rate of the national average, about 1 percent per year above inflation.

The arithmetic is based on your past earnings records, which you'll see on the printout. As you may already know, the government makes mistakes. Make sure its numbers agree with your records so you can get what you're entitled to. Do it now, since after three years records generally cannot be corrected. To be cautious, request and check the statement every three to four years.

When I married my second husband, he went to my employer and arranged to have me paid as a consultant rather than an employee. The money went into a corporate account that my husband used to pay our household bills for eighteen years—until we were divorced. I learned that as a result of my husband's arrangement, nothing had been credited to my Social Security account for eighteen years. Today, I work two jobs, seven days a week. I'm terrified because I know that one of them will force me to retire at sixty-five.—Nancy Silverman, 61, arts consultant, divorced, two grown children

The qualifying age for Social Security, which for years was sixty-five, will be going up a few months per year until it reaches sixty-seven in the year 2027 (or possibly before, according to some rumors from Washington). At one time, you got 80 percent of your benefits if you retired at sixty-two, but that number is sliding down to 70 percent in 2011. For each year you delay retirement until age seventy, your total benefits are increased. By 2008 this increase will rise to a maximum additional 8% to your yearly social security benefits.

Earning over a certain limit can reduce your benefits by as much as half under age sixty-five. The limit is raised until it disappears at age seventy.

Even if you have not worked yourself, didn't work long enough to qualify, or qualified for an amount worth less than half your husband's entitlement, if your husband qualifies you are probably entitled to 50 percent of his benefits at age sixty-five and 37.5 percent at age sixty-two. If you are widowed by someone who qualified or were married for at least ten years to someone who qualifies, you may also be able to collect, depending on your present age and marital situation. Both an ex-wife and a current wife may collect at the same time.

In any case, if your earnings were more than your spouse's (or ex-spouse's), and the amount to which you'd be entitled is more than 50 percent of what he would be entitled to, you will get the higher amount. To receive a pamphlet called "What Every Woman Should Know About Social Security" and/or ask specific questions about your entitlement, call 800-772-1213.

RETIREMENT SOURCE NO. 3: COMPANY OR SELF-EMPLOYED PLAN

In any of these plans, you put money aside before you're taxed on it and it grows without being taxed. Taxes are deducted only when you withdraw it. Withdrawals are permitted starting at age fifty-nine and a half and compulsory at seventy and a half or (in the case of a non-IRA) the April after you retire, whichever is later. Theoretically, when you begin your withdrawals you'll be retired and in a lower tax bracket, so your money will be subject to less taxes.

These plans are not an investment but rather a means of investment. Once they are established, the money you contribute is used to buy investments like stocks, bonds, mutual funds, or CDs.

EMPLOYER DEFINED-BENEFIT PLANS

At one time, more than 90 percent of large firms paid pensions to any employee who retired at fifty-five or older after having been with the company for a certain minimum period, usually ten to fifteen years. The employer funded the plan and guaranteed a certain monthly payment at retirement based on your salary and how long you'd worked—your benefit was defined. These plans are going the way of the panty girdle.

When a company offers a defined-benefit plan, after very few years you may be *vested*—in other words, the money your employer contributed is yours to keep—but at that point the dollar value is very small. If you change jobs frequently, over a period of years you may build up vesting with several employers, but you would have built up much more if you'd stayed in one place. That's why you have to look beyond the salary when you think about changing jobs, as one friend belatedly discovered:

> *You think the retirement plans you are offered will add up, but that's not so. After I was partially vested in my first job, I left to take another job at a higher salary. I got only a tiny, tiny amount of money from the pension fund. Then I changed jobs again, this time for a salary increase of $10,000. Because I hadn't yet been vested in the second firm, I got nothing at all. If I could do it all over again, I'd have stayed in the first job and put more in the retirement fund. Over the long run, the raises don't add up to anything. But the retirement fund can be huge.*— Jennifer Balbier, 47, cosmetics executive, single

Once you are vested, if you change jobs you may be able to freeze the amount in your pension fund, leave the money in place, and collect the pension at the appropriate age. The company notifies the Social Security

Administration, which may surprise you with news of long-forgotten pensions years later.

You may also put the money into your new employer's pension plan. If you're comparing the two plans, gauge how secure they are by asking the benefits office what percentage of the plan is funded. In other words, if it had to pay everyone off today, how much could it pay? If the answer isn't 100 percent, the plan is somewhat risky. Also, the less diversified the plan's holdings, the more risk is involved.

If you're not entirely happy with either plan, a third alternative is to move the money into a rollover IRA (see page 166). Do not take personal possession of the money for more than sixty days, or it may be considered a withdrawal. Certainly do not spend it. Altogether, penalties and taxes may reduce your investment by 30 percent or more. We were amazed to learn that only about 20 percent of people leave their retirement fund intact when they leave a job, and most will eventually regret it.

I was still in college when I started working for my former employer, and after twenty years, I decided I needed a break. I cashed in my pension to go on "Annie's Big Adventure." After penalties and taxes were deducted, I still had more cash than I'd ever seen all at once. I thought of it as "free money" and I bought some nice clothes, went on a cruise, and got a new car. Once I went back to work, I had to build my retirement from scratch. Now I realize that if I'd left the money in place, I'd have accumulated thousands and thousands of dollars for the future. I've only got a fraction of that, and I'll never make it up.— "Annie Deaver," 50, beauty supplies saleswoman, married, no children

If you leave and then return to a company within a certain time frame, you may be able to keep your pension intact. You may also be able to put in just 501 hours of part-time work annually to keep the pension growing. But if the formula for a pension depends on your last year of work, you may not want a part-time salary to be the basis for calculation.

If your husband is offered a plan with a survivor's benefit that passes to you on his death, it may not be in your best interests to accept.

When my husband was offered his government pension, we went over the options very carefully. Without a survivor's benefit, the payments to him were larger: men have shorter life expectancies, and the company would be paying for a briefer period. It made more sense for him to elect the larger amount, which gave us enough extra to buy a life insurance policy that provided even more income than the survivor's benefit.—Carol Safir

On the other hand, if the marriage falls apart, you may regret this choice.

We, too, decided to forgo the survivor's benefits for a larger pension. And when we got divorced a few years later, I discovered that decision was irrevocable. I wound up with no rights to the money.—"Janet Brody," 47, kindergarten teacher, married, two children

If the company goes bankrupt, the Pension Benefit Guaranty Corporation, a government agency, will step in with some protection. Even if your spouse dies before retiring and the company subsequently fails, you may have some benefits. But the real danger in a defined-benefit plan isn't bankruptcy. It's the likelihood that the plan doesn't have a cost of living increase or adjustments for inflation. Twenty years ago, a guaranteed monthly income of $2,000 may have seemed like a comfortable amount to live on. Less than twenty years ago, a postage stamp cost 15 cents. Today, the price has more than doubled.

EMPLOYER DEFINED-CONTRIBUTION PLANS

Most commonly today, employees are offered defined-contribution plans, which allow you to earmark a certain amount of money for investment that is sheltered from taxes until you take it out at retirement. Your employer may match a percentage of your contribution. What you contribute to these plans is always yours to take away, but whether or not you can take the employer's contribution as well depends on when you are vested.

The plans fall into two basic categories. The rarer of the two is a money purchase plan, which commits you to put aside the same amount per year—as much as 25 percent of pretax income to a maximum of $30,000. More common is a profit-sharing plan, which lets you vary the amount—up to 15 percent of your pretax income to an effective maximum of $22,500.

There are special plans for federal employees (federal thrift savings plans), for state and local employees (Section 457 plans), and for employees of nonprofit, charitable, religious, or educational organizations. The most common type of defined-contribution profit-sharing plan in the United States is a 401(k), which is offered by many employers. About 23 million people were participants as of fall 1996.

How the 401(k) works

Though the 401(k) is called a profit-sharing plan, it has nothing to do with the firm's profit. A certain percentage of your salary is deducted from your paycheck and put into a retirement fund. Though you do pay Social Security on the amount you defer, you pay no income tax on it until you take it out. Since the money you put away grows without being taxed, you will have more money in your pocket in the future.

Your employer can put money into your plan approaching or equaling what you put in. If you put in $1 and your employer matches it with 50 cents, you have earned 50 percent on your dollar instantly. Short of winning the lottery, you can't match those odds anywhere.

In most cases, you may begin to contribute to a 401(k) once you are twenty-one and have worked for your employer for either a full year or 1,000 hours within a twelve-month period. If you move from a division in a company where the plan isn't available to a division where it is, you get credit for all your time served. Your personal contribution is vested immediately.

The law requires that vesting begin after three years of service and that 100 percent vesting must take place after seven years. If a company is top-heavy with highly paid employees, the government tries to spread the good fortune around and requires that vesting in those companies begin after only two years and that employees be 100 percent vested after only six years.

In a few cases, mainly affecting unionized workers at very large corporations, vesting may go more slowly than the norm.

THE SIZE OF YOUR CONTRIBUTION

You can choose the dollar or percentage amount you want to contribute, up to a legal limit. For tax year 1997, that limit was $9,500. The figure is indexed to inflation, so it will change each year. Companies may set maximum and minimum limits of their own. There are additional limits for HCEs, "highly compensated employees." (The government determines the size of the salary that qualifies someone as an HCE. The figure is adjusted for inflation.) If at the end of the year the contributions of HCEs exceed their limit as a group, a portion of their contributions may be refunded and become taxable.

You may initially believe that you can't afford to make the maximum contribution you are allowed. Don't forget that what you're looking at is a pretax figure that amounts to much less once taxes are deducted. In other words, the $50 a week you could put away before taxes may amount to only $30 or so in after-tax spending money.

The biggest mistake you can make with a 401(k) is not participating. Even if you're saving for college tuition, it makes sense to put the money away in a 401(k). The money grows faster because it's tax-deferred, and you can borrow from the 401(k) for tuition payments. The second biggest mistake is not contributing the maximum. Only 5 percent do. But if you want to produce 80 percent of current income at retirement, you must have every penny working for you. A third mistake is to reduce your contributions.

In one wonderful year, my pension investments made 30 percent. I thought I could pick the hot manager and the hot investment to achieve my goals. So the next year I cut back on my contributions. And guess what? Between my saving less and my investment's indifferent results, in the past year my fund hasn't grown a penny.—"Helen Williams," 50, television production company executive, married, two children

If both you and your spouse have a 401(k), each should contribute the maximum, if possible. You'd each have a claim to the other's plan in the event of divorce. The point of contributing to both is simply to maximize the size of your retirement fund. But if you choose to put money into one plan only, get the better deal based on how much you can contribute, how much the company will match, where the better investment choices are, and where the employer's contribution will vest the most quickly.

Of course, if your investments go down, you may lose money. But if your employer matches your contributions, your losses are somewhat offset. And you can keep your risk low by diversifying and/or putting the money into a conservative investment.

INVESTMENT HELP FROM YOUR COMPANY

The company sponsoring the plan runs it with the assistance of the trustee, which is the group or committee that oversees the plan; the plan administrator, who handles the day-to-day activities; and the investment manager, an outside firm that buys and sells the investments.

Many companies with older plans try to comply with the law established for newer 404(c) plans, which limit the company's liability for any losses if employees are allowed to control their investments and helped to make informed decisions.

As an employee you must be given complete information about how the plan works and what your options are; copies of the prospectus of each investment option; information about fees and expenses for changing, buying, or selling investments; the current annual report; and a statement of your account. You are entitled to ask for a great deal more, including financial statements and information concerning the value of shares you already own and those that are available to you.

The law allows you to change the type and size of your investments quarterly, and the plan must offer at least three very diverse investment choices, such as a money market fund, a stock fund, and a fixed-income bond fund or *guaranteed investment contract (GIC)*.

GICs are also known as stable-value funds, fixed-income funds, capital preservation funds, or guaranteed funds. Because they are very conservative, GICs are the most commonly chosen investment option, but they haven't the same growth potential as an investment in stocks. Issued by an insurance company, a GIC usually charges higher fees than a fixed-income bond fund and produces returns comparable to a CD's. Since the "guarantee" in a GIC is only as good as the credit of the insurance company that issues it, before you buy, check the company's credit rating with one of the insurance rating companies (see page 175). A BIC is like a GIC but issued by a bank and insured for up to $100,000.

Most companies let you make your own investment choices without restriction. Few will require you to invest on an all-or-nothing basis or will limit how much you can put in a particular investment. If there is no investment option that especially appeals to you, choose the most conservative one. If your employer matches your contributions, there's virtually no way you can lose.

A booklet called "Protecting Your Pension" spells out the rules for pension plans, how to find out if they're being followed, how to find out if the money is being invested wisely, and what to do if you think there are problems. Request it from the Department of Labor, Pension and Welfare Benefits Administration, 200 Constitution Avenue N.W., Room N5625, Washington, DC 20210, or call 202-219-9247.

TAKING THE MONEY OUT

If you withdraw early from a retirement account, the company will withhold 20 percent for whatever taxes may be due. (If you owe less than 20 percent, which is unlikely, the difference will be refunded. You may owe more.) You will also owe a 10 percent penalty.

You will pay the taxes that have been deferred but no penalties for early withdrawal if:

- You become disabled.
- You take out money to pay deductible medical expenses that exceed 7.5 percent of your adjusted gross income.
- You are fired or laid off, quit, or take formal retirement at age fifty-five or older.
- You arrange to take out annuitized, roughly equal annual payments at any age from a plan at a company where you no longer work.

- You die. Heirs may withdraw the money without penalty, but the money may be subject to estate taxes. The law regarding the inheritance of pensions is very inflexible. Be sure the right beneficiary is listed on the form.

My ex-husband, the father of my sons, had a tremendous amount of money in his defined-contribution account. When he remarried, his prenuptial stated that the boys were to get the pension fund. However, the beneficiary on his plan wasn't changed. When he died, we discovered that unless otherwise stipulated, the law decrees that the widow must be the beneficiary. Since pension law supersedes all other law, the second wife got everything, and her position was that it was rightfully hers. I'm sure my husband would have been appalled.—"Beryl Marsh," 52, talent agent, married, two grown children

At age fifty-nine and a half, if you meet your company's retirement or withdrawal criteria, you can choose to do any of the following with the money:

Transfer it into a rollover IRA (Individual Retirement Account). If you don't need the money at this point, notify the custodian that you want to transfer it directly into a rollover IRA (see page 166). By putting your money into a rollover IRA, you allow it to keep growing while you continue to defer taxes.

Take a lump sum and pay the taxes now. You may have a one-time opportunity to income-average and cut down on the tax bite. Ask your accountant's advice as to whether this is the route for you.

Purchase an annuity from an insurance company that pays a fixed monthly amount. You can put it either into a regular annuity and start taking the money directly, or into a rollover annuity where it can continue to grow tax-deferred. (See pages 168–171.)

Arrange for regular payouts from the company. Some even allow withdrawals whenever you wish.

Arrange for annual distributions. The period and size of the payouts can be calculated by taking into account the age of one party or, for a couple, the ages of both.

Withdrawing a large sum in a single year or a large lump sum may cost you an additional penalty called an excise tax. (There is an amnesty rule on this until 1999.)

If you don't withdraw the money by age seventy and a half (or, in the case of a non-IRA, by April 1 of the year you retire, whichever is earlier), you will pay a penalty of 50 percent on the minimum amount that should have been distributed. Minimum distribution is also required for a 5 percent owner of a company, but not for someone who owns less than 5 percent and continues to work.

BORROWING AGAINST THE 401(K)

If their employer's plan allows it, many people borrow against a 401(k) to pay off other debts, to pay college tuition, or for other emergencies. The law imposes some restrictions, and your company may impose others:

- The maximum loan is usually $50,000 or half your vested amount, but there may be other limits.
- The minimum may also be determined by your company.
- You may be restricted as to the purpose of the loan, the number of loans you may take, and/or the size of the loan relative to your paycheck.
- You may be able to take a loan only against certain investments, or the loan may be spread equally among them. Most people use the balance of the vested amount as collateral.

Excepting a loan for a home purchase, which can be repaid in ten to thirty years, the loan must be paid back in five years. Club members were delighted to discover this easy and relatively inexpensive option for borrowing money, which has several additional benefits. If you use the money to increase the size of a down payment on a house, you may be able to negotiate a better deal and take out a smaller mortgage, saving interest in the long run. Interest on this type of loan is usually about the same as at a local bank and you may have to pay a service fee besides, but you're paying the interest to your own retirement fund. For some purposes (such as starting a business) the interest may be deductible. For others (such as paying off credit card loans) it is not.

However, there are some risks. If you're laid off or switch jobs you may have to repay the loan very quickly. If your investments go down during the loan period, you won't be able to duplicate your original nest egg. And though you repay the loan with after-tax money, once it goes into the plan it will eventually be taxed again, when it is withdrawn. Above all, when you're using the money, it isn't working for you. If you can borrow from a specific portion of the 401(k), use the one that is paying the least interest, like a GIC.

If the repayment isn't prompt, or if you borrow too much, the loan may be considered an early distribution and you will have to pay income tax and a 10 percent penalty.

The law does permit "hardship withdrawals" if you can prove you have no other source of money to pay medical or tuition expenses, to prevent an eviction or mortgage foreclosure, or to buy a home. (Forget that lake-side cottage; we're talking primary residences.) You may not be able to take any money that came from matching funds, the earnings on your contributions, or any contributions that weren't tax-deductible. You still have to pay taxes and a penalty, and you may be barred from contributing to your 401(k) for a year. But these sums don't have to be repaid.

IF YOU LEAVE THE COMPANY

Most people are downsized or change companies about five times in their lifetimes. It is very likely that you will leave a company where you have a 401(k). In some cases, the employer will remain the custodian on your behalf. You can't make additional contributions, but you can let the money accumulate until you reach age fifty-nine and a half. As an alternative, you can take your contributions—and if your account is less than $3,500, you may have to. When you are vested, you can take the company contributions as well. Have the money transferred directly to your new employer or, if you want more investment choices, directly into a rollover IRA (see page 166). Have it moved directly to avoid the risk of losing its tax-deferred status.

If you get a pension in a divorce settlement, and it's a defined-benefit plan with a guaranteed payout, leave it in place. If it's a defined-contribution plan, leave it in place or transfer it to a rollover IRA. Though you have the option of taking the cash, the pension is worth much more if it continues to grow tax-deferred.

> *When I got divorced at forty, retirement was the last thing on my mind. When my attorney asked if I'd remarry, I said, "Who knows? Probably." So I agreed in the divorce to cash out of my ex's pension. As it turns out, this was one of my dumber mistakes. I spent the money and I had nothing growing for me.*—"Ellen Martin," 52, dental hygienist, divorced, two children

WHEN THE COMPANY HAS PROBLEMS

Pension money is in a trust account. If the company goes out of business, it can't be attacked by creditors. If as the result of a merger or takeover you have to enroll in a new plan, you are subject to its rules. You can continue to shelter any investments that cannot be administered by the new plan by moving them into a rollover IRA.

Companies have occasionally dipped into a pension fund to cover business expenses. Usually, there are warning signs: the investments on your account statement aren't the ones you have chosen; the matching contribution from the company isn't indicated; the amount deducted from your paycheck doesn't show on the statement within fifteen days; the statement comes irregularly or late; and/or the balance on your statement drops out of proportion to market movement. It is also a bad sign if the manager changes often or for unexplained reasons or the annual report notes an unusual transaction loan to a company officer. For any of these reasons, or if the company is in serious financial trouble and/or you can't get answers to your questions, ask for help from the Federal Pension and Welfare Benefits Administration (PWBA), 202-219-8776.

Guidelines for Investing in a 401(k)

The general rules of investing apply to your retirement plan investments:

Do research. A 401(k) mutual fund may not have the same name as a fund available to the general public, but there will doubtless be a similar one in the same family. (Ask your plan advisor what other funds the manager runs.) Consult if possible with a broker or financial advisor who handles your other investments.

Take some risks. But you might be more conservative with a 401(k) than with a personal portfolio for three reasons: (1) You can't deduct losses. (2) When you cash in, you'll get the full tax hit, not just capital gains taxes. And (3) this is money that you can't afford to lose.

Diversify. About 42 percent of money in retirement plans is invested in employer's stock—a very bad investment strategy. You need fifteen to twenty stocks to be safely diversified, so one stock shouldn't represent more than 5 to 7 percent of your portfolio. Even a great company can have a bad period.

> *I had quite a bit of stock in my former company's 401(k), and I kept it even when I left. When you've been involved at a senior level and are part of the company's growth, you become attached and committed to the stock and may lose sight of how many factors can affect it. My stock lost two-thirds of its value. I would never put all my eggs in one basket again.*—Alice Shanahan, 49, vice president, retail, Waterford Wedgwood, two grown sons

Review your portfolio periodically. Check that your assets are properly allocated. Do this quarterly, if possible, and at least twice a year.

Keep some liquidity. If you reserve 5 to 10 percent of your 401(k) money in a money market fund or shares of a bank money market deposit account, you can buy when the market is rising. You also might want to park it there at a period when you believe the market may fall.

Stay for the long haul.

SIMPLE PLANS

These began in 1997, established at the request of small-business owners who felt 401(k) plans were too complicated to set up and prevented highly paid executives from taking a maximum tax deferral unless a lot of lower-paid workers were part of the plan. SIMPLE allows companies with fewer than 100 employees to establish a savings plan that resembles a 401(k) but is less costly and complex. The firm deposits 2 percent of each employee's pay into the employee's account or matches the first 3 percent that employees contribute to their accounts. There is a cap on the contributions of highly paid employees.

ALTERNATIVES TO EMPLOYER PLANS

Self-employed people and people who have a second job or are not covered by another pension plan may open up their own defined-contribution plan, such as an IRA, SEP, or Keogh. (In rare cases, a Keogh is set up as a defined-benefit plan.)

IRA PLANS

If you are not covered by an employer-sponsored retirement plan but earn money or receive alimony payments, you can save some taxes by opening an IRA. You and your spouse can each put away $2,000 tax-free annually whether or not both are working.

Even if you or your spouse is covered by a pension plan, you may still be able to make an IRA contribution. You can get the full IRA tax deduction if your adjusted gross income doesn't exceed $40,000 for a couple or $25,000 for a single person or head of household. As your income increases over this amount, the amount you can deduct is reduced, going down to zero when a couple earns $50,000 jointly or an individual earns $35,000. More than 76 percent of taxpayers qualify for IRAs that are fully or partly tax-deductible.

If your income is low enough you may be eligible for both a 401(k) and an IRA. Contribute to both, if you can. If you have to choose, compare the advantages. With a 401(k), there's less paperwork, you can make bigger contributions, the employer matches your funds, you can borrow against it, and you may be able to reduce taxes by income averaging at the time of withdrawal. But with an IRA, you aren't limited to the investments the company offers. Ask an accountant to help you decide.

Some of us had multiple IRAs, at different places, in different sorts of investments, but after we heard from the experts we realized that using one brokerage house account to put money in several places or one mutual fund "family" to invest in different types of funds makes more sense. You can keep track of your investments much more easily. It's also simpler to move from one type of investment to another in the brokerage account or from one fund to another within the family, though you may have to pay sales and other charges.

Date by which IRA must be established: April 15 for the previous year.

Date by which contribution must be made: April 15 for the previous year. Of course the earlier in the year you put it in, the sooner it's working for you.

Where account may be established: Brokerage house, insurance company, bank, family of mutual funds.

Minimum contribution required by institution: May be $100 or less.

Possibilities for investment: CDs, savings accounts, Treasury securities, mutual funds, annuities, and/or individual stocks. This money is already tax-deferred, so avoid tax-exempt investments (such as a tax-free municipal bond fund), which generally pay a lower yield.

Requirements to transfer an IRA from one institution to another: Follow the guidelines of the IRS code, or you may jeopardize the tax-deferred status of this money. When you make the transfer, the new broker or fund representative can supply applications to open a new tax-deferred account and authorizations for the current custodian to hand the funds over. If fees are involved, pay them out of pocket because they are tax-deductible. (Pay the yearly custodial fee by check, too, for the same reason.)

Rollover IRAs

If you are leaving one company and don't like the new employer's pension plan, or prefer a wider variety of investment choices, you can put your money into a rollover IRA. You can also set up a rollover IRA at age fifty-nine and a half, if you meet your company's retirement or withdrawal criteria and want to leave the money growing tax-deferred but have more investment choices. The money must be transferred from the prior custodian into a new tax-deferred account within sixty days or you will pay an early withdrawal penalty. Never mix regular IRA money with a rollover IRA. Someday you may join another firm with a qualified pension plan. If you add this money to it, you will have the benefit of professional investment advice.

Keogh plans

A Keogh is a pension plan for a self-employed person. Even if you already have a pension plan through an employer, you may be able to put away money in a Keogh as well if you earn additional money from self-employment. You may be able to open a Keogh in addition to an IRA.

Banks, brokerage houses, and insurance agents have prototype forms to establish a Keogh that your accountant can fill out. A special tax form, a 5500-C, is due every third year, and a 5500-R in intervening years. For a small plan that involves only you and/or a spouse you may have to file only 5500-EZ forms or be completely exempt from filing.

You can set up the Keogh as a defined-benefit plan and put away whatever you need to achieve an annual retirement income (starting anytime from age fifty-five) that is equal to the average of your highest earnings in three consecutive years.

Most people set up a Keogh as a defined-contribution plan, choosing one of two options. With a money purchase plan, you make a commitment to put aside the same amount each year—up to 25 percent of self-employment earnings to a maximum of $30,000—or you are subject to a fine and/or penalty. With a profit-sharing plan, you can put away up to 15 percent to an effective maximum of $22,500. If you don't want to commit yourself to putting away the larger amount because your income fluctuates, you can set up two plans, one of each type. But altogether you can't put away more than 20 percent to a maximum of $30,000. (The actual percentage you put away amounts to 20 percent rather than 25 percent and 13.04 percent instead of 15 percent because of required adjustments to your calculations.)

Date by which Keogh must be established: December 31 of the calendar year for which you're making the contribution.

Date by which contribution must be made: When taxes are filed.

Where account may be established: Same as for IRA.

Minimum contribution required by institution: Same as for IRA.

Possibilities for investment: Same as for IRA.

Requirements to transfer a Keogh from one institution to another: Same as for IRA.

Simplified Employee Pension (SEP) Plans

With a SEP you can put away 15 percent of self-employment earnings tax-free, to a maximum of $30,000. (The actual percentage you can put away amounts to 13.04 percent because of required adjustments to your calculations.) With a Keogh you can take out a lump sum at retirement and lower your taxes by forward averaging, but with a SEP you cannot. You also can't put life insurance into the plan or roll it into a employer's retirement plan. But it's very uncomplicated to administer.

Date by which SEP must be established: When taxes are filed, for previous year.

Date by which contribution must be made: When taxes are filed, for previous year. No requirement to contribute yearly.

Where account may be established: Same as for IRA.

Minimum contribution required by institution: Same as for IRA.

Possibilities for investment: Same as for IRA.

Requirements to transfer a SEP from one institution to another: Same as for IRA.

RETIREMENT SOURCE NO. 4: ANNUITIES OR NONQUALIFIED PLANS

Whether you're self-employed or work for someone else, the government limits how much before-tax money you can put aside. Once you reach the limit, you can contribute after-tax money to an annuity or a nonqualified plan.

NONQUALIFIED PLANS

Many employers permit you to put after-tax money into a nonqualified plan. Though the money you put in isn't tax-exempt, the earnings are tax-deferred. Your money can grow much faster when there are no taxes whittling it down. The penalties for withdrawal before age fifty-nine and a half are the same as for an early withdrawal from a qualified plan.

ANNUITIES

An annuity—which is sold by banks, brokerage houses, and insurance agents but is always backed by an insurance company—is the opposite of life insurance, whose payoff comes as a lump sum on your death. The point of an annuity, in contrast, is to create a steady stream of income during your life.

Technically, an annuity is a contract that the insurance company will pay you a set amount at a set frequency and continue the payments until your death, even after your initial contributions and the earnings are exhausted.

With a tax-deferred annuity, you contribute money over time. There is no limit as to how much you can put in. As with other tax-deferred plans, if you make withdrawals before age fifty-nine and a half, you owe the government a 10 percent penalty on the earnings plus whatever deferred taxes are due. And though many annuities permit 10 to 15 percent of earnings (not principal) to be withdrawn yearly without any fees, most have an early withdrawal penalty. If you take out more than 10 percent of the policy's value in any year, you'll have to pay a charge known as a *surrender fee,* a *back-end load,* or a *deferred sales charge.* The charge, often as high as 7 percent to start, diminishes on a sliding downward scale and may eventually vanish, though some companies will make you pay for as long as ten to twenty years. And there are other fees and expenses, similar to a mutual fund's.

If you die before collecting the annuity, your beneficiary gets the current value of your contract or the value of your original investment, whichever is higher. Once you've been adding to an annuity for a while, your investment may have grown substantially. So some annuities periodically *step up the basis* (or original investment) price on the death benefit so the guarantee applies to an amount larger than your original investment.

How annuities differ

There are two types of deferred annuities. A *fixed-rate annuity* is similar to a CD. It provides fixed rates that are usually guaranteed for one, three, five, or ten years and then reset annually at the renewal rate. The principal is 100 percent guaranteed against investment loss as long as the company stays solvent. Some annuities offer *bailout* provisions that let you drop out if rates fall below a certain minimum, but in such a case, the annuity usually offers a lower return. A *variable annuity* allows you to invest in a variety of vehicles, such as stock and/or bond funds managed like mutual funds. The annuity's returns will vary according to how well the investment performs. When you buy, you are shown an *illustration* that shows you the minimum return. You will also be shown an illustration that projects a much more optimistic return. The actual return will most likely be somewhere in between.

You may invest a lump sum (a single-premium annuity) or contribute periodically, at either fixed or irregular intervals. Sometimes people who receive a lump sum from a certificate of deposit, an insurance payout, or a retirement account put it into an immediate annuity that starts paying out right away.

At the end of the accumulation period, you can take the money out all at once, in which case taxes on earnings will be due immediately. Or you can take periodic payments—annuitization—in one of four ways:

Life income. You or a designated beneficiary gets a guaranteed income for your lifetime.

Period certain. You or a designated beneficiary gets a guaranteed income for a specific length of time. If you die before the period is over, the beneficiary is covered for the remainder of the period.

Life with period certain. Combines the above two. You or a designated beneficiary gets a guaranteed income for your life, or another person gets the benefit for a fixed period.

Joint and survivor. Two annuitants get guaranteed income for both lives. When one dies, the other is still covered. The payments to a surviving spouse have to be at least half what the couple formerly received but not more than 100 percent of what either received.

WHEN PURCHASING AN ANNUITY

Before you buy, consider the following:

The rating of the insurer. The insurance company makes the investments, deposits the money to your fund, and takes care of paying off you or your beneficiary. So the annuity is only as safe as the insurance company that is backing it. To make sure you're buying from a top company, check the insurance company's rating (see page 175).

The guaranteed rate offered for the initial investment. If you're offered an unusually high return, be on your guard. The company may be making risky investments or may be baiting you with rates you won't actually get. For example, the return may be lower if you try to withdraw money before annuitization, or the company may require that you annuitize though you may have preferred to take the money out as a lump sum. Check the insurer's renewal rate history and avoid one whose huge first-year rates have been followed by low renewal rates at a time when the economy is booming. Some companies offer guaranteed rates for up to ten years. At the end of the term, if you don't want to reinvest, you can take out your cash and/or move to another insurer.

The costs that are involved. Don't ignore the fees you will pay. Remember, you're buying this investment to make money, not just avoid taxes.

OTHER WAYS TO SAVE FOR THE FUTURE

You may be offered deferred compensation and/or an incentive savings plan. These are not pension plans but another means of funding your retirement years. With deferred compensation, you may have your employer put aside part of your salary to grow tax-deferred until it's paid out to you. You're taxed only as payments are made. Your rights to funds may not vest until retirement, disability, or death, but there are no contribution limits. The company cannot guarantee you this money or you will forfeit the ability to defer taxes, and if the company goes under, you are just another creditor. On the other hand, a highly paid employee of a very solid firm might find this option attractive.

Many of us in the club started our careers before retirement plants such as 401(k)s were in existence. In many cases, we worked at companies for many years and left with a very small sum, or nothing at all. Younger women (including our daughters) are fortunate not only for the obvious reason that they are starting to build for the future at an early age but also because they are learning something about investment choices from companies that are obliged to teach them.

When we had an expert speaker talk about retirement plans, many of us who were not ourselves covered came to ask questions about our husbands' plans. As with other investment decisions, sometimes our husbands hadn't given enough time or thought to managing their retirement plans. We offered at least to read the materials through and then have a discussion about how to proceed. Obviously, planning for the future affects everyone as a couple or as an individual, at every economic level.

C H A P T E R 6

BETTING AGAINST DISASTER

Buying Insurance

For months, I was confined to bed with a hip problem and couldn't work. I was in pain, terrified, and not thinking clearly. I didn't have much money in the bank. My only asset was some equity in my apartment, so I put it up for sale. My parents packed me up while I directed the proceedings from my bed. The experience was a nightmare. When I think about how just a little bit of insurance would have given me enough to hold on, I can't believe I never took it out.—"Judith Novak," 41, graphic artist, single

YOU DON'T PLAN TO FAIL; YOU FAIL TO PLAN

Of all the areas of personal finance, insurance was probably the one the club members found least intimidating. After all, life insurance and medical insurance seemed more familiar territory than pension planning. But as it turned out, there was a lot we didn't know or had overlooked.

Like most people, we didn't focus on insurance until an emergency had already happened. Not until the ceiling collapsed from a leak or a neighbor slipped in the foyer did we pay much attention to whether we were covered for water damage or personal liability insurance. Fortunately, we had an insurance expert among us: club member Gloria Gottlieb heads her own agency. As we started taking the initiative to investigate areas of financial concern, many of us consulted with her independently and informally.

Once she had prodded us into reading our policies, we discovered that many of them didn't give us the protection we thought we had. Equally important, a lot of the information was out of date. Our possessions had increased in number or value. In some cases, we had married a new spouse or shed an old one without changing our policies. A friend shared a story that illustrated how a catastrophe can result.

At forty, my cousin finally married Mr. Right. Shortly afterward, the couple adopted three young relatives who had been orphaned by a tragic accident. To celebrate, the new parents took their ready-made family on vacation, and planned to put their finances in order the minute they came home. But my cousin's husband had a massive heart attack and died. The beneficiary to his insurance was his first wife, whom he had divorced after a brief, childless marriage. Though by law, the second wife was entitled to a portion of his estate, it wasn't nearly enough to provide for her and the children.—"Ronnie Robert," 52, personnel director, married, two adult children

FINDING AN AGENT

Before you can deal with your insurance, you need to find an insurance agent. Many of us admitted that we were inclined to mistrust agents in general. We were never sure whether they were recommending a policy because it was truly in our best interest or because the sale would qualify them for a reward from the insurance company. In part our suspicions were due to the fact that we simply didn't have enough information to evaluate the worth of what we were being offered. Gloria had some very practical advice:

One way to reduce your concerns is to deal only with the most successful insurance agent you can find—someone associated with a big firm and/or who seems to have a large clientele. The less desperate the agent is for the sale, the more likely he or she is to guide you to the best decision.

If we can manage to find pediatricians and gynecologists and dentists we have faith in, we should be able to find someone to handle our insurance. Your stockbroker may be licensed to sell insurance, or may recommend an insurance broker. Or get a recommendation from an attorney, or a financial advisor you respect or whom a friend thinks highly of. However, friends' intentions are often better than their judgment, so rely on your own instincts in making the final choice. Insurance agents are required by law to have a certain amount of expertise and to hold licenses to sell specific kinds of insurance (life and health, property and casualty, and so on). Many hold several licenses. Some may also be licensed to sell stocks and bonds. As a result of recent legislation, agents must attend continuing education courses to keep their licenses in force. An agent who also has a title such as CFP (Certified Financial Planner) or CLU (Chartered Life Underwriter) has passed an exam that tests his or her knowledge of insurance and how it is connected to tax law, accounting, and related financial issues.

You should go to an independent agent, who represents the products of several companies rather than only one company. Similar products may have different price tags and different specific advantages, and as with any purchase, you should be able to comparison-shop.

When you meet with the agent, bring along copies of all the policies you have—even the ones you are embarrassed about because you think it was a mistake to buy them. An insurance agent is paid by commission, so refer back to Chapter 2 for the guidelines in this kind of situation. Don't hesitate to ask what the agent's commission will be on any insurance product that is being recommended. Get a second opinion on the purchase. And ask as many questions as necessary. The only people who find questions annoying, we've discovered, are people who don't have the answers.

Reputable agents will sell you policies only from companies that are financially strong and likely to still be around in two or three decades, when you or your heirs might collect on a policy. All insurance companies are rated for quality by a number of services whose publications you can consult at the library; or call them for a phone or written evaluation. They include A. M. Best (900-555-2378); Standard & Poor's (212-208-1527); Duff & Phelps (312-629-3833); Moody's (212-553-0377); and Weiss Research (800-289-9222). Some impose a charge for this service.

We found that a so-called bargain in insurance, like all bargains, may not be the most sensible purchase. A low-priced policy may not be from a top-rated company.

READING THE POLICY

Curling up with your insurance policy may not sound like a terrific way to spend the evening, but make yourself do it. Our club members have learned that we must read every policy from cover to cover. Mark the key points with a highlighter so you know what's included and—more important—what is not.

If there is anything that isn't clear, ask your agent to clarify it. If it's a medical policy, does it cover routine pediatric visits? If it's property insurance, will it cover a suitcase stolen when you are on vacation? Gloria prepared checklists for reviewing every kind of insurance (and you'll find them at the end of each section). If you aren't covered for a particular kind of situation, maybe you should consider replacing the insurance with another kind of policy. If an agent assures you that you have coverage in an area about which you are unsure, get the promise confirmed in writing.

When you have read through your policy, note the date on the cover page. You should review it every year. Make it one of the jobs you do when the seasons change, like turning the mattresses and checking the batteries on the smoke alarm. (If you don't have such a seasonal list, start one now.) Here's why a review is important:

> *Years ago, a friend took out a policy that combined life insurance with a daily hospital benefit. Recently, he was hospitalized and his wife had the policy reviewed. The agent called the husband in the hospital. "How fond are you of Leslie?" she asked, mentioning the man's former wife, whom he had divorced thirty years before. "Not especially," he said. "Then why is she the beneficiary of your life insurance?"*—Gloria Gottlieb

In the twenty-seven years he'd been married to his current wife, our friend had never brought his old policy up to date. Believe it or not, this is very common. In fact, the very same thing happened to another friend of ours, and in her case the consequences were terrible:

> *When my husband died suddenly, his ex-wife was still on the policy as a beneficiary and she was the one who collected. I was left destitute, and it took me years of hard work to get back my bearings.* —Harriet Mosson, 54, president, Liz Claiborne Dresses, divorced, one adult child.

LIFE INSURANCE

> *"I don't need insurance, I have my husband." Famous last words.*—Gloria Gottlieb

People find many different uses for the proceeds of life insurance: to pay off debts (such as mortgages, credit cards, banknotes, or margin loans), to buy out a partner's interest, to make a gift to charity, or to cover the cost of a child's education. But most commonly, it's a source of cash to pay estate taxes and to replace the lost income of the person who has died.

LIFE INSURANCE FOR INCOME REPLACEMENT

Although many of us in the club have jobs, of the women who are married, in almost every case the husband is the primary breadwinner. Naturally, they have concerns about what would happen if their husbands died. Would there be enough money so that they (and the children) would be able to live just as they currently do? Single club members have the same concerns about the people who are dependent on them.

To address these concerns, you first have to know what your current living expenses are. If you haven't already completed the calculations of yearly income and expenses (Chapter 3), do it now. Even if one person were to die, the family expenses wouldn't change significantly.

The next thing to determine is how much Social Security benefits you (and your minor children), or your dependents, would be entitled to. In

Chapter 6, we explained how to find out (see pages 150–151). Add to that figure the total income that you can expect from your current investments. The difference between your total expenses and your total Social Security and investment income is the amount that life insurance must make up.

Suppose the family expenses are $50,000 and the Social Security and other investments would produce $25,000. The survivor would need another $25,000 a year. A total of $250,000 worth of life insurance would run out in less than ten years, assuming inflation continued to rise between 3 and 4 percent. Ten years from now $25,000 would buy a lot less than it will today. On top of that, since on average a woman is widowed at fifty-six, chances are she'll be around a lot longer than ten years.

What is enough insurance? Ideally, it would be a lump sum large enough to generate the amount of the missing income through investments. The usual gauge is that it is reasonable to expect a 5 percent after-tax return on investments. To produce $25,000 on that basis, you'd need an initial lump sum of $500,000. But in order to take into account the effect of ongoing inflation (estimated at between 3 and 4 percent), you'd need even more.

To calculate our personal needs, we got expert help. You can get it from a financial planner, possibly an accountant and/or tax lawyer and your insurance agent. The size of the nest egg you will need will almost certainly be very large, and the only way most people can amass this amount is through a large life insurance policy.

Those of us in two-career households realized we needed life insurance coverage in proportion to the amount of the family income we earn. Parents with young children in a household in which only the father works have another consideration. They must prepare for the expense of the child care if the mother should die or if the father dies and the mother has to go to work. Obviously when the children grow up, this need disappears—another example of why life insurance needs should be reviewed regularly.

Life insurance to pay estate taxes

Those in the club who had been widowed told us that they hadn't been prepared for the amount of cash they needed after a spouse died. There were funeral expenses, probate costs, and estate taxes to be paid within a few months. A $100,000 estate typically has $5,000 in probate costs and state taxes of $1,500 (though these figures vary by state). An estate of $600,000 may pay $31,000 for the former and $27,000 for the latter. There may also be other debts and liabilities to pay off.

And though a husband and wife generally inherit each other's property tax-free, if the second to die leaves an estate over $600,000, federal taxes will most likely be due. These start at 37 percent and slide upward to as much as 55 percent. Uncle Sam is very impatient. He wants his money within nine months of the death. If heirs inherit assets that don't generate enough cash, the assets may have to be sold.

Even some of the very richest people don't plan for a situation like this. One of the most famous examples was Joe Robbie, the onetime owner of the Miami Dolphins. (Insurance agents love to tell this story.) Robbie left a tremendous estate, but his assets weren't liquid. To pay the millions due the government, his heirs were forced to sell the team. Elvis Presley's heirs were singing the blues after they were forced to sell off his property at bargain basement rates to raise the money for taxes. The sales shrank the value of his estate by 73 percent. Because of a similar problem, John D. Rockefeller's estate shrank by 64 percent. We were pleased to discover that with a little planning we could be smarter about money than a Rockefeller. The solution is to buy *survivorship* (also called second-to-die) term or permanent life insurance for the purpose of paying taxes.

Term insurance and permanent (whole life) insurance

There are two basic kinds of life insurance: *term insurance* and *permanent insurance*, also called *whole life insurance.* There is only one kind of term insurance, but there are several types of permanent insurance.

Term insurance

Term life insurance is very simple to understand. It gives you a limited amount of protection for a specific period of time. Gloria said we should think of term insurance as being similar to a rental arrangement. Like rent, the premium is due regularly and the rates go up periodically. At the end of the term, the deal is off; you have no further rights and no further obligations. In fact, if at any time you want to terminate the policy, you just stop paying.

The ideal candidate for term insurance is a young breadwinner with a family to support. Term insurance offers a lot of income replacement at a very low cost, but you have to shop carefully. All term policies cost relatively modest amounts at the beginning and a great deal more over the years, but they rise at different rates and to different levels. Choose one that remains the most affordable over time.

Term insurance makes no sense at all for people without dependents. There are insurance agents who will try to sell it to you anyway; and some of us had fallen for such a pitch—more than once.

> *I got totally carried away buying term life insurance policies. Someone would come and try to sell me one, and I'd agree to it. At one point I had four term policies. I kept buying them because I knew my parents had them.*—Jennifer Balbier

Whenever you take out term insurance, agree to pay the small extra charge that guarantees that the policy is renewable. Otherwise, if you get a terminal illness, you may have no coverage. But never prepay a policy. When you buy insurance, you're gambling the company will have to pay up before you've invested a great deal. Why would you let the insurance company hold on to your money?

Some club members had term insurance coverage as an employee benefit. Their employers permitted them to buy additional coverage for a spouse or raise the amount of their own coverage at relatively low rates. Most of them had the option to convert the policy to an individual policy if they left their jobs, but most would not exercise the option because the cost was relatively high. On the other hand, for someone who becomes uninsurable due to ill health this is a terrific opportunity.

Some of our members were also offered insurance coverage through their professional organizations. The rates are usually lower than if you apply as an individual. Also, it's usually easier to get coverage: while most policies require a medical exam, it may not be necessary if you come in as a member of a group.

You may be tempted to lie about a medical condition if you are afraid you may be denied life insurance as a result. Don't do it. Gloria warned that if you don't mention an illness on the application, and you have a subsequent problem, the policy may be void. An experienced life insurance agent can help you get the best possible coverage whatever your circumstances.

Permanent (whole life) insurance

There are two main selling points for permanent or whole life insurance. One is that the cost of the premium stays level—the same—and eventually may even disappear. The other is that the policy builds up cash value. After a few years, the amount of money you have paid in premiums earns enough interest to pay the future premiums, and the amount you continue to pay becomes a savings account. You can even take out a loan against the cash value of the policy.

> *Women think they just keep putting money into an insurance policy. But, if you need to, you can borrow against it and pay it back, and you haven't lost any of the face value of the coverage. Once you realize that this kind of policy is a financial vehicle, having it is a great comfort.* —Laura Pomerantz

There are a couple of catches. One, the face value of the policy may be reduced by the amount of the loan. (If you take out a $10,000 loan on a $100,000 policy, the insurance return may be reduced to $90,000). Two, you have to pay interest on the loan even though it's your own money you're borrowing. And while the loan is unpaid, you also lose interest on the cash value of the policy. But if you need cash in a hurry, this is quicker and a lot less complicated than taking out a bank loan. Also you're the one who decides when (or if) you want to pay it back. The club members who have whole life policies love the loan feature and say they feel it is like having money stuffed in a mattress for an emergency.

Permanent insurance traditionally produced a very conservative return on your investment, about 5 percent even in boom times. Because customers demanded more attractive deals, insurance companies came up with new types of permanent insurance policies:

- ***Variable life.*** This lets you choose among different types of investments.

- ***Universal life.*** This combines term insurance and a savings account invested in fixed-income investments. Its most unusual feature is that you can change the face amount of the policy (and thus the premium) from year to year, which is good if you're a self-employed person with volatile income.

- ***Variable universal life.*** This combines a variable premium with a variety of investment options. You can switch among them as conditions change.

Let your broker take you through the choices, and make sure you understand them. Whichever you choose, the broker will show you an illustration. Despite the name, there are no pictures, just columns of numbers showing how much money you'll have to pay on the policy and for how many years, plus the cash value your policy will accumulate based on current investment rates.

Some of the club members said in the past they had been confused by the illustrations. You are always given one illustration that shows what will happen if interest rates are high, and another that shows a worst-case scenario, if interest rates bottom out. In the former case, the premiums vanish quickly, after only a few years; in the latter, the payments go on forever. Since agents tend to accentuate the positive, some members who had bought this type of policy had unrealistic expectations about when the premiums would vanish and were disappointed when they discovered that because interest rates were low, they would have to keep paying much longer than expected. In the future, they plan to ask for illustrations using figures that are neither very high nor very low, so that they can have realistic expectations.

When you buy permanent insurance, you're paying high commissions (as much as 86 percent of the first year's premium) as well as administrative costs and fees. Also, the insurance protection is relatively costly. If you have to cash in within the first couple of years, the charges could eat up your entire investment. Some people think you're better off buying cheaper term insurance and putting the extra money into conventional investments.

On the positive side, permanent insurance, unlike term insurance, does give you some return on your money. More important, many people love the forced savings feature. Without it, they say they would never put any money aside.

In the last few years, *low-load whole life insurance* has become available. The commission may be half the going rate, the ongoing charges may be smaller, and you may be able to cash in the policy without any charges. But the companies have small sales forces, so they can't sell a lot of product; and a company that doesn't sell a lot of product isn't as solid as one that does. (When insurance sales via computer become more popular, a small sales force may not be a factor.) Second, and more important, you don't get much service with this kind of feature. When policyholders call with questions and are told, "We can't give advice," about 90 percent ultimately cancel and find new insurance. And getting reinsured is not always a certainty.

> *I was careless about the premiums and let my policy lapse. Meanwhile, I had developed a chronic illness and then found I was uninsurable.*—"Dorothy Lake," 44, manicurist, divorced, one child

THE CONVERSION FEATURE

Some of our club members had spouses in their sixties for whom term insurance premiums were becoming so high that they refused to pay. The women looked into the possibility of converting the term policies into permanent insurance. In such a case, the premium may be lower than buying a new policy, since the rate is based on your prior rating class, which may have been established years ago. Also, when you convert, your health and occupation won't be considered. For someone with a chronic or terminal illness, this can be a tremendous opportunity.

> *My husband took out a term policy years ago for the benefit of our kids, who were little. Now they're grown, and in the meantime, he's developed adult-onset diabetes. Thank goodness, he was able to convert the term policy to whole life and make me the beneficiary without having to go through a physical. Since he's at great risk, he might have been uninsurable.*—"Jill Washington," 44, clerk, married, two children

Some club members with grown children did another kind of conversion: they converted their whole life insurance into an annuity. The money is invested to give you continuing payments for your lifetime. Or you can cash it in and use the money for investments.

A LIFE INSURANCE CHECKUP

Your policies should be reviewed yearly, on the anniversary of the policy. Although the agent should call you, don't hesitate to take the initiative yourself. After all, who cares more about your money, you or the agent? Schedule a meeting. Before you get together, jot down any changes that might affect your insurance coverage. For example, have there been any additions to the family?

Club members with growing families were delighted to discover the possibility of making a "class gift"—not a gift to your alma mater, but a gift that affects a class of beneficiary. For example, if you name "my grandchildren" as beneficiaries on a policy, each newcomer is automatically entitled to a share even though not specifically named. (This is handled differently in different states, so check with your agent.)

Other points to cover in your review:

- Is the right name on the beneficiary line? Is it clear who the beneficiary is? One of our friends comes from a big Irish family. There are twenty-two O'Brian first cousins, and even more second cousins, among them five Mary O'Brians. When the patriarch of the family leaves money to Mary O'Brian, who collects? To avoid confusion, the beneficiary on a life insurance policy should be identified by a Social Security number as well as a name.
- Has the premium been paid? Is the policy in force? If payments aren't timely, the policy may be valueless. Premiums may be paid annually (which is the cheapest way), semi-annually, quarterly, or even monthly. A company is required by law to give a thirty-one-day grace period. If you pay within the month beyond the due date, the policy won't be canceled. And if you die, your heirs will get the money, less the amount of the missing premium. But if the grace period has come and gone and you still haven't paid, your beneficiaries may be in trouble.

My husband was exceptionally devoted but careless about paying bills. "I have to get that life insurance premium off on Monday," he told me as we prepared to go away for a weekend. Saturday night he died of a heart attack. He had missed the grace period by a matter of three days. I never did get that quarter of a million dollars on which my husband had paid premiums for many years. Thank goodness friends helped me get a steady job to support myself and our seven-year-old daughter.—"Suzie Childs," 53, newspaper reporter, widowed, one child

- Are there loans against the policy you have forgotten about or aren't aware of? If the policy is being stripped of value, you should be aware of this.
- Should the policy be replaced?

My husband took out a term policy when our son was born, fifteen years ago. Each year the rates went up, and by now they're $5,000 a year. Quite casually, our agent mentioned that another carrier offered far lower, level premiums that would save us thousands. We immediately attempted to make the change, but over the past year my husband had developed some medical prob-

lems and couldn't pass the physical for the new policy. So we're stuck with the large and growing premiums of the old policy. I'm mad at the agent for not staying on top of our situation, but I'm also mad at us for not doing the same.—"Wendy Lewis," 54, freelance writer, married, one child

When the policy pays off

Whoever is designated as a beneficiary to your life insurance gets the money free of income tax. If you name your favorite niece the beneficiary of a $250,000 policy, she collects that amount when you die, no strings attached. But that $250,000 is considered a gift from the estate, and taxes on it will be deducted from the estate before the heirs divvy up the rest. If a trust is the owner of the policy (and this is something you can set up with a lawyer), the beneficiary collects the money and your estate avoids the taxes. We explain this in more detail in Chapter 7 on pages 230–231.

If the beneficiary is a child, you must name a guardian or trustee since an insurance company isn't allowed to make out a check to a person under eighteen.

The owner of the policy and the person insured by the policy aren't necessarily the same person. Ownership can be a tricky issue.

My husband bought a large policy, named the kids as beneficiaries, and made me the owner instead of himself, in order to protect the cash value against any creditors. He figured if he really did need the cash, I could make the loan against the policy. When he died, the policy paid off and I gave the money to the kids. Since his estate was well under $600,000, had he owned the policy, the money would have gone to the children tax-free. But, since I was the owner of the policy, the IRS considered that a gift from me and I was obliged to pay a lot of money in gift taxes.—"Fiona Shayle," 60, volunteer, widowed, two children

Young marrieds often don't get around to buying life insurance. This club member was in that situation:

I was only twenty-seven, with an eight-month-old baby, when I was widowed. At that age, I certainly didn't expect my husband to die, and neither

did he, which is why he didn't have much life insurance. If I had known better, I would have made sure he had more. Prepare for the worst. Before I married my second husband, I made sure the insurance policy was in place, which turned out to be a good move; though he was relatively young, I was widowed a second time.—Harriette Rose Katz

Buying insurance can be a relatively inexpensive way for a wife to protect herself if the husband has no policy or one that is too small. To own a policy on another person you must have an insurable interest in his or her life, meaning that the death of the person will affect you economically. Though you can't take out a policy on your neighbor, a wife can hold a policy on her husband, just as a child can hold a policy on a parent or a businessperson on a partner.

And an ex-wife can own a policy on her ex-husband, just as one of our club members does, in order to give herself continuing financial security when he dies. She chose to pay the premiums herself so she knows he can't cash in the policy, discontinue it, or change the beneficiary. Once the policy is taken out, changing the beneficiary is easily done.

One favorite trick of a philandering spouse is to buy insurance with his wife as the beneficiary, then afterward substitute his girlfriend as the beneficiary. If you have any suspicions, make sure you know where the policy is and whose name is on it.—Gloria Gottlieb

Checklist for Life Insurance

When you are buying life insurance, go over all of the following:

1. Premium schedule (frequency and amount of payments; total dollar cost; number of years premium must be paid; if and when it vanishes).
2. Amount of death benefits.
3. Cash value schedule (information about increased amount of cash value year by year).
4. Loan provisions.

5. Dividend information. Premium payments may earn dividends: do they reduce the premium, are they used to add cash value to the policy, or are they used to purchase additional insurance?
6. Is the policy renewable? Is a fee involved to make it renewable?
7. Can it be converted from term to whole life?
8. Name of owner.
9. Name of beneficiary.
10. Provisions for the grace period.
11. Reinstatement policy. If there is a lapse in payment, how can the policy be reinstated?
12. Incontestability clause. If you die within two years of taking out a policy, the insurance company may contest the beneficiary's right to collect—unless the policy has an incontestability clause.
13. Automatic premium loan feature. If you forget to pay, will the company take the cash value to pay the premium so your policy doesn't lapse?
14. Assignment clause. May a bank be the beneficiary?
15. Waiver of premium clause, so that if you become sick, the policy is paid for.

MEDICAL COVERAGE

Women are more concerned about medical coverage than men, but if they are on their own, they often have a harder time affording it. After sixty-five, Medicare comes to the rescue, but a younger person should have at least hospitalization and medical/surgical coverage. The former pays for room charges, nursing care, operating room fees, various tests, and so on. The latter covers doctors' fees associated with hospitalization and certain other costs.

Most new plans combine basic coverage with major medical coverage—supplemental coverage that begins when regular coverage runs out, typically in the case of catastrophic illness. Your individual policy determines how many days of hospitalization are covered, the maximum amount that will be paid for medical costs in your lifetime, and many other limitations. Review it carefully.

CHECKLIST FOR MEDICAL INSURANCE

1. Deductibles. The deductible is the amount you must pay out of pocket before the insurance coverage kicks in. There may be both an individual and a family deductible on your policy. If the deductible is $250 per person and $500 for the family, the family deductible may have to be met before each individual is qualified to make claims. Each calendar year, you have to meet your deductible all over again.
2. Co-insurance. Even after you meet the deductible, you may not be reimbursed for every penny. There may be a co-payment provision that specifies the percentage of costs you must pay. Typically, a company may pay 80 percent of the expenses and you pay 20 percent up to a certain amount, after which the company pays 100 percent. With an HMO, you may simply pay a small co-payment.
3. Lifetime benefit. Is there a maximum you can receive? In the case of a medical catastrophe, this will be important.
4. Does the policy cover routine physicals, preventive care such as breast cancer screenings, immunization, outpatient care, chiropractic, psychological services, nursing care, radiology, allergy care, pediatric care, preventive dental care for children?
5. Laboratory services. What is excluded and what is included?
6. Emergency care. To what extent is it covered?
7. Hospital care. What is included?
8. Surgery schedule. What are exceptions, limitations, or other restrictions? Second opinion required? Allowed?
9. Network doctors. An HMO, or health maintenance organization, may hire its own physicians and run its own facilities or contract with health care providers and facilities to provide services to members, who pay a small fee. You may be limited to the doctors hired by the plan or within its "network." What is the company's policy about payment if you go to a doctor who is not in the network?
10. Exclusions. Certain illnesses and types of care may be excluded, such as plastic surgery and drug or alcohol rehabilitation. If there are many exclusions and you are buying your own insurance, see if your agent can suggest another carrier with a better policy. If there are many exclusions but your employer is paying for most of the insurance, obviously you will go along with the plan. But you should be aware of

what items won't be covered. Otherwise you may be in for a rude shock.

My husband needed emergency surgery and the doctor ordered private nursing care at the hospital, which cost $1,000 a day for three shifts—payable only by check. I later discovered our policy pays for nursing care outside the hospital only. It's important to know what is and isn't covered, especially with HMOs and managed care. After my husband recovered, we had our agent come in for an annual review to advise about any changes in coverage and bring all employees up to date on their benefits. Every business, family, and individual should do the same.—"Debbie Muir," 53, real estate operator, married, one child

There is always some room for negotiation. The company representative may have the discretionary ability to approve or disapprove certain payments.

I am a district attorney. When I developed breast cancer and needed radiation, I was told that the insurance wouldn't cover the cost of my wig. I went to the benefits coordinator, pulled off the wig, looked him in the eye, and said, "Do you expect me to go into court like this?" That man got in touch with the insurance company, and the payment for the wigs was authorized.—"Elena Settler," 35, married, two children

Before you go to a doctor who is not connected with your HMO or PPO (preferred provider organization), find out what the company's policy is or you may find yourself with a medical bill for which you won't be reimbursed.

Shortly after managed care insurance was put in place in our small firm, I was told I needed surgery. The nurse asked me for the referral from the primary care doctor. I didn't know what that meant. My referral to the surgeon had come from my internist, but he wasn't on my HMO as my primary care doctor. Because I didn't know the rules, I almost scheduled a surgery that would have been disallowed because it hadn't been pre-approved. I would have had to pay thousands of dollars out of my own pocket.—"Charlotte Adler," 29, librarian, married, two children

Read your policy. Have your agent explain it. Know what it covers. We can't stress this enough.

IF YOU LEAVE THE COMPANY

If you are fired or downsized, under a law known as COBRA (Consolidated Budget Reconciliation Act of 1986), you have a right to continue your medical insurance for 18 months by paying for it yourself. Under certain other circumstances—for example, if you are divorced from or widowed by someone who covered you under his insurance—your coverage may continue for 36 months if you are willing to pay. The cost may astonish you.

One way to cut costs when you have to pay for your own insurance is to increase the amount of the deductible. Catastrophic medical coverage may come with a deductible of $5,000 or $10,000 and relatively small annual payments. Since medical coverage is so costly, you may be better off paying for routine medical visits out of your own pocket and insuring yourself only for a major illness. Since many routine visits aren't covered anyway, you may come out very much ahead with this approach.

HUSBAND-AND-WIFE COVERAGE

When spouses work for separate employers, both may be offered medical insurance. There are at least three reasons to consider paying for double coverage. The companies may coordinate payments so that one picks up whatever portion of a medical bill the other does not. One plan may cover expenses that the other does not cover. And in a worst-case scenario, there could be a problem if one spouse became seriously ill, could no longer work, and then hoped to be covered by the other spouse's insurance. The expenses for the pre-existing condition of the ill spouse might not be reimbursed. Discuss the pros and cons of double coverage with the benefits specialist at your place of employment.

DISABILITY INSURANCE

Disablility insurance protects your most valuable asset: your ability to earn money. It works when you can't.

The very fact that disability policies are relatively expensive is an indication that companies are frequently obliged to pay. Six out of ten people will need some disability assistance in their lifetime. At thirty, your chance of being disabled for a period is five times greater than your chance of dying, at forty it's four times greater, and at fifty it's three times greater. And women are more often disabled than men, generally due to stress-related disorders and muscular/skeletal problems.

The primary reason to buy disability is income replacement. If you are unable to work due to illness or accident, the policy will pay you a certain amount of money for a certain amount of time.

> *As a makeup artist, I knew I was out of luck if I couldn't use my hands. I always had disability insurance.*—Laura Geller

Most people aren't this prudent. But look at the situation this way: if you had a machine that could produce $30,000, $100,000, or more a year, surely you would insure it against breakdowns for a certain period of time. Think of yourself as that machine. Being out of work even temporarily can be a disaster if you don't have the funds to replace your salary. Find a way to afford disability insurance. Cut back somewhere.

When we discussed disability in an informal group, each of us in the club realized we could name at least a couple of personal acquaintances who had been unable to work for an extended period due to injuries or long-term illnesses like Lyme disease or Epstein-Barr virus. Temporary disabilities affect many people who are generally in good shape.

My husband and I were both physically fit, healthy people. Between us, we collected disability insurance three times before either turned forty. I had a six-week recovery period from surgery for cancer of the mouth and a bout with a bad back that kept me in bed for six months. He had a toe-to-groin cast for nine months as the result of a bad skiing accident.—"Gillian Lord," 42, X-ray technician, married, one child

Social Security will cover only permanent disabilities, and many claims are denied. Workman's Compensation Insurance protects you for a maximum of six months and only if you are injured on the job. If you're disabled off the job, you're covered by State Mandatory Disability Insurance. That, too, lasts just six months. Even if you ultimately get this sort of coverage, it may not come through for months (or even years). Having disability insurance would provide at least some income in the meantime.

In buying a policy, one of your biggest concerns should be who defines the disability—your doctor or the doctor designated by the insurance company. (Different companies have different rules.) Some coverage will pay in case of an accident but not in case of sickness. Some companies won't pay unless you are completely disabled. The definitions may be very inflexible. One of us had even heard of a firm that doesn't consider mental illness a disability. (Needless to say, we immediately put this firm's stock on our Don't Buy list.)

Own occ (occupation) protection in a disability policy covers you whenever you are incapable of performing the duties specifically required by your chosen profession. With own occ, if a dentist has an accident that destroys a nerve in her hand and she can no longer perform as a dentist, or a saleswoman loses her voice, the coverage would pay. However, with *any occ* coverage, the company might take the position that they could work in an unrelated field: the dentist could make a living as a teacher and the saleswoman as a clerical worker. Some coverage gives you own occ for one to five years, then changes to any occ.

The amount of disability insurance you can buy is based on what you're earning when you take out the policy. A freelance writer whose income varies widely made a point to apply for disability during a top earning year. But you might wind up applying in a bad year, when you are most concerned about possible loss of income. You can always try to raise your coverage by having the policy reviewed when you're doing better.

In no case will the coverage replace more than 60 percent of your normal salary. If you make $6,000 a month, the coverage will not exceed $4,000 a month. The insurance companies don't want to encourage claims for disability when none exists. They are also very restrictive about issuing policies. You can't apply unless you are working, and not everyone who applies will qualify.

The waiting period before the money starts coming, the size of the benefit, and the length of time it continues all affect the cost of the policy. If you agree to a waiting period of ninety days, your coverage may cost as much as 50 percent less than if you will wait only thirty days. Some policies don't pay until you have been disabled 180 days.

Coverage for residual or partial benefits may be optional. The former gives you supplemental income if you can do some work but not up to your normal capacity. The latter gives you an additional three to six months of coverage if you're partially disabled.

A COLA—cost of living adjustment—may add 25 percent to the cost of the policy. The adjustment may be calculated according to a specified rate or tied to the consumer price index.

For the best protection, you should have a policy that cannot be canceled. Otherwise, the insurer could give you the boot the minute you file a claim. It should also be guaranteed renewable, which means that if you pay the premium, it can't be canceled. And hikes in the premium should be limited to occasions when the company is raising premiums on all its policies.

Less than a quarter of small companies give employees disability insurance, but club members who worked at large companies reported that they could purchase it through a payroll deduction. One didn't like her policy and, at Gloria's suggestion, asked to get credit for the amount of the premium to apply toward a better policy of her own. You can also buy supplementary insurance.

If you collect disability insurance, the income from the insurance you paid for personally is tax-free. The income from company-funded disability is taxable. If you leave a company, under the COBRA regulations you can keep your disability insurance current, like your medical insurance, by direct payment for a limited period. A friend of ours didn't know about this and let the insurance lapse by one week, then wound up disabled and without coverage for a year and a half.

Many policies supply only 50 to 60 percent of your income. Some won't pay disability that equals more than a certain percentage of your wages, even if you have taken a private policy in addition to your company policy for extra protection.

Since it's supposed to guarantee work income, disability coverage may be extremely expensive or totally unavailable once you reach sixty-five, the usual retirement age. Younger people should take out the most disability insurance, because if you have a long-term disability you may never be able to build a pension fund.

CHECKLIST FOR DISABILITY INSURANCE

Review each of these points when you are buying disability insurance. If the policy is too restrictive, you may want to look elsewhere for your insurance.

1. How is disability defined and by whom?
2. Own occ or any occ coverage?
3. Amount of coverage you can purchase?
4. Elimination period before money comes in?
5. Length of benefit period?
6. Do you get residual or partial benefits?
7. Cost of living adjustment included?
8. Guaranteed noncancelable?
9. Guaranteed renewable?
10. Premiums waived while you are collecting?
11. Raises in premium limited?
12. Notification policy: your policy may require you to notify the company within a certain period in order for you to collect.

PROPERTY INSURANCE

Property insurance protects you, your income, and your property—your house, your furniture, your car, your furs, your jewelry, your collectibles—against loss or damage.

Homeowner's policies usually cover damage to the house itself plus attached structures or outbuildings and the contents. They may reimburse certain living expenses if the house becomes uninhabitable due to damage. There are six different forms of homeowner's policies, of which these are the most common:

An *HO-1* covers damage from fire, lightning, storms, explosions, riots, vehicles and aircraft, smoke, theft, vandalism, and glass breakage. It excludes damage from a burst water pipe, replacement of appliances in the event of fire, and certain other problems. An *HO-2* is similar but also covers damage from falling objects and the weight of snow and ice on a deck or roof; water or steam pipe damage; damage from a hot water heating system; and injuries to electrical appliances, devices, and wiring. An *HO-3 (special form)* and *HO-5* provide additional, increasing amounts of coverage but exclude flood, earthquake, war, and nuclear accident. Earthquake insurance in most cases may be purchased separately. Low-cost flood insurance from the Federal Insurance Administration can be purchased through your local insurance agents.

Renters can buy an *HO-4*, which doesn't cover the building itself but does cover personal property and provides liability insurance to cover you if someone sues for an injury or damage that occurs on your premises or as a result of your actions. An *HO-6* is designed for condominium owners. Though the tenant association carries insurance on the structure, the condominium owner must insure fixtures and all additions and alterations to the unit as well as other personal property and have liability coverage.

As a rule of thumb, in homeowner's insurance the replacement value of the contents is considered to be half the value of the house itself. So if you have a $200,000 homeowner's policy, you're automatically covered for $100,000 worth of contents. Some policies require you to carry insurance equal to 80 percent of the replacement value of your house in order to give you full value for your loss.

Gloria pointed out to the club members that to get full replacement value you need a *new for old* rider. Let's say you paid $5,000 for a sofa a few years ago that now is priced at $6,000. If something happened to the sofa and you didn't have the rider, you would get back only market or depreciated value—the amount that the (used) sofa would currently be worth. In other words, very little. However, with a new for old rider, you get the $6,000 you would need to buy the sofa today. This sort of coverage is expensive but worth the difference.

There are many exclusions in homeowner's insurance. Your home office may not be covered. Claims for jewelry, silver, and firearms may be limited to $1,000 or less. Claims for cash, stock certificates, coin collections, and other items are also limited. If you want coverage for these or other items of value, such as furs or a camera, which are considered "unscheduled personal property," you have to make special arrangements. Each can be covered by a rider.

Such coverage is relatively inexpensive but requires documented proof of the item's value—a receipt or an appraisal (which may cost a few dollars). One club member asked Georg Jensen, the silversmith, to give an estimate of the cost of a ten-piece place setting and some serving pieces. The estimate cost $50, Georg Jensen appraised the silver at $24,000, and the member pays $46 per year for the rider. If you don't know where to get an appraisal, your insurance agent can help.

Check your homeowner's coverage carefully. It may or may not cover damage or loss of property outside your home. Whenever an item is damaged or stolen, whether you are at home or away, call your insurance company to inquire if you are covered for the loss. But always ask what impact making a claim will have on your premium. Sometimes it's less expensive to replace the item than to pay a higher premium year after year.

Once you have made arrangements for property coverage, you receive a binder, temporary coverage that goes into effect immediately and lasts until the insurer accepts or rejects your application. Rejection is unlikely but possible if you live in a neighborhood or a type of building that is considered too high-risk.

Review your policy periodically to adjust it for changes in property values and inflation.

AUTOMOBILE LIABILITY INSURANCE

Car liability coverage is usually described in three numbers, such as 100/300/50, which translates to $100,000/$300,000/$50,000. The first number is the limit for bodily injury per person per accident; the second is the limit for bodily injury per accident; and the third is the limit for property damage.

Imagine you are involved in a serious accident and three people sued you for medical expenses, lost wages, and so on. You are entitled to legal defense paid for by your insurance company. If you win, you're off the hook. Suppose, however, that you lose. Two of the injured are suing for $100,000, and the third wants $150,000. Since you're covered for $100,000 per person per accident, the first two would get what they want. The third would get $100,000 too, since you're covered only for $100,000 per person and $300,000 per accident. You've reached both limits. The plaintiff who asked for the additional $50,000 might sue you for it personally.

Some states set a minimum for your liability coverage, but the maximum is up to you. Someone who believes you have a great deal of money may sue for a larger amount than he would otherwise. Your age, driving record, and other factors determine the cost of your insurance. Adding thousands of dollars of additional coverage doesn't raise the cost a great deal.

Liability coverage is third-party coverage—it covers only the other driver's losses. To cover your own losses, you will need first-party coverage, which includes:

- ***Collision coverage.*** This pays the cost of repairing damage to your vehicle, whether or not you were at fault. (If the other driver is at fault, your insurer will pay for a lawsuit.) Since you won't be reimbursed for repairs that cost more than the car's value, some people don't bother with collision coverage on an older car. Sometimes you can reduce the cost of your premium just by selecting a high deductible.
- ***Comprehensive coverage.*** This pays for any losses to your car or property inside it due to theft, fire, or vandalism. It also covers damage from falling objects and broken glass. Cut costs by selecting a high deductible.

- ***Medical coverage.*** This is no-fault insurance. Whoever is injured can collect no matter who is to blame. The state may require a certain minimum. If not, and if you already have medical coverage, this is redundant.

Car insurance policies also include uninsured motorist's coverage and underinsured motorist's coverage, which protect you in case of an accident where the other driver has no insurance or an insufficient amount to cover the damages. For your own protection, you may want to take out more insurance than the mandatory minimum.

UMBRELLA LIABILITY INSURANCE

Homeowner's property policies include liability coverage. This protects you if you or a family member is sued for negligently injuring someone or damaging property. It also pays for medical expenses if someone is injured on your property.

To protect yourself against a catastrophe—some personal event that would exceed your auto liability or homeowner's liability protection—you need umbrella liability coverage. The friend of a club member was ruined many years ago when a child attending a barbecue at his home was badly burned and the family sued. Nothing could have protected the man from the psychological consequences of the event, but if he'd had umbrella liability insurance he would have been spared the anguish of going into bankruptcy. As we in the club are very well aware, sympathetic juries often award enormous settlements in liability cases. Umbrella insurance can provide insurance for up to $10 million at relatively low cost.

Umbrella liability insurance also covers gaps in your other policies. For example, a club member's decorator was sued by someone who slipped while coming to a business meeting in her home. It turned out that the homeowner's policy didn't provide liability protection for her home office but the umbrella coverage did. Another advantage of umbrella liability is the fact that if you're sued, the insurance company will defend you in a lawsuit before paying. Without the policy, you would have to pay for legal expenses out of pocket.

LONG-TERM-CARE INSURANCE

I've had long-term-care insurance for a long time—not because I was smart, but because my friend's mother broke her hip, became bedridden, and needed full-time nursing care. She exhausted all her savings. I looked at what happened to her family emotionally and financially and took out insurance.—Margot Green

The popularity of long-term-care insurance is a recent phenomenon. Long-term care is custodial and/or skilled care for a person who needs assistance for daily living at home or in a nursing home. It also provides coverage for post-surgical (or other types) of rehabilitation; for prolonged rehabilitation for accident victims (like Christopher Reeve); or for assistance to someone with a debilitating illness.

There are four levels of assistance. The highest and most expensive is skilled round-the-clock care provided by licensed professionals working under a doctor's supervision. Intermediate care may also be provided by a licensed professional such as an RN or a physical therapist, though not necessarily on a daily basis. Custodial care involves nonprofessional assistance with routine activities such as walking, dressing, bathing, eating, getting in and out of bed, taking medication. Home health care, a relatively new concept, involves a licensed practitioner such as a nurse or lab technician making a home visit to provide services formerly offered only at a hospital.

Those of us in the club with older parents had almost all mistakenly assumed that Medicare will pay for this kind of help, then discovered that it would not. Medicare is designed primarily to fund acute medical care for people over sixty-five who are entitled to Social Security benefits or who qualify under the Railroad Retirement Act. Once you have paid a deductible and initial co-payment, Medicare Part A covers most hospital expenses, including cost of the room, nursing staff, some skilled nursing home care, and certain at-home medical services. Part B pays for doctors' fees, with some exceptions. According to one survey, Medicare covers only about 74 percent of actual hospital-related bills and 54 percent of doctors' bills. Ten standard voluntary supplemental policies—so-called Medigap insurance—are available to help cover the difference. Some of these cover catastrophic illnesses.

Medicare also pays for hospice care for the terminally ill and may cover some costs of full-time skilled home care and/or a physical therapist. But it pays nursing home fees only under certain restrictive conditions. Of the billions spent on nursing home care annually, Medicare covers less than 5 percent. Yet a large number of older Americans may at some point be in a nursing home.

Medicaid covers some costs, but Medicaid is welfare. In theory, you have to use up your assets before you qualify for it, but seniors with very limited assets qualify right away. Wealthy seniors used to see a lawyer and become "poor" immediately by transferring their assets and/or establishing trusts for their own benefits. However, as of January 1, 1997, as part of the Health Insurance Portability and Accountability Act, some such transfers were criminalized. To wade through the consequences of this, you will have to consult with an attorney who specializes in elder law.

Meanwhile, the most straightforward alternative to having your assets whittled away by medical and nursing home costs is long-term-care insurance. Since January 1, 1997, this type of insurance has been treated like accident and health insurance for tax purposes. The premiums—and long-term-care services—became legitimate medical deductions for anyone who itemizes. Self-employed people can take a partial deduction. This makes the purchase of long-term-care insurance much more attractive. However, residents of certain states may not be able to purchase policies that qualify for the deduction. Your insurance agent can guide you.

Premiums are based on such variables as age of the applicant, size of the benefits (from $50 to $300 daily), and length of coverage (three years to a lifetime). Don't be penny-wise about purchasing these policies. The price differential between limited coverage and lifetime care may be only 10 percent.

We were all startled when one club member reported reading that the average woman today will spend more years caring for her aging mother than she will have spent caring for a child. When possible, we are recommending that our parents take out this kind of insurance and definitely considering it for ourselves.

CHECKLIST FOR LONG-TERM-CARE INSURANCE

There is a tremendous variation among policies. Go over any policy you are considering with the agent line by line.

1. What is the cost now? In five years? In ten?
2. What is the daily dollar benefit?
3. How long does the benefit continue? Is there a maximum?
4. What is the waiting period for the benefit? Does coverage begin on the first, 21st, 30th, 60th, or 90th day?
5. Does the policy cover care both at home and in a nursing home?
6. What qualifications must be met for the policy to become effective? Is a hospital stay, a skilled nursing home stay, or any kind of prior nursing home stay a prerequisite for any type of coverage, and how long must the stays last?
7. What level(s) of care are covered: aide/practical nurse/skilled nurse? What is the maximum paid for each level?
8. Is there an inflation rider? (Payments go up tied to inflation.)
9. Is there a waiver of premium rider? (Premium is not charged in certain circumstances.)
10. What is the renewability policy?
11. What, if any, are the limits on pre-existing conditions? Is Alzheimer's disease covered?
12. Does the policy pay a fixed dollar amount or a percentage of care expenses?
13. Will it keep paying up to a predetermined amount of dollars or length of time; or until a qualified care provider has made a certain number of visits?
14. What medications are covered? Are experimental medications covered?
15. Are there age restrictions?
16. Does the policy provide benefits if you move?
17. Are there any other limitations, exclusions, or conditions?
18. Are alcohol-related, drug-related, or other types of diseases excluded?

Remember that you get a free thirty-day look period for this policy, during which you may cancel.

ANNUAL INSURANCE REVIEW

Along with your life insurance policy, review your other policies. Did you buy any new possessions that require additional coverage? Is your child nearing an age where the medical policy will no longer cover her? Are there any other changes in your health, your family situation, and your financial status that require some adjustments?

> *My husband's insurance contained a rider that excluded a pre-existing condition—problems with his back—for two years. At the end of that time, he confirmed on the phone with his broker that the waiting period was over. He went into the hospital for some minor elective surgery and came out paralyzed. Then we discovered that the agent had failed to get the insurance properly in place. We sued, but never got the full amount.*—"Melissa Bryant," 56, travel agent, married, three children

There are three secrets to being thoroughly protected by insurance. The first is, review your policies. The second is, review your policies. And finally, review your policies. This will do more to keep away worry lines than any cream on the market.

CHAPTER 7

WHAT YOU NEED TO KNOW ABOUT YOUR HUSBAND'S MONEY

Planning His (and Your) Estate

A cardiologist worked with a lawyer on careful planning in anticipation of large estate taxes. But the doctor failed to mention an important detail: he and his partner of twenty-five years had signed an agreement that if one died, the survivor would get the $3 million practice with no money changing hands. After the cardiologist's death, his wife and other heirs were hit with a bombshell: there was $800,000 in estate tax due on his $1.5 million "gift" (the value of half the practice)—and it would have to come out of their share of the inheritance.

You personally may not be dealing with a problem of this magnitude. Indeed, if your estate is under $600,000*, you have no estate tax issues at all. But there are several nonmoney concerns that are part of estate planning that we in the club were very concerned about—and they may well involve you, too.

One is *guardianship.* If you have responsibility for a minor child (or an incapacitated adult), you must name someone to take your place if the need ever arises. You will have to make this decision when the children are young, but at some point they will be mature enough to discuss whom they would choose to live with if you weren't available to care for them.

*As we go to press, the government is considering raising this figure.

You should instigate such a conversation. Many teenagers know (or know of) another child who has faced such a predicament and have thoughts to share. Hear what your children have to say, even if some of their wishes can't be accommodated. (The parents of their best friends may not be willing to serve as their guardians.) Revisit this topic every so often, since as children grow older, relatives move out of or into the area, and relationships alter, naming a different guardian may be appropriate.

A second estate issue is *health and incapacity*. If you (or your spouse) are disabled, who would take over the business and financial duties, from writing checks to managing investments? Who would make decisions about medical procedures? What kind of life-sustaining measures do you want to authorize in the case of a terminal illness? These choices should be put down in writing.

A third issue is *property*. How are the house, car, and other assets owned? Who holds the title? And at death, how will they be transferred?

Moreover, even if your estate falls within the $600,000 limit and is not subject to federal estate taxes, state taxes may apply. For example, in New York, when the second spouse dies, state taxes become due on any estate over $115,000. You have to plan accordingly.

Carlyn McCaffrey, a club member and an estates and trusts attorney, pointed out that the sooner you deal with all of these issues, the better. We agreed that the more remote and distant they seem, the less emotional the discussions will be and the more logical the planning. If circumstances change, the plans can always be modified. Do not make the mistake of postponing these conversations until someone is terminally ill. Although the need is then urgent, talking becomes even more difficult.

> *After my husband became sick, he and I avoided any serious discussion about how I would take care of things if he died, since that sent the unspoken message that he wasn't going to make it. Fortunately, my husband had already put our affairs in order. But if this is not the case, and a woman is in a similar situation, she must find a way to get her husband to sit down and talk.*—Lucy Feller

Sometimes last wishes aren't clarified until a person is on the deathbed—an awkward scenario that has been described as burying a person who is still alive. After some experts talked to us, club members vowed we would not let that happen to us or a spouse.

STARTING POINT: THE WILL

A will is the legal document that directs what should be done with your property when you die. It should state how and to whom you are leaving your money and possessions and appoint *fiduciaries*—responsible parties, including executor(s), guardian(s) if there are young children, and trustee(s) if necessary—to help see that everything is done as you wish. What constitutes a will is determined by state law. For example, in New York a will must be written, signed, and then witnessed by two people who are not beneficiaries.

A will is subject to *probate*, a court procedure that confirms that the will is authentic, approves it, and ensures that bills are paid and assets are properly distributed. There are several problems connected with probate. The process can be slow and/or expensive, depending on the laws of your state. If you have residences in two states, the process can be even more cumbersome. Even more disturbing is the invasion of your privacy. Probate makes the will a matter of public record that unscrupulous people can scan and then approach the survivors at a vulnerable time. One way to avoid probate is by setting up a *revocable trust*, also called a *living trust* (see page 224). You will still need an ordinary will to appoint a guardian and to dispose of anything that has not been placed in trust.

If you die intestate—without a will or trust—your heirs will discover that the state has provided a will for you. For example, in New York, if you are married but have no children, everything goes to your spouse, and vice versa. If you have both a spouse and children, the first $50,000 goes to the spouse and the rest is divided equally among the spouse and the children. If there are minor children and you haven't named a guardian, the other parent will be named the guardian of their person but the surrogate's court will select a guardian of their property—for example, the proceeds of any life insurance. You could leave a very awkward situation behind. To exercise control over what happens to anything that is precious to you, you need a will.

A will also gives you an opportunity to be very specific about your last wishes. You may, for example, specifically disinherit someone. If you simply leave a child out of the will, the state law will not assume you mean to disinherit. Johnny might successfully convince a judge that the omission was an oversight, though it's hard to imagine simply "forgetting" a child. If your intention is to leave Johnny nothing, you must say so in your will. You may even specify that anyone who challenges the will will be automatically cut out of it. But it is virtually impossible to disinherit a spouse completely. Generally you must leave a spouse at least the minimum that the state law requires. If you want to leave him nothing, you have to divorce him first.

LETTER OF INSTRUCTION

The lawyers who spoke to our club suggested that in addition to the will we also prepare a letter of instruction and/or lists to tell our heirs in greater detail anything they need to know. (If you've followed our suggestions in the Resources section for putting your papers in order, you've already gathered this information.) This is an excellent means of tying up a lot of loose ends, because you can deal with all of the following:

IMMEDIATE MATTERS

As part of the letter, or attached to it, include a copy of the Master List from the Resources section, which contains information about all your financial contacts. Provide a list of where personal papers can be found. Give your heirs specific instructions about the people they'll be dealing with. For example, write, "I always dealt with Harry's firm and they have my will; but when Harry died everything was turned over to a new associate whom I don't know very well. You can either stay with that person or find someone more convenient or more suitable. The insurance agent, Sam, is very knowledgeable about our personal insurance and also about the insurance for our property in Perth Amboy." And so on.

ESTATE-RELATED MATTERS

Provide information regarding your wishes about a funeral and burial. List any money market accounts and other liquid investments in the name of your spouse (or other family members) to provide cash for immediate needs. Remind heirs to make life insurance, pension, Social Security, and other claims once they have the necessary papers. If you have established a trust, describe it in your own words, so that they understand its intent. If you have given the trust beneficiaries the right to change trustees, say so here.

GUIDE FOR DEALING WITH BUSINESS ASSETS

A self-employed person must arrange with a colleague for a plan of succession and a formula for compensation. Otherwise the biggest asset—a business or practice—is lost to the heirs.

> *The fact that my husband had done no estate planning hurt me and the children tremendously. It also gravely affected my husband's clients. Fortunately, our accountant found a lawyer who could take over all the cases, and we received a percentage of the billing. Until that was worked out, we were in a desperate situation. We had been living comfortably, and suddenly there wasn't a dime coming in.*—"Dorothy Boyce," 42, housewife, widowed, four children

If you have made plans for a buyout or sale, explain the arrangements in your own words for the sake of your heirs. Although one of the club members knew vaguely what her husband's plans were, she asked him to use this letter as a vehicle to explain them in a way she could understand.

SMALL PERSONAL BEQUESTS

Fights over personal items are the most common cause of long-standing family rifts. Use this letter to state which personal effects you want specifically to leave to anyone. Although some of them may be disappointed at your choices, at least they won't be angry with one another. One club member has placed colored stickers on the bottom of each of her possessions and broken the code in the letter of instruction. One daughter will someday learn that the green stickers under the china and other items will indicate that they are hers, and another will learn that the blue stickers under the glass paperweights and the chest of drawers mean that those have become her possessions.

STATEMENTS FOR POSTERITY

You may take this last opportunity to summarize your life and its meaning, to express affection, and/or to give advice. Think carefully about your message. We know two brothers who were devastated by a well-intentioned last note from their mother. They were hoping to hear some words of satisfaction about their achievements and character, and instead she left them rules of conduct.

CLARIFICATIONS

If children have been treated unequally or you think your trust plans may leave the beneficiaries puzzled, explain your reasons in the letter of instruction. But let your estate planner review the way you've worded your explanations. Some of them may have unintended legal consequences.

Our advisors told us that more and more people have decided to leave a videotaped final message to clarify issues and/or raise the points discussed above. Some lawyers even have a taping setup just for this purpose that their clients may use in privacy. The tape is left with the will. Although this is not for everyone, there are club members who think a tape might be useful.

WHERE THE WILL IS KEPT

The lawyer who prepares your will will probably offer to keep the signed original. There should only be one in existence. Otherwise, if it is known that there is a copy and it can't be found when you die, in some states the courts will presume that that will has been revoked. For informational purposes, you may give unsigned, conformed copies—"conformed" means that names of signatories are typed into the appropriate spots—to your trustee, your children, and/or other trusted individuals. After a death, heirs may request the return of the signed will from a lawyer if they wish, and proceed to an attorney of their own choosing. Make sure they know this.

Don't keep a will in a safe deposit box. (See Resources, I and II.)

POWERS OF ATTORNEY

Often a power of attorney, a living will, and a health care proxy are prepared at the same time as the will.

A *power of attorney* gives another person the right to sign papers on your behalf. Assign your power of attorney only to someone you thoroughly trust, because it conveys broad rights. (There is a commonly used power of attorney form that lists the various options.) You may sign a *limited power of attorney*, which restricts that right to a single transaction or a single type of transaction.

Both a limited and an ordinary power of attorney become invalid if you become incompetent, which is exactly when you might want someone else to be able to sign on your behalf. So you can sign a *durable power of attorney*, which remains in effect even in this case. Or you can have a *springing power of attorney*, which comes into effect only if you're physically or mentally incompetent, and you can attach restrictions and conditions. For example, it may spring only if you are disabled. Or it may give someone the power to take reasonable care of you and pay bills but not to dispose of your assets.

Like a will, a power of attorney should not be kept in a safe deposit box, which may be sealed if the bank discovers that you have lost your mental capacities. (We did wonder how the bank would find out.) Of course, such a situation is just when such a document may be needed. So give copies of your power of attorney to your lawyer and the person to whom you've delegated your power.

Review these documents from time to time. You may decide to withdraw or reassign them.

> *When my husband and I were selling our former dry cleaning business, I signed a power of attorney giving him the right to sign on my behalf but not limited to that transaction. Ten years later, when we were on the verge of separating, I went away for the summer and came home to find a different name on the mailbox. He had used my power of attorney to sell the house we owned jointly.*—"Ellen Simpson," 48, owner of retail dry cleaner, divorced, two children

LIVING WILL

A living will is a legal document that allows you to state your desires regarding the use of extraordinary medical measures or procedures—such as a respirator, feeding tube, and intravenous therapy—that would delay death when your condition is terminal. It can also specify whether surgery should be attempted, pain medication can be used, or organs can be donated. It's the document that allows your family to permit the doctors to pull the plug.

Preprinted living will forms are available from your personal attorney, doctor, hospital, or state medical association. A living will must be signed by you and two witnesses.

Give signed copies of the living will to your doctor, your lawyer, your grown children, and whomever you've entrusted to make this decision for you. People with very serious medical problems may wish to carry a copy of the living will. If they are taken ill, in the absence of such a document, medical personnel are forced to use life-sustaining measures that may not be desired.

HEALTH CARE PROXY

A *health care proxy,* also called a *medical durable power of attorney,* authorizes someone to make decisions about medical procedures on your behalf when you cannot. It is different from a living will in several ways. It appoints a person to act on your behalf to make all medical decisions rather than just those that come up toward the end of your life, and it can include specific instructions about any treatments you do or don't wish to have. If you do not formally name someone as your agent to do this job, a health care provider or institution may make decisions for you or a court may appoint a guardian.

The most frequently changed item when wills are redrawn is the name of the agent on the health care proxy. Obviously, you will want to think long and carefully about whom to entrust with the burden of responsibility these documents delegate. Name both an agent and an alternate. Sign four original copies: keep one, send one each to your agent and alternate, and send one to your doctor.

Those of us in the club who had recent experiences with hospitalizations noted that it is customary nowadays for a hospital to give a newly admitted patient (or the family) living wills and health proxies. If the hospitalization is planned and the situation isn't serious, dealing with these forms isn't a problem. But the last thing you want to do is wave these forms under the noses of elderly or gravely ill patients. They may not even be competent to sign. Don't let this happen. Collect blank forms from a hospital, and when you're together in a calm situation have everyone in the family—from grandparents to grown children—sign the forms and exchange copies with one another.

A *uniform anatomical gift form* specifies that you want one or more of your organs donated at your death. The states determine the nature of the form. In New York, for example, it is part of your driver's license.

WHEN A SIMPLE WILL ISN'T ENOUGH

If your estate—or, in the case of a couple, the estate of whoever is the second to die—will be smaller than $600,000,* you can have a simple will, sometimes known as a sweetheart will, in which you simply leave everything to one another. You can leave an unlimited amount to a spouse, provided the spouse is a U.S. citizen, and no federal taxes will be due. Federal

*As we go to press, the government is considering raising this figure.

estate taxes apply and affect the beneficiaries only when the second spouse dies and the estate is larger than $600,000.

Ross Kass, of Jablons, Kass & Greenberg, an accounting firm, told our club that most people are richer than they think. They look in their bankbook, and there's nowhere near $600,000 in the account, so they rule out the need for estate planning. But when you add together the value of a home, personal effects including jewelry and antiques, even the potential value of goodwill to a self-employed person's business—and especially if there are life insurance proceeds or pension benefits from the death of the first spouse—many people have $600,000 and more. Your beneficiaries may have to pay taxes starting with the first cuff link or earring that brings the worth of your estate over the tax-exempt limit.

Federal taxes on estates are huge. They start at 37 percent on estates that range in size from $600,000 to $750,000 and rise to 55 percent on the affected portion of an estate of $3 million. Depending on what you spend, how well your investments do, and the effects of recession or inflation, the total of the assets you own this very minute will change before you die. Most likely they will increase. A good attorney can help you leave money for the enjoyment of your own relatives rather than for the enrichment of Uncle Sam.

The computer programs that do estate planning and write your will are good, but they are based strictly on numbers. Almost certainly, you have some concerns that aren't strictly financial. For example, club members had a range of opinions about the age at which their children could be relied on to manage (and so inherit) money. Some of us wanted to provide for our children in different ways. One might be better off; another might have special medical needs. An attorney can put together a plan tailored for you.

FINDING AN ESTATES AND TRUSTS SPECIALIST

As club member and attorney Carlyn McCaffrey explained, trusts and estates lawyers have two jobs. One is to draw up the documents so that the people you care about receive your assets in the manner you wish with as little hassle and as few taxes as possible. The other is to carry out your wishes by guiding your executor and/or beneficiaries through the process of administering your estate after your death, paying your final bills and taxes, and distributing your remaining assets according to plan.

A good attorney needs strong people skills along with legal know-how. Estate planning involves some very sensitive topics: your money and your feelings about the people you're leaving it to, their strengths, their weaknesses, and the nature of their relationships with one another.

If a husband and a wife use the same lawyer for estate planning, as they often do, the lawyer represents them both and has an ethical responsibility to treat them equally. As we have pointed out before, sometimes a wife feels that her husband, not the couple, is the client. Try to build your own relationship. Call the lawyer with any questions you might have, both to clarify the issues and open a line of communication. The more contact you have, the more your lawyer will be inclined to give your concerns as much weight as those of your husband.

If that fails to be helpful, tell your husband you want to go to another attorney. Since the estate planning should be reviewed every couple of years, each new planning occasion provides a logical opportunity to consult with someone new. In any event, it is sometimes useful to get a second opinion. If you see a new attorney whom both you and your husband like, perhaps you can make a switch.

A lawyer in another specialty may be able to give you a referral to a colleague in trusts and estates. Or get a suggestion from the development officer of your favorite charity, who presumably deals with many lawyers in the course of administering trusts.

The lawyer's fee will depend on what is customary in your part of the country, which firm you use, and what your estate planning involves. Obviously, the fancier the neighborhood, the more prestigious the firm, and the more complicated your situation, the larger it will be. For estate planning and drawing up the will, you may pay a set fee or hourly rate. For handling the estate, you may pay a set fee or a percentage of the estate. If the estate is large but well organized, a set fee may be preferable. Once you've negotiated a deal, ask for a written confirmation, also called an *engagement letter*. There may be extra charges for such tasks as preparing tax returns or supervising a property sale.

WHEN YOU MEET WITH THE LAWYER

Before you meet with the attorney, you should have decided whom you will name as beneficiaries, whether you want them treated equally, and whether they will receive the money outright or in trust. You should also be prepared to name an executor, trustee, and/or guardian.

You should have the following information handy:

- Date of your marriage.
- Copy of prenuptial agreement(s), if any.
- Personal information for each child: age, whether married, occupation, and occupation of spouse.
- List of your assets: cash and money market funds, marketable securities, residential real estate, interest in closely held businesses, personal belongings, cash value of life insurance, pensions and IRAs, and so on.
- List of liabilities: mortgages, outstanding loans, and so forth.

If you expect an inheritance that will substantially affect the size of your assets, mention it to the lawyer. Don't withhold any information during preliminary discussions, because otherwise you won't get the most accurate advice. Besides, a conversation with an attorney is "privileged," meaning that nothing you say can be used against you, as any regular viewer of TV crime dramas knows. (However, a client-accountant conversation is not privileged. So if you suspect your late husband may have been underreporting cash or any other financial irregularities, have your attorney hire an auditor.)

As the attorney asks questions to gauge your financial and family situation, you'll have a chance to see how well his or her style suits you. If you're not compatible, find someone else. This should be a comfortable relationship.

Carlyn McCaffrey estimates that 70 percent of the people who come to see her for the first time have done no prior estate planning. Not infrequently, a wife will set up the meeting or come in for a consultation first and then bring her husband for a follow-up.

She pointed out that in a good marriage, both spouses have the same concerns: to provide for one another and the children. But there are some situations—for example, a second marriage, if the interests of a spouse and the children from a first marriage are antithetical—that call for his-and-her attorneys.

No matter whom you hire, you yourself are ultimately the most concerned caretaker of your own interests.

I was in shock after my husband's sudden death. As a result, the lawyers took to making decisions without consulting me, even though I was the executor. They thought they were doing me a favor, but I felt put down in the same way I did after my first huge job promotion, when my boss said, "Now don't let the fellows fill your pretty little head with figures." Finally, I took charge once again. Now I ask questions. I call often. I use my fax machine like crazy. I check the bills closely and ask that they be explained. I like my lawyers, but I realized that I couldn't look to anyone else to be my protector. I have learned that the only one who is truly interested in my welfare is me.—"Ruth Nusser," 55, merchandise and marketing consultant, widowed, grown daughter

IF YOUR HUSBAND WON'T SEE A LAWYER

If your husband won't take care of estate planning, or if he says he already has and is unwilling to discuss it further, consult an attorney by yourself. You may be able to present your husband with some information that gets his attention and inspires him to have everything reviewed. Your perseverance may have a positive payoff.

The assets were all in my husband's name, not because he was trying to do me out of anything but because he just hadn't made the time to deal with the planning and paperwork. I brought up the subject of estate planning periodically, though without being unpleasant. Finally, to celebrate our anniversary, he made the time. We went to an attorney together, and everything was done correctly.—"Barbara Golden," 42, high school principal, two grown children

OTHER KEY PLAYERS IN THE ESTATE-PLANNING TEAM

Depending on how complicated your situation is, your estate lawyer may consult with the other professionals in your life.

Your life insurance agent will help you work out what insurance you need for income replacement and who should own the policy.

Your accountant can give the lawyer an accurate picture of your assets and will ultimately be in charge of the many, complicated income and estate tax returns to be filed, especially if the estate includes a privately owned business and/or rental real estate. For a complicated estate, the accountant may prepare a spreadsheet listing your assets and how they are owned (jointly or individually). The accountant can also project what the taxes would be if you died today in a common accident, if you died at retirement age, and if you lived your complete life expectancy. Your accountant should review your estate plan after it is worked out.

Your financial planner may be able to provide additional useful information and should review the proposed plan.

If you're appointing a bank or trust company as an executor and/or including a gift to a charity, representatives of the bank or trust and/or the development office of the charity should be part of the planning.

THE ROLES OF THE EXECUTOR AND TRUSTEE

The executor is the person who has a short-term responsibility to close out the estate by collecting what's due, paying what's owed, distributing assets, and filing tax returns. An executor can be a spouse or other family member, friend, professional, or institution. Executors' fees are set by law in most states, usually on a sliding scale dropping from 5 to 2 percent.

Sometimes these are very large. In Florida the executor collects more than $55,000 on a $2 million estate. If an attorney acts as your executor, you won't be charged both executor's and attorney's fees. Even if the attorney might be willing, the court may not allow it.

A trust is a legal arrangement by which someone allows the *trustee,* a person or institution, to hold title to money or property for the beneficiaries. A trustee may be chosen from the same pool as the executor. When naming the trustee, always list several successors, in case your first choice cannot or prefers not to serve. A trustee's chief responsibility is to make investment decisions, which may include reviewing investments periodically, collecting income, and in some cases handling bookkeeping and accounting. If the trustee is an institution, it may provide detailed statements of assets and/or prepare all tax returns. A trustee's fee may be based on custom in your area or on the amount of assets in the estate. Sometimes the fees are established by state law.

The trustee also has broad discretionary powers to distribute income or principal. An heir may appeal to the trustee for cash for unforeseen medical expenses, to start a business, or buy a home, which most probably would be approved. But a request to finance a Corvette might not pass muster. Club members know of parents who have made provisions that would allow a trustee to turn off the spigot on funds if a child acted irresponsibly. On the other hand, some parents have given the right to a child to serve as co-trustee for his or her share on reaching the age of twenty-one. As a precaution, though, they have specified certain decisions in which the senior co-trustee has the final say.

One reason to review estate plans regularly is to see if the trustee and/or executor should be changed. Some states don't permit a nonresident to be an executor, so you will have to name someone else if your executor plans a move. Or you may no longer have a relationship with the bank or individual you formerly named. If you make a bank a trustee, be sure to give a relative the power to change the trustee. The banker in charge of handling the trust may turn out to be less than an expert at making investments.

Never make an in-law a trustee. In-laws tend to come and go, yet a trusteeship may keep you linked to someone with whom you no longer have anything in common.

My husband got along just great with my sister's husband, Jack. Unfortunately, my sister didn't. They got divorced and Jack went off to Hawaii. Because Jack had once worked in a bank, my husband had named him a trustee and never got around to making a change, when he suddenly died of pneumonia. Now my fate is in the hands of a guy who, as far as I can tell, is at a nonstop luau. We have a terrible time getting him to respond to our calls, and I resent that he has so much power over my life.—"Chris Sanford," 35, telemarketing worker, widowed, two children

PROBATE ESTATE VERSUS TAXABLE ESTATE

The *probate estate*—the estate dealt with in the will—may not be all-inclusive. For example, a beneficiary form, not a will, controls the disposition of pensions and insurance. The laws of the state may determine how jointly owned property is passed on. Property in trust may also follow other rules. The authority of a will may also be restricted by contracts you've signed, such as partnership buyouts and marital agreements, or overruled by state inheritance law.

The *taxable estate* includes much more than the probate estate. (Uncle Sam isn't particular about where he gets his money.) Whether or not they are mentioned in the will, all of the following are part of the taxable estate:

- What you own individually, from your furniture to your jewelry to your business interests.
- Your share of jointly owned property, from a house to a bank account. Only 50 percent of property owned with a spouse is considered to be in the estate of the person who dies. But 100 percent of property owned with someone else will be included in the taxable estate—unless the survivor can prove he or she contributed to its cost, and how much.
- Whatever you have transferred to someone else but kept control of. This may include:

  Anything in a *living trust* that is set up to allow everything you own to pass to another person without probate.

Anything in a *life estate,* property that has been transferred to a future heir but you have kept the right to use until you die.

Anything held in a *joint and survivor annuity,* a common way to pay out a pension plan. It gives the pension holder a fixed income for life and some to the spouse on the pension holder's death. Money due the pension holder is part of the estate.

- The proceeds of any life insurance policy whose ownership has been transferred within three years of death.
- The total of gifts you have made in your lifetime, with a few exceptions. Here's how that works:

TAXABLE AND NONTAXABLE GIFTS

The doctor whose story we told at the beginning of this chapter didn't realize that anything you give away may be considered part of your taxable estate. Similarly, if you own a life insurance policy for $50,000 and your niece is the beneficiary, the $50,000 is considered part of your taxable estate. She gets the money tax-free.

Many of the club members were surprised to learn that a person who gets a taxable gift doesn't pay the taxes. The giver (or giver's estate) does. In other words, your gift to one person may have the undesired and unintentional effect of reducing what you leave to someone else. You have to plan if you don't want this to happen.

Be sure to take advantage of all the opportunities to make tax-free gifts:

- Thanks to the unlimited marital deduction (and with few exceptions), spouses can give one another any amount tax-free.
- During your lifetime, you may make as many $10,000 gifts per year to as many people as you choose with no taxes owed by either you or them. A couple can each give $10,000. As a couple you can give each of your children (or anyone else) $20,000 per year. In this way you can reduce taxes on your estate without doing any paperwork.

- During your lifetime, you may also pay unlimited amounts for educational or medical benefits without tax consequences. A grandmother may pay a child's tuition or a parent may pay an adult child's medical insurance policy, so long as the check is made out directly to the school or insurance company. Otherwise, support to your children in excess of $10,000 a year becomes a taxable gift once they reach whatever age the state mandates—twenty-one in New York, for example, eighteen in California.
- Gifts made to charity with certain limitations are free of taxes.
- A total of $600,000 to person(s) not your spouse is also tax-free. During your lifetime and at death, you get a tax break called a *unified credit* of $192,800. That is exactly the amount that would be due in estate taxes if you gave away assets amounting to $600,000. But the unified credit cancels the obligation to pay the $192,800. That's why people say the first $600,000 in any estate is tax-free. Unification occurs when the total amount of your taxable estate is calculated. All the assets you owned at death are totaled and added to the total of taxable gifts you have made *during your entire lifetime.* Any gift tax already paid is deducted from your final estate tax bill.

Whenever you make a gift of over $10,000 to any one individual, you are obliged to file a gift tax return. We asked Carlyn how the government could find out about unreported gifts. She explained that one technique is to review lists of properties that have been transferred each month to see if gift taxes have been paid. Also, if an estate is audited after a death (which is likely if the estate is sizable), further investigation is possible. If the person was a business owner, the heirs will be asked who got the business. Then the government may take its own turn at giving that person the business!

An eighty-year-old mogul had a long-standing relationship with twins, former Playboy models. Over the years he presented one with jewels, fur, a house, and cash worth more than $3 million and the other with $1 million worth of goodies. The IRS found out somehow. They characterized the girls' "presents" as payments for "illegal services"—and went after them for taxes. The girls maintained that the presents were gifts. Daddy Bigbucks sided with the IRS, *but the courts excluded his testimony as being self-serving, on the grounds that if they were gifts, his estate, rather than the girls, would then be liable for the taxes. The case was taken to the appeals court.*

Someone with a great deal of money may gift assets during his or her lifetime that have the potential to grow. Even though taxes will be due, it may make sense to remove the asset before it becomes even more valuable and even larger estate taxes will be owed. However, assets that have already increased in value should be held, to take advantage of the new *tax basis* that will apply when the owner dies. For tax purposes the value of the assets is considered to be the amount they are worth on the date of death or six months afterward, whichever valuation date is chosen. Say your uncle bought a painting in the 1960s for $1,000. When he died in 1990, on the date of his death the painting was worth $12,000. He bequeathed it to you. The estate, if it was larger than $600,000, may have had to pay federal estate taxes on the painting, but you didn't. Then suppose you didn't like the painting and sold it the next year for $15,000. You would pay taxes only on the $3,000 profit, not on the entire $15,000.

But suppose your mom gives you a hundred shares of Amazing Uplift Lingerie that she bought at $20 and which is now selling for $80. Her gift comes to $8,000, which is under the tax-free allowance of $10,000 per year. No problem there. But if you decide to sell that stock at $100, you have to pay taxes on the difference between $20 per share—*her* original purchase price—and $100.

WHY TRUSTS ARE ESTABLISHED

Aside from the probate problems we have already discussed, a will takes a long time to settle. Assets may be tied up during the probate process and may lose value. Most important, when assets are passed by will, only a relatively small amount escapes taxation. That is why people turn to trusts. Any type of property can be transferred into a trust, including real estate, bank accounts, stocks, bonds, and insurance policies.

A trust can be used for any or all of the following reasons:

- To save estate taxes. Though the estate of the second spouse to die can pass on a total of $600,000 free of federal estate taxes (though there will still be state estate taxes), with the use of a trust a couple can bequeath up to $1,200,000 free of taxes.
- To protect family assets. The person who dies can set up a trust to assure a second husband or wife income for a lifetime and then return the bulk of the estate to the children from a first marriage.
- To plan for incapacity. In the absence of a trust (or the appropriate power of attorney), if you become incapacitated a court-appointed person will manage your affairs.
- To keep your affairs private.

I set up a trust for my son, who's divorced. I don't want his ex-wife to know how much money he's going to inherit because she'd start hounding him for more child support.—"Alexis Whyte," 55, art collector, widow, two grown children

REVOCABLE AND IRREVOCABLE TRUSTS

If a trust can be canceled, it is also known as revocable. A *revocable,* or *living, trust* (also known as a *grantor's trust*), is set up and starts operating while a person is alive. You put assets into it for your own benefit, act as your own trustee, and designate a beneficiary, but while you are living all income tax is paid as if the trust did not exist. The trust substitutes for a will, and the property in the trust passes directly to the beneficiary, escaping probate. When you die, there are no interruptions, delays, or expenses in bequeathing your money. If you become incapacitated, a living trust makes it a simple matter for your designated co-trustee to manage your assets.

A living trust is very flexible. You may take money out as you wish, change the trustee or any beneficiary, add or remove assets, change or add to the terms of the trust, or cancel it entirely. Along with the trust, people often create a type of will known as a *pour-over will.* It comes into existence at death and "pours" into the living trust any assets that weren't already there. Then the trust can manage all the assets at once.

An *irrevocable trust* makes outright gifts that can't be taken back. The purpose is to remove assets from the taxable estate and/or shift income to a family member in a low tax bracket and/or provide for the ongoing care of a spouse, children, or grandchildren. Examples are a marital deduction trust, trusts for children and other family members, a life insurance trust, or a trust for charity. *Inter vivos* trusts may be established while you are alive, and *testamentary* trusts are established by a will after death. At least two kinds of irrevocable trusts are commonly used in estate planning for spouses.

BASIC ESTATE PLANNING FOR COUPLES

One major piece of estate planning for couples is to ensure that there is enough cash to cover the immediate expenses of the survivor, pay estate taxes without having to sell off stocks or deplete other assets, and provide the surviving spouse with enough money to live on. It is likely that your husband will be the first to die. If he has put aside enough emergency cash to cover expenses for three to six months and purchased life insurance as explained in Chapter 6, these immediate needs will be taken care of.

The other piece of estate planning has to do with how the marital property will be passed to the survivor. State laws have a lot to say about what the surviving spouse (and in some cases the children) are due. Federal law applies only to retirement funds (IRAs, pensions, annuities) and profit-sharing funds.

In the nine *community property* states, Arizona, California, Idaho, Louisiana, Nevada, New Mexico, Texas, Washington, and Wisconsin, property that you acquire during marriage is community property. If your spouse dies, you're entitled to retain your half but nothing else. He may bequeath his half to whomever he chooses.

In other states, property owned with another person may be held as a *tenancy in common.* You each own half as an undivided interest, and in your will, you can bequeath your half to anyone. Or it may be held as a *joint tenancy* with the right of survivorship. You each own half, but you can't leave your share by will to anyone except your partner, who gets it automatically when you die, no matter how the will reads. *Tenancy by the entirety* is the same as a joint tenancy but applies only to married people. The property passes automatically to you when your spouse dies but it is included in the estate for tax purposes.

State laws govern the other assets as well. As we mentioned earlier, a surviving spouse (and in many states, the children) usually has a right to a fixed minimum percentage of the estate. In New York, for example, the surviving spouse gets at least one third of property owned at death, jointly held property, property held in revocable trust, and property transferred subject to a retained life estate (meaning the owner kept the right to use it). You can't disinherit a spouse if the state grants a fixed minimum because state law takes precedence over a will. Furthermore, a prenuptial or postnuptial agreement takes precedence over state law. It's unfortunate if you change your mind once the bloom is off the rose.

> *When I became engaged to my second husband, I made the emotional decision to give him my only asset, the beach cottage where we fell in love, and made that promise in the prenup. At this point, I'm looking at things more realistically. My husband is well fixed, and I'd prefer to leave the house to my daughter. But he's being prickly about my "reneging," and I can't change the deal. State law will grant him an automatic piece of my estate, and the prenup takes precedence even over that. When you sign a prenup, you've in effect done your estate planning.*—"Renee Ellis," 45, actress, married, one child

Carlyn pointed out to us that when there is no property, or when all your assets have been used up paying the estate taxes, rights to an estate are meaningless. The point of estate planning is to make sure those rights have maximum worth. The children or other beneficiaries of a married couple benefit at minimum from the fact that a person can leave $600,000 tax-free. Estate lawyers can increase that benefit by using a device called a *bypass trust.* When one spouse dies, his or her assets go not to the survivor but into the trust, where they are used for the benefit of the survivor during his or her lifetime. The trust may be set up so the spouse may dip into the principal for special purposes, such as medical expenses. When the surviving spouse dies, the assets in the trust bypass his or her estate and go to the other heirs, usually the children. Since the money is in a trust, it isn't taxed as part of the estate.

Say Sally and Harry have such an arrangement. When Harry dies, the bypass trust is established with $600,000. Sally receives the income it generates. Then she dies. The children get up to $600,000 of her estate, tax-free, *plus* whatever remains in the bypass trust. Result: the kids get as much as $1,200,000 without paying taxes on it. Of course, if the first spouse to die has no assets, the bypass trust has no point.

My parents' will was written properly and included a bypass trust, but the attorney hadn't been careful about determining what was owned and how. My dad, a physician, had $2 million in his name, mostly from his practice and the real estate it owned. Being unlicensed, my mother couldn't co-own the practice, but she could have held part of the real estate. However, when she died of a stroke, her assets consisted of $83 in her checking account. We will never get the benefit of a tax-free transfer from her bypass trust because there was no money in it.—"Joyce Mayer," 30, medical writer, married, two children

Even if a bypass trust hasn't been established prior to death and/or the assets haven't been properly allocated, there is the possibility of setting one up. The surviving spouse may "disclaim" assets, at which point they go into a bypass trust.

After the first $600,000 is placed into a bypass trust, the remainder of a spouse's holdings may be given outright to all the beneficiaries or left in a *marital deduction trust.* A marital trust may give the surviving spouse a "life estate with a power of appointment." This means the spouse gets both the income from the trust and the right to decide who gets the assets from the trust when he or she dies. The spouse and trustee both have a lot of freedom in using the principal, and may even agree to terminate the trust, but the trustee has the ultimate management and control. Since the money is being used for the benefit of the spouse, there are no estate taxes until it passes to the next beneficiary.

Another kind of marital trust is a *QTIP* (qualified terminable interest property) trust. This is as common a feature of a second marriage as a despised former spouse. It allows the grantor of the trust to exert control from beyond the grave. Like the other kind of marital trust, it is set up for the spouse to get the income during his or her lifetime. But at death, the spouse's rights (or "interest") terminate and the property goes to beneficiaries named by the grantor of the trust. These beneficiaries are often the offspring of the first marriage. If Wife Number Two is about the same age as her stepchildren, they may inherit when they're relatively old—or possibly never. Since this kind of a trust often allows the beneficiary some access to the principal, she may even fritter it away. As an incentive to keep it intact, her husband may leave part of the money to her children as well as his own. The trustee's rights may be broad or narrow. In this case, too, there are no estate taxes until the assets pass to the next beneficiary.

IF THERE'S A TRUST IN YOUR FUTURE

Trusts can be an excellent way to shelter your money from the government. For the person who establishes the trust, it can also be an excellent way to shelter the money from your heirs, by limiting its access.

Club members have many widowed friends who complain about being subjected to a trust that was set up to give them little or no control over the money or investments and no say in the disposal of the property when they die. They can't disinherit stepchildren, no matter how obnoxiously they may behave. Of course, the very purpose of such a trust was to limit control. (When women are the ones who have the money and create the trust, the issues are exactly the same, but the positions of the genders are reversed.)

Though a trust may be restrictive, it has many benefits:

- If a trust guarantees you money, you don't need the protection of a prenuptial.
- Future creditors can't attack what's in a trust for you.
- A trust can protect beneficiaries from control by a subsequent spouse.

- A trust can protect beneficiaries who have no expertise from making foolish investments.
- The trustee is available to give you impartial financial advice. He or she isn't trying to sell you a financial product. (However, bank trustees may not necessarily be financially savvy.)
- A trust can help you keep control over trust investments and allows indirect control over trust distributions.
- A trust can provide for a spouse before giving control to other beneficiaries.
- The contents of a trust you set up during your life are private. If you have a child with a drug problem, you can set up a trust that doesn't release an inheritance until the child has been drug-free for a certain amount of time. Your stipulation is not publicly known.
- Unlike the assets in a will, the assets in a trust aren't overseen by the court. You have some control over them.

If you know there will be a trust in your future, ask at least for the rights to invade the principal and to replace the trustee. If your husband won't agree to this, then do your best to protect and add to any assets in your name so that you will have some funds over which you have total control. During his lifetime, let *him* do the spending and keep your own money intact.

In some states, you have the right to receive money outright rather than in a trust. You can "elect against" the trust and take whatever the state law authorizes. However, in signing a prenuptial you may have given up this right.

ESTATE PLANNING CONCERNS FOR SINGLES OR SIGNIFICANT OTHERS

If a person without husband or children dies without a will, the property goes to his or her parents and, if they are not alive, to the parents' descendants. There is a hierarchy of relationships spelled out by the law, and your property may be divided up among distant relatives if they can establish that they are heirs. If you have other plans for what should be done with your assets, you had better put them in writing.

You should establish a living trust so there is someone named to take over your affairs if you are incapacitated.

To provide for a life partner, you may leave money outright, in which case it is a gift and taxes must be paid by your estate. Or you may establish a trust.

People who are cohabiting may be able to protect the survivor's right to remain in the present housing through a trust or will. (In certain rent-controlled or rent-stabilized housing, an unmarried partner has no right to remain in the premises if the leaseholder dies.)

OTHER GIVING TECHNIQUES

There are many ways to minimize estate taxes with which a professional can help you. Following are some of the most common:

A grantor retained annuity trust allows you to give away assets while keeping a temporary interest. You have the right to a fixed annual annuity. Since this isn't an outright gift—it's considered a gift of "remainder interest"—the calculation of the value for gift tax purposes is low.

A qualified personal residence trust is a way to reduce the amount of estate and gift taxes on a residence you leave to your heirs. You transfer the residence, or an interest in the residence, to a trust. You keep the right to live in it for a specified number of years, after which it is transferred to the children or retained in trust for the benefit of spouse and children. There is a gift tax, but for the purpose of calculating the tax, the value of the residence is reduced by the value of the retained interest. If the person who transfers the property outlives the term of the trust, there will be no more gift or estate taxes to the beneficiaries.

Life insurance trusts, if correctly set up and administered, can permit you to leave the entire proceeds of a life insurance policy on your life to any beneficiary. The key is the effective use of your annual $10,000 gift tax exclusion. First, you transfer your life insurance policy (or the money to buy a policy) to the trustee of your life insurance trust. This must be an irrevocable trust, meaning that you can't change your mind about who will receive the proceeds, although you can give some flexibility to the trustee to make changes. You must make later cash additions to the trust so the trustee can pay the premiums.

Your original purchase of the policy or its transfer to the trust and transfers of the premium amounts each year afterward are all gifts. Normally, the annual gift tax exclusion protects only current interests. Since the beneficiaries of this life insurance trust won't get the proceeds until your death, this isn't a current interest. But if you give your beneficiaries the right, at least for a limited period of time, to take your gifts out of the trust, the exclusion does apply. So each year, you and your trustee go through a little charade. You give the money to the trustee, who notifies your beneficiaries that they have the right to take the money out of the trust for thirty days afterward. Of course, you would be horrified if the beneficiaries took this invitation at its word and spent the money on a ski vacation in Aspen. The beneficiaries are supposed to leave the money just where it is so the trustee may use it to pay the insurance premiums.

Properly set up, a trust can provide protection that might not otherwise be anticipated.

My brother-in-law made a terrible mistake. He had a very large life insurance policy on himself with his wife as the beneficiary and their two children as the secondary beneficiaries. When the children were away at camp, both parents died in a fire at home. His will appointed us the guardians of the children, but because it hadn't been spelled out, the surrogate's court became the guardian of their property, which included the proceeds of the insurance. There were substantial estate taxes due on this money, and a stranger is now making decisions about how it is spent. Had my brother-in-law set up an irrevocable life insurance trust, he could have named someone familiar with the home situation as trustee to dole out the money as needed. Equally important, the proceeds would have been tax-free.—"Arlene Nova," 50, film producer, married, two children

An UGMA—Uniform Gifts to Minors Act—account lets you put away money for a child who will receive it at age eighteen or twenty-one (depending on the state). You cannot be both the custodian and the source of the income. Otherwise, if you set this up and die before the child is eighteen (or twenty-one), the full value of the money is taxable in your estate. So the child must inherit the money with no strings attached and is perfectly free to spend it on tattoos and nose rings. Needless to say, there were certain members of the club who had a lot of reservations about this kind of trust. A new vehicle has recently become available with a standard form that permits you to stipulate at what age the child can get the money. Ask your financial planner for details.

A charitable remainder trust (CRT) lets you sell a highly appreciated asset without paying capital gains taxes, reinvest the full amount, and increase your lifetime income. Here's how it works. Suppose you bought a stock that has grown greatly in value. On one hand, it provides little or no dividend income. But if you sold it, you would pay such large capital gains taxes that you would be left with a relatively small amount to reinvest. So you get virtually no benefit from this investment. With a CRT, you transfer the asset to a trust for both you and a charity. The charity sells it without paying any capital gains tax. The money stays in a trust and is invested. An amount of money (an annuity) goes to you and/or another beneficiary for life or a term of up to twenty years. The annuity can be either a fixed amount or percentage of the value of the trust each year. If what you gave away is sizable enough, the annuity may be big enough to buy a life insurance policy that replaces its entire value to your heirs. There are some restrictions about the type of gift that qualifies for this technique. You can change the trustee and change or add other qualified charities as beneficiaries.

A generation-skipping trust minimizes the tax bite to a wealthy family that will pass a lot of money down from generation to generation. Normally, money would be taxed as it passes from generation to generation: from father to son, then from son to grandson. This trust permits up to $1 million to go directly from a grandparent to a grandchild, so it is taxed only once. Different states have different laws regarding this kind of situation.

There are many other kinds of trusts and innovative ways to reduce taxes. For example, the IRS will let you make loans to your children at bargain rates without paying a gift tax, with some limitations. If your children can invest to earn a return higher than the IRS rate, they will keep the profits free of gift taxes.

Never give away more than you can spare, but maximize the possibilities by working with an estates and trusts lawyer.

ADDITIONAL TAXES

In addition to federal estate taxes and possible state estate taxes, there may be income tax due on certain inheritances. And if you've contributed more to a pension plan than the tax laws allow, there's also a 15 percent excise tax. Carlyn McCaffrey calculated that for a New York City resident with more than $1 million in a pension plan and $10 million in an estate, combined taxes can add up to 103 percent of the pension plan.

You won't owe estate taxes if you are the beneficiary of a spouse's tax-deferred pension plan, such as a 401(k), but you will have an income tax obligation. You can postpone the payment until you are seventy and a half by putting this money into a rollover IRA, but eventually you will have to pay. Remember, this is money that hasn't yet been taxed.

> *When my father died, the attorney said we wouldn't owe any taxes on my inheritance—that any taxes on the estate would come out of the estate. But he didn't explain to us that there were* income *taxes due on any money that was put aside in tax-deferred savings, which includes pensions. My father worked for the city and we wound up with a $78,000 windfall, which we immediately spent on renovations for our home. Then we got hit with a $25,000 income tax bill. We simply didn't have the cash, and we had to take a home equity loan; by the time it was approved, we had incurred penalties on top of the taxes.*—"Gail Keller," 40, interior designer, married, no children

However thorough you think you've been, have your will and estate plan updated every few years. The laws and your family circumstances may change. And a small detail can change everything. For example:

> *When my sister found out she had terminal cancer, she set up a trust with income available for her teenage son's health and education. He would get the principal gradually during his twenties and thirties. But my sister failed to change the beneficiary of her main assets—$300,000 in life insurance, $100,000 in a retirement plan, and $20,000 in an IRA—from the child to the trust. So the well-laid-out trust has nothing in it and my nephew, who is completely out of control, will be free to squander the money when it comes into his hands at eighteen.*—"Joan Farley," 45, high school teacher, married, two children

Had a good estates and tax lawyer been called in, many of the horror stories you hear about estate problems would not have happened.

CHAPTER 8

TRANSITIONS

What to Do When Things Change

When Emily married Chandler, her family paid for the wedding, and subsequently she paid for everything else, including the Connecticut home that he chose. He had great taste and—thanks to Emily's share of the fortune her family had made in the furniture business—the couple had the money to indulge it. But Chandler soon took up with another woman, and then a second. Emily filed for divorce. It was her misfortune to be living in one of the several states where the court may assign to either spouse all or parts of the estate of the other, even if it's acquired by gift or inheritance. Chandler demanded half of everything, including Emily's share of her family business. Moral: if you've got more than he has, be careful where you move.

Many of the experts who spoke to our club made the point that taking care of personal finances isn't only a matter of choosing the right mutual fund or` knowing what kind of disability insurance to buy. You must also be able to anticipate and cope with major transitions—from marriage to divorce to widowhood—that alter your life completely. And this is true whether you're used to living on a large amount or from paycheck to paycheck. Change is always hard.

Between the experts and our own firsthand experiences, we've learned many things that Mother never told us. We'd like to share them with you and urge you to pass them on.

WHAT YOU OUGHT TO KNOW ABOUT MONEY BEFORE YOU GET MARRIED

Your view of marriage: a way to celebrate your love.

The state's view of marriage: a civil contract that creates a personal and economic partnership.

The duties and rights of the marriage contract are spelled out by state law. At one time, the husband provided financial support, in exchange for which he had control of all the family's property, including his wife's. Her role was to provide the household services: housework, child care, and sex. That understanding has changed. All of the states have modified their statutory contracts so that both parties have financial obligations.

State law also defines marital property. Whatever is yours before you say "I do" is separate property. Whatever you acquire afterward may or may not be marital property. In some cases, marital property may even include the increased value of separate property. For example, in New York, if you had $5,000 in your brokerage account on your wedding day and had parlayed it into $6,000 by your first anniversary, that $1,000 gain could be considered marital property, especially if you've been actively managing it. However, gifts and inheritances received after marriage are considered by most states to be separate property if not mixed with marital assets. If Aunt Judy leaves you money that you want to keep as a private nest egg, put it into a separate account.

The distinction between what's his, what's yours, and what belongs to both of you becomes extremely important in the case of death or divorce. As this wife learned, it isn't always clear:

> *I thought I could at least count on having my jewelry and the beach house since they were gifts from my husband, but now I find that all gifts exchanged between spouses are marital property and the judge can put them into the "pot" to be divided.* —"Marge Pettit," 40, secretary, separated, two children

When you're planning to get married, it's hard to imagine your relationship could deteriorate to the point where he's trying to claim ownership of your ring and you're trying to get your hands on his Jeep. But we've seen it happen—many times. Naturally, when you're thinking wedding bells and "happily ever after," you don't want someone raining on your parade. However, we would suggest that you bring an umbrella. You never know.

As a group, we have made most of our major mistakes by relying on Mr. Right to come to the rescue. Maybe the man you plan to marry actually is one of the greatest guys in the world. Maybe he really does intend to be incredibly responsible about your personal finances. He probably intends to remember all your anniversaries, too. Our collective hunch is that you shouldn't count on it. Even if he tries, the chances are that someday, for one reason or another, he won't be around at all. (Remember that 85 percent of women die single.) Don't just prepare for a rainy day. Build yourself a tornado cellar.

If you protect yourself, you will rarely be disappointed and you will have fewer fears. If the marriage is happy and enduring—as many are—every one of the following things you have done in your own interest will ultimately benefit you both.

1. BE PREPARED TO EARN YOUR OWN MONEY.

We can't emphasize this or repeat it enough. If you are working, keep at it if at all possible. Being without a means to earn your own money neutralizes you and takes away your control. If you can't work full-time, work part-time. Read, study, volunteer—do whatever you can to stay marketable. A marriage may not be forever, but your skills will be.

A study of battered women in Minnesota revealed that 85 percent of those who had the means left their husbands while 85 percent of those women with no financial support stayed to endure more punishment. Money doesn't just buy more and better things; it brings you independence, respect, dignity, and freedom. Ask the women who have some:

> *I don't have to go to my husband for money. If I need $200 or $300—it's mine. I make the decisions.*—Sylvia Weinstock, 67, cake designer and baker, married, two adult children

When my brother lost his job and needed money to get back on his feet, I was so grateful that I had my own bank account to dip into. Maybe my husband would have made me a loan, but I didn't want to be obligated to him on my brother's account. My mother's mother was a suffragette. And my mother, thank goodness, told me time and again, "Always have a way to earn money by working from home." I took her advice. I made enough money giving private lessons to put my kids through school and bail my brother out and treat myself to things I wanted.—"Colleen Mackey," 53, private speech coach, married, one child

I used to think a woman should have as much money as her husband. Now I think that's wrong. She should have more *money. Having your own money means being able to tell your husband that you are staying with him because you love him, not because you need him.*—Gloria Gottlieb

If you aren't already working, prepare yourself for a career. Go to college, or night school, or community college, and have a goal in mind. You don't know what bends may lie in the road ahead.

You think life will be one way, and it turns out to be another. My education was much too narrowly focused. I took only art courses. It never occurred to me to take a business course. That was so shortsighted. Even artists have to know about marketing. I tell my daughter that everyone needs business knowledge. I believe the most important thing is to help her develop skills that she can use to support herself.—Audrey Landau

Don't spend all your free time at the health club. Don't enroll in courses like New Age Astrology. If you haven't got a degree, work toward it or study something you can turn into a business opportunity. The courses that lead you toward your goal will also bring you in contact with people from whom you can learn social and business skills and with whom you can network for a possible future job. Alternatively, find volunteer work that gives you some valuable business experience.

I learned a lot about management when I was the house committee chair of our country club with a budget of nearly $1 million. I hit the ground running.—Enid Rosenthal, 58, volunteer, married, two adult children

2. SHARE THE RESPONSIBILITY FOR FINANCES FROM THE MOMENT YOU'RE MARRIED.

Unfortunately, the average marriage doesn't last a lifetime. Women must take the initiative by becoming educated about financial matters and getting involved in the couple's financial planning and long-term wealth-building strategy, no matter what their financial status.—Christina Rizopoulos Valauri

Get involved in your marital finances when you're young and your relationship is still flexible. Planning your investments and doing your research is a wonderful interest that you can share throughout your marriage. Work with your husband on gathering your papers (see "What Belongs in Your Home Financial Files" in the Resources section at the end of this book). Learn how to use computer software for personal finance, and share the obligation to do the bookkeeping. Make all decisions a fifty-fifty deal. Make all purchases in both your names. Meet with your advisors as a twosome. This is important for you as a couple and for you personally.

My mother-in-law objected to the fact that I took care of the money and said that wasn't the role of a wife—but when her husband passed away, she knew very little. I'm glad I won't be in that boat.—Enid Rosenthal

3. IF YOU CAN'T WORK AT A PAYING JOB, BE A WIFE WITH A CAPITAL W.

Be a working partner. Doing your share should make you feel more entitled to a partner's share of your husband's earnings. Even more important, in the event of divorce, a judge will feel the same way.

In the nine community property states—Arizona, California, Idaho, Louisiana, Nevada, New Mexico, Texas, Washington, and Wisconsin—

when divorce occurs, each spouse gets a vested interest in the joint property. In some states, such as California, the interest is half. In equitable distribution states, if there is a divorce and the parties and their lawyers can't reach a settlement, the courts divide the property in a way meant to be fair. Equitable distribution is not necessarily equal. The judge takes into account the husband's and wife's ages, employment history, health, income, and length of time they've been married as well as what the tax obligations will be, how much alimony is being paid—and the contributions of each spouse. If you want a fair share and your contributions are not financial, you should be able to point to your nonfinancial contributions and say that you've spent the bulk of your time caring for the home and children to free him up to do his job.

Playing tennis and taking bridge lessons don't count. What counts is whatever a wife does to relieve her husband of other responsibilities so he can concentrate on work. Even if you have help with the children, don't delegate everything. Take primary responsibility for school pickups, activities, sports, and doctor's appointments, so your husband will have no concerns about the quality of the children's care.

Travel with your husband, know what's going on in his business life, be available to have discussions and act as a sounding board. It would be helpful if you could prove you entertained your husband's employer, customers, and/or business associates on his behalf. You may not have to make the cheese straws with your own hands, but you should be initiating, planning, and overseeing social events.

Recently, a New York State Supreme Court ruling granted support to the wife of a partner in a prestigious law firm plus half the value of his partnership in return for having shouldered the household responsibilities. The husband spent most of his waking hours at work, the judge wrote in his decision, because "the wife's contributions to the marriage enabled him to do so." (The decision was appealed by the husband, but the wife prevailed.)

WIFE STYLE

Though Carol Levin, one of our club's founding members, had held high-level positions in the Chicago and Dallas city governments, she left a paying job to raise the kids and handle the home front while her husband, Jerry, rose through a series of corporate positions to become the CEO of Revlon. He frequently acknowledges that he wouldn't be where he is without her as a partner. We asked her suggestions for making a marriage into a partnership:

"Divide the work: there should be certain jobs he does and certain jobs you do. For example, I'm in complete charge of where we live. When we've moved for business reasons, I'm the one who buys and sells the houses, sometimes without first consulting him. I also furnish our homes and keep track of things. I run the departments of Lost Shoes and Disappearing Underwear.

"Get interested in the parts of his jobs that you can get interested in. When Jerry was at Pillsbury and they bought Häagen-Dazs, the board of directors sent me a special commendation, because I was so helpful working with my husband to court the owners of the company. [Jerry says, 'Carol's being a cosmetic and hair junkie is particularly useful to me in understanding Revlon's products. But she recognizes she can influence my opinions and is careful about discussing products with employees.']

"Don't rely on him to get a life of your own. Build your own network. Reach out however you can. When we moved to Chicago I called a great many people to ask for recommendations for nursery school. Jerry said, 'Why are you calling all those people when you've chosen the school already?' I said, 'I thought this was a better way to start a conversation than simply saying, "I've just moved here and I don't know anyone."'

"Choose a role model. When my husband was at Pillsbury, Janet Spoor, wife of then-chairman William Spoor, set a great example. She made everyone feel welcome. She was open and friendly and genuine. She was as sincerely concerned about whether the bus driver had a nice lunch as about any other detail. [Jerry says, 'Carol is entertaining, funny, and intelligent. She cares. She ensures key Revlon affairs are stylish, well organized, tasteful, and fun. This is an enormous plus for me as a CEO.']

"Find something that gives your own life meaning. I don't believe a person should be living a privileged life without giving something back. I'm very deeply involved with four charities that mean a lot to me."

4. Marry him before he finishes professional school. And encourage him to go for an advanced degree.

Professional licenses, certifications, fellowships, and advanced degrees, if acquired during the marriage, are considered marital property in New York State and assigned a cash value in a divorce. In other states, the courts may recognize them as a valuable asset and take them into account in settling the amount of spousal support and dividing property, so the effect may be the same. Of course, if you're the one with the professional degree, the opposite advice holds: marry *after* you've finished professional school.

5. Encourage your husband to maximize his pension contributions.

This is something he will feel he is doing for himself, since it's the best way to build a nest egg, so he will probably do it willingly. If there is a divorce, you'll probably get a significant share. (And during the marriage, he can't name another beneficiary without your consent.) If you stay married, you'll have a nice cushion for your future together.

6. Start a collection.

If possible, build your tangible assets by buying art, furniture, rugs, and other collectibles that have a resale value. Attending flea markets and auctions in a quest for acquisitions can be a wonderful shared interest and (if you buy the best quality) a substantial shared asset. Unless your husband can prove he used separate funds to purchase these items, they will be considered marital property.

7. Share a bank account.

If a man has opened an account in his name before the marriage and during the marriage he keeps it in his own name, it's his money. But if his wife makes even small contributions into that account (and keeps a record of them), the funds are commingled. If the marriage stays together, this maneuver has no impact, but in the event of divorce, the court might consider the account as a joint asset, in which case it can be divided.

8. Always keep your own reserve fund.

Don't give it all away, as this woman learned from bitter experience. Trim and still beautiful in her sixties, she has the appearance of someone who's been cared for all her life when, in fact, that's not at all the case:

> *When my second husband's business began to falter, we had to sell our home and move into a small apartment. The house was half mine, so I banked my share. But over time, he'd ask for a thousand dollars here, a couple of thousand there. Instead of thinking, "This is my nest egg," I said to myself, "This is my husband. How can I not help?" and I gave him most of my money. I took a job, so I could contribute more. One day I came home from work and found his closets empty, his luggage gone. His lawyer contacted me and said he'd gone overseas. To this day, I've never seen him again. My advice: hang on to your own money. Don't be moved if your husband says, "I thought you loved me, but you won't give me any money. What kind of wife are you?" I was dumb. I gave in.*—"Helene Jenner," 60, retired social worker, single, two grown children

9. Keep written records of your arrangements.

Never lend a significant amount of money—even to your husband—without getting a promissory note. There is nothing dirty about this request. Men routinely demand it, but women don't, since they're afraid their husbands will get angry. An honorable person should not only be willing to sign but should also respect you for standing up for yourself. Without protection, you can be terribly harmed.

When Eliot, a handsome man who ran his father's very successful family business, started dating me, I couldn't believe my luck. He had a lovely penthouse in the city and a French provincial country home, both decorated by Marco, the city's top designer. Shortly after we married, Eliot told me he wanted to start his own company, but all his assets were in the family business. I lent him the money, and when he failed, I lent him more. By the time he'd made a third start, I'd given him $70,000, my entire savings. Then he stunned me with two announcements. He was going back into his family business, and he had fallen in love with Marco. Crushed, I asked at least for my money. His position was that I had simply made investments that hadn't worked out, and he owed me nothing. Since I had no proof that it was a loan, the law was in fact on his side.—"Marilyn Morgan," 40, magazine editor, divorced, no children

You don't need a lawyer to draw up a written agreement. Just copy the following, inserting the pertinent details:

For consideration received, I, ____________ [his name], promise to repay $______ [amount] to my wife, ____________ [your name], with ______ [percent interest] on ______ [date] or upon her request.

10. DEVELOP YOUR OWN CREDIT HISTORY.

If the marriage ends, you will need borrowing power of your own.

My husband had left me for another woman. Within the week, I was at the bank and my ATM card didn't work. A bank officer said, "You are no longer a customer here." My ex-husband had wiped out the account. My second husband is wonderful, but I will never be in that position again. I will always have at least one bank account and one credit card in my name only. Though I work for my husband, I insisted on a paycheck so I could always show a stream of income and have Social Security credits. My experience was a painful way to get more savvy.—"Randee Bank," 34, medical office manager, married, two young children

Even if you stay together, having your own credit rating can be valuable.

Now I'm a landscape gardener in Boca Raton, but at one time I lived in a mansion that was the equal of any of my clients'. My husband, Sam, and his father, Fred, were running a wildly successful retail business. But when the economy fell apart, so did the company. We discovered that Fred had been selling off portions of it without sharing the proceeds. Sam had to come up with cash to pay huge income taxes on the profits. We didn't have the money and we lost everything, including Sam's credit line. I had no ability to help. Today, I've built up a business and a credit line of my own, and Sam has reestablished his. I've learned how important credit is. Now I figure if anything happens to my company, he could supply the credit to bail me *out.* —"Rosalie Palmer," 49, married, no children

If you have a credit card in your own name, you already have a credit history. Check with the credit bureaus to see what they're reporting about you (see page 283). If you don't have credit, you need to build a history with a major credit card such as Visa or MasterCard or a card from a chain such as Sears. A card from an individual store or a gas company credit card won't do.

If you and your husband share a major credit card, you can write to the company and ask that all joint account transactions be reported in your name in addition to his. Once you have a joint history, you can usually get a card issued in your own name, though the credit bureau will still indicate that your spouse is the income source and you won't have a rating good enough to take out a loan.

You may be able to get a credit card if you open an account at a brokerage house or bank, using stock certificates sitting in a drawer, municipal bonds in the safe deposit box, or a passbook savings account. Or perhaps you have some government savings bonds you can turn in for this purpose. (And when you do, keep the receipt so if the IRS asks where the money came from, you can explain.) Your credit line is tied to the balance in your account.

Still, without a steady income source, you may have a problem getting a significant amount of credit.

> *My stocks and bonds had been in a safe deposit box, but after the divorce, I turned them over to a brokerage house. There were hundreds of thousands of dollars there, but when I tried to buy a house, I couldn't get a mortgage. Why? Because the bank wanted to see an income stream. So my broker had to put my money into investments that didn't have as much growth potential but paid bigger dividends and interest.*—"Kathy Gerrard," 50, political organizer, divorced, no children

Buying a condominium or co-op may also be impossible without an income stream.

If you do manage to get a card, start charging on it. Don't pay it off all at once. Making regular payments is a better way to build a credit history. But don't apply for a card if there is a good chance you'll be turned down. The rejection shows on your credit report and tends to make other institutions gun-shy about extending credit to you.

11. Don't make a habit of forging each other's names for the sake of convenience.

We have a friend who couldn't get her own checks accepted when she signed them herself. The only signature the bank accepted was the one her husband routinely forged for her.

12. Never sign anything unless you understand it completely.

Don't be bullied into signing any document under pressure—or, worse, allow your name to be used on a document you haven't even seen.

His accountant just handed me blank income tax forms to sign. I never saw the completed returns.—Nancy Silverman

My husband didn't involve me at all. He simply signed my name. And he had no problem getting away with it. Since there were other occasions when he had signed for me, the lawyer told me that my consent was presumed. —"Kimberly Korman," 30, restaurant hostess, divorced, two children

If your husband asks you to sign an income tax return, look at it. If there is something you don't understand—or if you don't understand any of it—go over it with an accountant. As we said in Chapter 2, if the government believes the full amount of taxes hasn't been paid, either because of an effort to defraud or simply because of an honest mistake, you're as responsible as your husband is once you've signed a joint return. The "innocent spouse" defense is rarely successful, almost never if the wife is educated, and particularly if she has benefited from any unreported income. If the returns you sign report an income of $40,000 and your husband is treating you to Alpine ski vacations and cruises to the Greek islands, the tax court system will not believe you didn't know something was going on. In cases where fraud is suspected, the IRS can pursue the case without any time limitations. Whether or not you are now divorced is irrelevant.

In the separation agreement, Fred agreed to pay the government what he owed in back income taxes. Then he disappeared. I opened the mail one day to find that since the government couldn't find Fred, they were coming after me. My friend Harriet's former husband wasn't unscrupulous, just naive. He invested in a tax shelter that the government disallowed. Faced with an enormous, unexpected bill from Uncle Sam, he packed up his fly rod and ski boots and took off for Canada. Harriet arrived at the bank to find that the government had put a lien on all her accounts.—"Sondra Lerner," 38, painter, single

Fortunately, this may change. Congress is considering a taxpayer's bill of rights that obliges the IRS to tell either spouse if attempts are being made to collect taxes from the other. The bill also demands a study of the liability rules to see if there are ways to protect the rights of separated and divorced spouses. Meanwhile, protect yourself.

13. Ask for a bond instead of a bauble.

On your birthday, tell him you'd like a municipal bond or a few shares of a mutual fund. In your name, of course. You're a lot better off with an asset in a brokerage account than one in your jewelry box. A cash gift has more value than a thing gift. Tell him that the reason you want the investment rather than anything else is because you want to learn more about money to benefit both of you and having your own assets will get you more involved.

Some men only want to buy a gift that can be put on display. If you have a choice, ask for stones. A modest pair of diamond stud earrings or a small stone pendant may cost the same as or even less than more elaborate costume jewelry, but if you ever have to sell, you'll find that the gems have much greater resale value.

While jewelry given during a marriage is considered marital property and a husband would be entitled to a share in the event of a divorce, there is nothing to stop you from selling it while you are married and using the proceeds as you wish. One woman we know did so with brilliant success.

> *A friend was married to an extremely clever businessman who made a lot of money but was a drug abuser. When her efforts to get him into a rehabilitation program failed, she sold her diamond engagement ring and earrings and invested in a real estate deal in Florida. It was a lucky deal, and she tripled her money. She used it to make the down payment on a fixer-upper in the Hamptons, renovated it, sold it during the real estate boom at a huge profit, and bought a wonderful place for her own use. That's what her stones bought her.*—Vivian Serota

Obviously, most people don't have the kind of jewelry that could reap such a bonanza. But our point is that diamonds aren't really a girl's best friend. Stick with mutual funds.

14. TRY TO ACQUIRE AS MANY ASSETS AS POSSIBLE IN YOUR OWN NAME, INCLUDING TITLE TO REAL ESTATE.

Real estate broker Marilyn Kane, forty-eight, featured on a 1995 *People* cover as "the ex-wife who nailed America's worst deadbeat dad," recalls that her husband stopped sending support after abandoning the family, canceled the credit cards, and notified the parking garage that she no longer had the right to use the car. Most women don't know that their names are not on the ownership certificate of the family car. How many women go into a showroom with their husbands and insist that their names be on the lease or sales agreement? But beware: putting property into your name may not insulate it from being marital property, though it does give you control.

WHAT YOU OUGHT TO KNOW ABOUT MONEY IF YOU'RE CONSIDERING DIVORCE

We pondered whether to take a holiday or get a divorce, and we decided that a trip to Bermuda is over in two weeks, but a divorce is something you always have.—Woody Allen

Your view of divorce: getting rid of an undesirable lug.

The state's view of divorce: a method of dividing your property.

In community property states, any property acquired during a marriage except by gift or inheritance theoretically belongs equally to both husband and wife. So does any debt obligation, no matter who incurred it. A creditor can collect the debt from any community property asset.

In some equitable distribution states, any property acquired during a marriage except by gift or inheritance is considered marital property, but control belongs to the person whose name is on the title and the spouse has no rights until there is a death or a divorce. If your husband buys a winning lottery ticket in his name, he can spend the proceeds as he wishes (but in the event of divorce, the proceeds are considered marital property); if his name is on the title of the house or the boat, he can sell it or give it away without your say-so. Whoever takes on a debt during the marriage is the one who is obliged to pay it. But the other spouse may take on equal responsibility by co-signing a loan or putting his or her signature on the income tax form. If there is a debt, the judge may reduce the value of the marital property that is distributed by that amount.

The state may require the wealthier spouse to pay alimony or support if the other spouse can't meet reasonable income needs of his or her own to maintain the standard living acquired during the marriage. A Park Avenue wife may successfully contend that she is used to a standard of living that qualifies her for both a property settlement and a generous living allowance. Now that the obligation for support is mutual, women may have to pay an ex-husband. High-profile recent examples include Joan Lunden, Joan Collins, Roseanne, Elizabeth Taylor, and Jane Seymour.

The amount, type, and length of the period of support can vary. While the divorce case is being fought, a spouse may get temporary support. While pursuing the education or training to be self-supporting, a spouse may get rehabilitative support for a certain number of years. "Permanent" alimony or maintenance terminates at remarriage (unless the agreement otherwise states) or at the wife's death. In New York, there is a trend to award permanent alimony to wives in long-term marriages who have not worked, lack marketable skills, and have enjoyed lavish lifestyles. The court order should provide for life insurance or an annuity in an amount to cover the support obligation.

Whether or not alimony is affected if you move in with someone depends on your state's law about what constitutes cohabitation and the terms of your agreement.

The person who receives alimony pays taxes on it. The person who pays can take it as a tax deduction. So what constitutes alimony becomes important in a settlement. If the nonresident spouse has title to a house and pays the mortgage, that's not alimony. But if the resident spouse has the title and the nonresident pays the mortgage, it is.

There is no tax on or tax deduction for child support. Depending on the state, this may end at eighteen or go on until the child graduates from college or turns twenty-one. Of course, the parties may agree to any kind of arrangement: the support may continue until the child is twenty-three, finishes graduate school, or whatever else they decide. Child support is usually paid to the custodial parent, even when the child is away at camp or boarding school or vacationing with the other parent, unless your agreement says otherwise.

If circumstances change—inflation is driving costs up and you haven't got a COLA (cost of living adjustment), unanticipated expenses crop up, or that little basement business your ex started has gone public—you can return to court to change the deal or seek help from the state's child support agency. Your husband also can appeal to reduce child support if his income has gone down through no fault of his own.

Once you are seriously contemplating divorce, there are several steps you should take:

1. Start gathering the papers.

Do this as quickly as possible. Getting information from banks, financial institutions, credit card companies, and so on is often expensive and sometimes futile. The more information you have in hand before you alert your husband to the fact that you want a divorce, the easier it will be for your divorce lawyer to assess your case. Moreover, there may be some documents that are so revealing that they will give your lawyer an early leg up on the negotiations.

Removing the original documents from the files is not a good idea. They may get lost. And once your husband discovers that they are missing, you've tipped your hand. Instead, start photocopying all of the following:

- Biographical information on both of you, including the following:
  - Date and place of marriage
  - Length of time you have lived in the state
  - Existence of a prenuptial agreement
  - Children of prior marriages and custodial arrangements
  - Current employment and income
  - Education/degrees/training
  - Job history and income potential
  - Joint assets and liabilities
  - Separate or personal assets and liabilities
- Checkbook registers and/or stubs.

- Bank statements and canceled checks. If they are missing, you can get duplicates of the monthly summary (but not canceled checks) from the bank.
- Business income tax, personal income tax, gift tax, and estate tax returns. If they are missing, you can request copies from both the IRS and state tax office for the past five years (though they won't send backup information). If you signed them, you're entitled to have a copy sent to you, even if your husband is at another address.
- Savings account passbooks.
- Credit card statements. If they are missing, contact the credit card companies to send duplicates. You should also have a copy of a recent credit report (see page 283), to show any transactions.
- Deeds (originals or copies) to any real estate.
- Papers concerning any trusts.
- Brokerage account statements. You can request statements for joint accounts from your broker. The year-end statement or the 1099 will report all transactions, but the monthly statements show trading activity.
- Life insurance policy information. You can request copies from your agent. A summary may be sufficient: name of the issuing insurance company, face amount, whether it is term or whole life, cash value.
- Pension plan information:

  Beneficiary. A spouse is automatically the beneficiary unless she or he waives the rights. Waivers have been forged.

  Value. If your spouse has a defined-benefit plan, your attorney or a CPA must calculate its worth. If he has a defined-contribution plan such as a 401(k), it is subject to a QDRO (qualified domestic relations order). You are entitled to a portion unless you have specifically signed away your rights, and you may get the money immediately if you roll it over into an IRA. The 10 percent penalty for invading these funds before age fifty-nine and a half doesn't apply in the case of divorce.
- Deferred compensation arrangements.
- Financial statement. One may have been prepared for a recent mortgage or business loan.
- Appraisals on any real estate or personal property. One may have been done recently for insurance purposes.

- Spouse's business tax returns. If it's a family business, your lawyer will want as much as possible of the following information:
  Type of business
  Number and name of shareholders, percentage of ownership of each
  Bank statements and tax returns
  Loan applications
  Income and balance sheets
  Financial reports
- Payroll stubs. These may reveal if part of his earnings is being put into a savings and retirement fund.

2. Start searching for a divorce lawyer.

Club member and matrimonial lawyer Diane Steiner offers this advice:

- Do not use your family attorney or any attorney recommended by your husband or connected to your husband as a colleague, business partner, golfing partner, friend, or friend of a friend. Never agree to use the same lawyer as your spouse. Get someone whose loyalties are exclusively to you.
- Don't use a general practitioner. Choose a matrimonial law specialist with good credentials and references, and—if your case will be complex and the assets are substantial—make sure your lawyer has years of matrimonial experience. After you meet, look at "Reviewing Your Impressions" on pages 62–64.
- Going through a divorce is one of the most depressing and traumatic experiences you will ever have. Choose someone nonjudgmental, someone whom you're willing to entrust with your deepest, darkest secrets. Your lawyer should always return a call on the day that you make it. For that reason, meet with your lawyer's partners and/or associates so you feel comfortable enough to call on them if your attorney is in court, at a deposition, or otherwise engaged.
- A divorce mediator may help resolve issues of visitation and custody. But when it comes to matters of money, mediation may not be the best choice. You may capitulate when you should not.

- Do not look for a shark—even if you're out for blood. Look for a good negotiator whose goal is to reach closure with maximum benefit and the least possible cost.

I went to someone because I thought he'd give my husband a hard time. As it turned out, he wasn't particularly nice to me, either. Also, he was so hated by my husband's lawyer (and most others in the matrimonial bar) that the fees escalated while they exchanged nasty letters and failed to come to terms. When I hired someone who didn't need to show off, we settled the case in two months.—"Donna Clark," 38, photographer, three children

3. Check out your Social Security entitlement. (See pages 150–151.)

4. Start estimating how much money you need to live on.

After the divorce, you'll need enough to cover everything—federal and state taxes, living expenses, health care costs, educational expenses, child care if you return to work, and any other special needs. Ultimately, you'll need an accountant to go over your estimates.

5. Start covering your backside.

- Stash whatever money you can into a sperate account.
- Open your own safe deposit box.
- Don't co-sign any loans from now on.
- Retrieve the power of attorney.

6. Try to negotiate a formal separation agreement.

You are not legally separated until you have executed a formal separation agreement, which can lay out the following:

- The division of your possessions: real property such as residences or land; personal property including furniture, art, jewelry, cars, investments, and bank accounts; and intangible property such as businesses, limited partnerships, trademarks, and so on. The worth of your personal property is calculated at fair market value, which is the price it would get at a tag sale—no more.
- The division of your debts. Even if you've signed a bank loan jointly, your husband can agree to be responsible for it. But no matter what he signs, the bank won't release you from the obligation. (If it can't find him, it will find you.)
- Support issues.
- Custody and visitation issues, including who can take the tax exemption for the child(ren).
- Insurance (life, health, and disability).

The court under some circumstances can modify the child support and/or custody terms in a separation agreement if doing so is in the best interests of the children. It can change support terms that affect adults only if the agreement in a subsequent divorce decree provides that it can.

7. Get your agreement fast, while he's still feeling guilty.

—"Nancy Dann," 50s, artist, divorced, two grown sons

Often the first offer is the best offer. But a woman who is feeling hurt and vindictive and being poorly advised by a lawyer who tells her to hold out for more may keep pushing beyond the breaking point. Provoked, her husband may retaliate by offering less—and that's what she gets. Your demand must be reasonable and in line with what's customary. In New York, for example, it is unlikely that women who have short-term marriages will get alimony for more than the number of years the marriage lasted.

WHAT YOU OUGHT TO KNOW ABOUT MONEY WHILE DIVORCE ACTION IS PENDING

1. CHANGE THE DOCUMENTS.

Change beneficiaries on your savings account, insurance policies, and brokerage account. Ask the personnel or benefits department for copies of the change forms.

Draft a new will.

Remove his name from the safe deposit boxes, car titles, and/or titles of other personal property.

Send a letter to your stockbroker, mutual fund firm, and bank advising them not to make any transactions affecting your money unless your name is on the request along with your spouse's. Once you've sent such a letter, if there is a mistake and he's allowed to make off with the money, the firm or bank is liable.

If there are any trusts created in your name, make sure his name is removed from them and that he resigns from them as trustee. Get him to give up his rights as part of your negotiations.

If there are any trusts in the children's name that may have been previously established, decide whether or not you want him to continue as trustee.

If you have not already done so, ask him to return any power of attorney you may have given him, and destroy it.

2. DEAL WITH YOUR CREDIT SITUATION. WITH DEBTS DO YOU PART.

If your soon-to-be ex went on a spending spree to annoy you or simply because he flipped out, you can go to court to get a restraining order preventing him from further dissipating your marital assets. His creditors may come after you anyway.

If he's trying to go into bankruptcy, he's still legally obliged to pay your maintenance and/or child support, but obviously collecting it may not be easy. Even if your husband has agreed to take on all remaining debts, you may need legal assistance in enforcing his ability to pay the debts.

Write to all creditors to close your past accounts, and ask for new ones. Tell your ex-husband that you're doing this so that he will be able to do the same. Ask for a credit report after three months (see page 283) to make sure the information the credit bureau is giving out is still accurate. If there are joint accounts still open at this point, contact both the creditor and credit bureau to close them.

See the suggestions on pages 244–246 about getting credit. Alimony is considered income, so you may eventually be able to use it to get credit if you have none. Since your former spouse is the source of the alimony, his credit history will probably be required.

To repair a damaged credit history, it may help to put a 100-word letter in each credit report explaining why payments were delayed in the past and where you will get an income flow to manage credit card debt in the future. Then be sure to establish a pattern of regular payments. If you're repeatedly late, creditors aren't anxious to extend credit; and if you have a balance that was "charged off"—you never paid it—you may not get credit anywhere without a five-year history of on-time payments.

You could open a savings account that comes with a credit card. Though your line of credit is equal only to your balance, this is another way to establish a good payment history.

3. ASK FOR DISABILITY INSURANCE. (IF YOU WORK, GET SOME YOURSELF.)

If your alimony or child support is dependent upon his salary, try to get your husband to agree to purchase disability insurance to protect his payments to you.

When a proposal for a divorce settlement comes in without a disability policy, I urge my client to try to do better. Go back, I say. No way. The husband breaks his back going down a slope in Aspen and then he hasn't got the cash to make the alimony. I'm always going to raise this issue with my clients.

—Debra Franklin, insurance agent

4. Settle the health insurance question.

Your spouse's health insurance will probably cover the kids until they're twenty-one. But there is no specific coverage on medical insurance for an ex-wife, though your case may be an exception.

I was lucky. My former husband works for a top-notch firm with excellent benefits. His medical plan includes his present family as well as "up to one ex-wife." (Fortunately, he only has one, so he didn't have to choose.) He agreed to pay the premium, and I'm covered just as if I were an employee.—"Marlene Ring," 38, media buyer, single, one child

If his company has more than twenty employees, it has obligations under the Consolidated Budget Reconciliation Act of 1986, known as COBRA. The spouse of a covered employee, should she become widowed or divorced, is allowed to apply for continued coverage at the group rate in her name for another three years. If there is a change in your situation (a divorce, legal separation, death), contact the insured person's employee benefits representative within 60 days. If you are entitled to this continuing coverage and your ex-husband refuses to pay the premium, pay it yourself. You lose the COBRA benefit if you remarry and the new spouse has a plan that covers you or you get a job where you are covered by another plan.

5. Make sure he has plenty of life insurance—payable to you.

The court can oblige him to keep you as the beneficiary of existing life insurance. If there is no life insurance and you depend on his support and believe he can pass the physical, ask if he will agree to your taking out a policy. Pay the premiums yourself until alimony payments stop so you will be assured of continuing support even if he dies. Or, if he agrees to pay the premiums, get authorization to contact the insurance company to determine if the premiums are currently paid. Have the insurance company notify you before the policy lapses or if he changes the beneficiary (which he can do if he owns the policy). You can sue, but the process will cost you a lot of money and the results can't be guaranteed.

6. Bring in an accountant to look over the deal.

Have an accountant look over the agreement regarding maintenance and child support and explain all the tax implications to you.

> *My attorney and I calculated I needed $50,000. After a long negotiation, my husband offered $50,000 taxable maintenance. I didn't really understand the consequences. I wasn't sophisticated about money, I was under a lot of stress, and I just wanted to get the whole thing over with. One year later, I realized I had only about $38,000 after-tax income—nowhere near enough to live the way I'd planned. The court wouldn't allow me to renegotiate because I'd had legal representation and the deal had been explained to me. Unfortunately, it hadn't been explained well enough.*—"Rita Barber," 41, nursery school teacher, divorced, mother of two

There also may be tax consequences down the road in connection with the division of your property. These women learned how much bad planning may cost:

> *In 1972, my husband bought a huge amount of Columbia Pictures stock at less than $2 a share. When Coca-Cola took over the company, his shares were exchanged for Coca-Cola stock, which shot up until it was worth many, many times what he paid. I got a lot of this stock in our settlement in 1995. When I sold it shortly afterward, I assumed I'd pay taxes on the difference between the price of the stock when I got it and the price that I sold it at.*

Wrong. I paid taxes on all the profits from the date my ex purchased it. If I'd realized how much I would have to pay, I'd have taken the settlement in another form.—"Lauretta Vickers," 48, record company executive, divorced, two grown children

I took our home in the divorce settlement. The market got soft, and I had to hold it four years before I got an offer at much less than I'd expected. Meanwhile, I'd spent a huge amount keeping it maintained in salable condition. And since we'd bought the house at a fairly low price, there was a tremendous capital gains tax to pay.—"Harriet Pace," 39, freelance writer, remarried, one child

I got the house as a residence for me and the children, with the arrangement that I wouldn't sell it until the youngest went to college. My ex and I would split the equity and share capital gains and closing costs. The minute our second child moved into a dorm, I put out the "For Sale" sign. We got $270,000. We'd paid only $100,000, so I thought this was a great deal. But the income taxes on $85,000 (my share of the profit) plus the transfer taxes, closing costs, and recording fees left me with only $60,000. My ex was smart enough to have kept our vacation home, for which we'd paid a lot more money. When he sells, the tax impact on him will be much smaller.—"Sherry Louis," 42, office manager, divorced, two grown children

The accountant should go back over three years of jointly signed tax returns to look for any liability before you sign any agreements. Here's why:

During our marriage, my husband had invested in tax shelters the government later disallowed, and after the divorce it demanded back taxes. He and some partners fought the case but lost, and the penalties at that point were significant. My husband sued me *because I refused to pay a 50 percent share. And the lawyers said I couldn't use the "innocent spouse" defense. They said no judge would believe an educated person didn't understand what she was signing, even though that was absolutely true. I should have had an accountant take a look at our joint tax returns prior to the divorce.*—Betty Broder

Your accountant should help you deal with any financial decisions that have to be made immediately as a consequence of the divorce.

7. Bring in an estate tax lawyer to look over the deal.

In divorce papers, one couple agreed to "mutually give up any right, title, or interest in and to any earnings . . . pension plans, profit-sharing plans . . . or property of the other," which seems extremely clear. Yet in subsequent proceedings, the judge ruled that because the agreement didn't specifically mention the plan in question, the ex-spouse was entitled to it. An estate tax lawyer may anticipate problems that the matrimonial lawyer may not.

8. Get a guarantee of future payments.

Never accept payments due at some future date without security. Money you are counting on may disappear:

> *The minute my divorce settlement was negotiated, I bought a new apartment. It was a bit of an extravagance, but I was working and I knew that I'd have alimony coming in for the next few years. I'd just settled in when I got the bad news. My husband had gone bankrupt. And although alimony and child support must be paid even in the case of bankruptcy, the obligation to pay an equitable distribution award can be discharged.*—"Sybil Allen," 52, television producer, single, no children

9. The house may not be your most valuable asset. Plan carefully.

Many women have emotional ties to their homes and make the mistake of taking the house instead of another—and perhaps more beneficial—asset. If you're both over fifty-five and qualify for the once-in-a-lifetime $125,000 exclusion from capital gains tax for the sale of a primary residence, get divorced before you sell. At that point you each qualify for the exclusion of $125,000 (for a total of $250,000).* But don't count on that exclusion if you're not using the house as your primary residence:

> *My husband had custody of the kids and the marital residence until the children graduated. I moved away, and six years later, when they went off to college, we sold. I planned to roll over the gain into a new residence or (since I was over fifty-five) to exclude the $125,000 gain. However, I was shocked to discover that since my primary residence was in another state, I had to pay full taxes on the entire gain.*—"Judy Baxter," 52, health care professional, unmarried, two children

10. Remember that it's in your economic interest to have him do well.

Unless you have an outright cash settlement, don't carry out any of your revenge fantasies because, in the end, you may harm yourself:

> *Wives who think they can blackmail their husbands by calling the IRS are cutting off their noses to spite their face. They are dependent on the husband for their support. If that husband ends up in prison without money, that support is gone.*—Diane Steiner

*The government may raise the amount of this exclusion significantly in the near future.

WHAT YOU OUGHT TO KNOW ABOUT MONEY AFTER THE DIVORCE BECOMES FINAL

1. Deal with any name change.

If you're going to revert to your maiden name, which can be done as soon as the divorce becomes final, notify the Social Security office, get new credit cards, and replace any other documents that may be affected. Keep copies of any documentation of the changes.

2. Get help if your new responsibilities are overwhelming you.

Sometimes newly rich divorcées want to just put the money in a mattress and not make any decisions. Even Diana, Princess of Wales, can't afford that—and she got the equivalent of $22.5 million tax-free in her divorce settlement. If she didn't invest a cent—or spend a penny—her fortune would sink to about $5 million in buying power by the time she reached eighty-five. And if she continued to spend the $1.2 million per year royal watchers estimate she does ($12,000 for personal fitness trainers and health clubs; $15,000 for psychotherapy, aromatherapy, colonic irrigation; it adds up), she'd be down to her last pound in her early fifties. Still, she would have a couple of decades before the wolf appeared at the door. The average divorced woman may be just months away from disaster.

If you don't have a financial advisor already, find one (see Chapter 2) and begin to implement a plan.

WHAT YOU OUGHT TO KNOW ABOUT MONEY BEFORE YOU MARRY AGAIN

In the first marriage, you commingle the finances. The second time around, usually (but not always) what's his is his, and what's yours is yours. That's not the only difference. The second wife often doesn't have the protection of life insurance because either her (older) husband is uninsurable or the premium is unaffordably high. There also may be antagonistic stepchildren who are trying to protect their interest in their father's assets. Problems with stepchildren are the number one cause of divorce in second marriages. And finally, the woman entering a second marriage may have her own money at this point, thanks to her late husband or ex-spouse or acquired in the course of a successful career. This makes it even more important that you take steps to protect yourself.

1. Consider a prenuptial agreement.

You may not even want your husband-to-be to know that you color your hair, let alone reveal to him the details of your bank account. But though drawing up a prenuptial agreement is not very romantic, it is necessary if you have unequal assets and/or children and stepchildren to consider. As a plus, if the kids feel secure and satisfied with the financial arrangements, all the relationships may be less stressful, and the marriage may be more secure.

It is increasingly common for business partners to insist on prenuptial agreements if a partner is getting married in order to protect corporate entities from the inquisitive eyes of divorce lawyers. Cooperatives and condominiums may also require one, in order to be assured of the financial stability of both parties in the event of a divorce.

The spouse with less money takes a risk in signing a prenuptial, which almost always limits the amount of the other party's obligations. If your husband becomes extremely wealthy during your marriage, your prenup may not entitle you to share in the windfall if you are ever divorced. You will be limited to the cap agreed on in the prenuptial, even if state law would have entitled you to more.

The same is true when a spouse dies. Each state guarantees the survivor a certain minimum claim to the estate. If you're cut out of a will, you have a claim. But you may have given up that right in the prenuptial, and such an agreement has a higher authority than state law.

On the other hand, if you have few assets you may be content to have a prenuptial that guarantees you at least a certain minimum.

And since a prenuptial is always designed to protect the wealthier party, if you're the one controlling the purse strings, of course you want it.

No matter how uncomfortable it may be to hash out the details, not having a prenuptial exposes you to situations that may be even worse. In some cases, it may break up a marriage before it begins. If you need help in negotiating, bring in the therapists and counselors—maybe even a minister or rabbi—to join the financial advisors, your attorney, and his attorney.

A prenuptial should include all the following:

- Complete disclosure of everything from finances to furniture.
- Plans for splitting personal and other property if you separate.
- Agreement as to who pays for what during the marriage, if you're keeping money separate.
- Plans for housing. Will you keep both homes or neither? Who will buy the new home? What are the tax consequences of selling current homes, and when should it be done?

My ex and I agreed to sell our home. My share of the profits was $150,000, and my new husband and I bought a new $200,000 home. If I paid for half—$100,000—then $50,000 of my gain wasn't reinvested. The accountant told me it was advisable to own a bigger portion of the new house. Fortunately, my husband agreed—but I spent a lot of time worrying that he would refuse that arrangement. —"Alexis Miller," 46, artist, remarried, two children

- Disclosure of any debts from the past or any history of bankruptcy. You're not just marrying him, you're marrying his financial history. If you're uncomfortable asking, your lawyer can do it.
- Disclosure of any other financial obligations. Are there kids for whom your shared money must pay? Alimony? Parents to support?
- Plans for life insurance. Is a current policy in his kids' name? Will he change the beneficiary or buy additional insurance naming you?
- Plans for medical insurance. Will his medical policy cover you? Your children from a prior marriage? Even if you are covered, should you keep your policies in effect?

- Plans for retirement. What arrangements have been made about the pension plan?
- Agreement regarding issues of the various children and stepchildren. Is a trust necessary to protect the interests of your children from a previous marriage? Have they been provided for in a will? Are there upcoming college tuitions? What about health coverage? (On medical insurance, a child is no longer a dependent if he or she becomes twenty-three, marries, doesn't live with the insured or surviving or divorced spouse, or doesn't qualify as a dependent on the income tax return of any of those people. The COBRA law makes an ex-spouse and children of the parties eligible to receive for the first three years after divorce any group-rate health insurance provided by her ex-husband's employer.

Remember that you may destroy a prenup after you're married and renegotiate a post-nup.

> *My husband was twice wounded, three times shy when I became his third wife, and he was quite concerned about providing for his young children, so our prenup wasn't very generous to me. But I loved him, and over time, the marriage got stronger and the kids and I became very close. I got him back to the bargaining table twice, and eventually he undid most of the limitations.*
> —"Natalie Ames," 60, personnel director, married, two stepchildren

Furthermore, although a spouse can waive the right to alimony, if the judge thinks that the agreement was unfair when made and unconscionable at the time that the action is commenced, he can order payments anyway. Also a prenup that's signed shortly before the wedding may be contestable by a spouse who claims she was forced to sign under pressure. But don't count on such reversals—you need much more to show duress.

One item can't be covered by a prenuptial. A doctor who wanted to protect her pension for her children had her fiancé give up all rights to it in the prenuptial pact and even made sure he signed a special waiver form provided by her plan administrator. Catch-22: only a spouse can waive those rights. To be enforceable, the waiver of a pension has to be signed *after* the marriage.

2. Change the documents.

If you're going to change your name, notify the Social Security office, get new credit cards, and replace any other documents that may be affected. Keep copies of any documentation about the changes.

Change beneficiaries on the savings account, insurance policies, brokerage account, and retirement and pension accounts. Ask the personnel or benefits department of his and/or your employer for copies of the change forms.

Add your name (or his) to car titles and/or titles of other personal property.

3. Redo the will and give each other durable power of attorney.

4. Take special care with estate planning.

If you buy real estate together as joint tenants, the survivor inherits automatically. You may prefer to buy as tenants in common.

If you own the house and want the children to inherit it, you may want to ease the transition for a spouse and allow him to remain in it rent-free for a year after your death, letting the estate pay the carrying charges. If you want to allow your spouse to stay in it for life and then have it revert to your kids, put it into a QTIP trust. (See page 228.)

Finally, when you bequeath personal effects, remember that they include the furnishings of the house. Make sure your will clearly spells out what goes to your spouse along with the home.

5. Never get involved in situations of control that concern former family members.

In situations that affect children from a previous marriage, leave it to the attorneys.

I was Wife Number Three. There were children from both the first and second marriages. My husband hadn't expressly said where he wanted to be buried, and both sets of children started squabbling. I was supposed to handle the money for one of the children who had a drug problem. Instead of leaving this in a lawyer's hands, my husband entrusted it to me. The other kids mistrusted me already and raised a great hue and cry about this.—"Cassandra Davis," 45, cabaret singer, widow, two grown children

HOW NOT TO REMARRY

After years of marriage, Anne's husband leaves her for another, younger woman. She's devastated, and then Steve comes into her life. He's crazy about her and promises to take care of her forever. On her birthday, he buys her a gold bracelet from Cartier. On the next birthday, he gives her diamonds. He again promises to take care of her forever. He offers to marry her and doesn't even want a prenuptial agreement. It is obvious to her that he has a huge amount of money. She tells herself that he must love her very much if he isn't asking her to sign a prenuptial.

Mistake Number One: Not getting a prenuptial. If he says, "I don't want a prenuptial because I love you too much; let's not spoil our love affair by discussing money," watch out. Often, a man who doesn't want a prenuptial is a man who doesn't want to disclose his finances either because he has more than he wants her to know about or significantly less.—Diane Steiner

Next he tells her he'll sell his house and move into hers temporarily, until they buy one together. After a time, her daughters are getting married. She asks him to make plans to move so she can have the proceeds from the house to give her daughters. They find a house that she loves: great location, great grounds, swimming pool, the works. The day of the closing, she's getting dressed and he says, "Don't bother to come." "Why?" she asks. "Because your name isn't going to be on the deed. For estate-planning purposes, everything should be in my name." Years later, she explains why she didn't protest: "I had two children. I was in my sixties. My first husband threw me over for a younger woman, and I was scared. I didn't want to make a scene for a couple of hundred thousand dollars. I figured over the years I could change his mind." She never does.

Mistake Number Two: Letting him put everything in his name.

Meanwhile, she's also given her husband her entire nest egg to invest, all the money she made from the sale of her house. She never looks at it. Ten years later, she discovers that he's put the money into tax-exempts that paid only 2 to 3 percent per year. She's lost a tremendous amount of potential appreciation.

Mistake Number Three: Leaving all the investment decisions to him.

Now he's become ill, and his care is costing a fortune. He tells her to cut back on her spending and insists that they sell the house. It develops that his disease is progressive and terminal. Finally, she discovers that her husband sold his business years before they were married and put all the proceeds in trust for his children. He has lived on the income and occasionally dipped into the principal, but at least officially, he can't get into it. When they divorce, neither can she.

Mistake Number Four: Not knowing the details of your husband's assets.

WHAT YOU OUGHT TO KNOW ABOUT MONEY BEFORE YOU MOVE IN TOGETHER

The number one pitfall of moving in together without any commitment is that your partner may simply up and leave with no provisions for your care. Imagine: you put up with the snoring for all those years and won't get a dime for it. No matter how close you feel, you cannot assume you and he are on the same moonbeam.

> *I thought Bert and I had the same goals when we moved in together: love, affection, a long-term partnership. To celebrate his sixtieth birthday and our tenth year together, I gave him a surprise party. Later, we were sitting on the sofa, in front of the fire. He was wearing the Polo robe I had given him. He thanked me for a wonderful evening and even more wonderful ten years. I felt so close to him. "Bert," I said, "we've shared our lives. Maybe now is the time to combine our assets. If we pool our money, we can probably save more, make decisions together—" He sat bolt upright. "What do you mean? We always said, 'No strings.'" I told him we weren't getting any younger, we really had to think about each other's future security. He just looked at me, shocked. "This wasn't the deal," he said. "We're separate entities. My future is my future. If you're in it, great, but I have to tell you, what's mine is mine." I felt devastated and betrayed. I wound up sleeping in the living room, and the next morning I went to an attorney to see how I could protect myself.*—
> "Ellen Fowler," 54, cleaning products wholesaler, divorced, two children

If you can't get him to take out a marriage license, there are in fact a couple of ways you can attempt to legitimize your relationship for the purpose of your future security.

1. PACK YOUR BAGS.

In the majority of states, you aren't legit without the license and unless an authorized person ties the knot. But under *common-law marriage* in Alabama, Colorado, Georgia, Idaho, Iowa, Kansas, Montana, Oklahoma, Pennsylvania, Rhode Island, South Carolina, Texas, Utah, and the District of Columbia, you may be considered legally married if you do such things as share a checking account with both your names on it; live in the same apartment; have a lease with both names on it; share medical insurance; introduce one another to others as your spouse; and/or register as Mr. and Mrs. in a hotel. Simply living together doesn't suffice. New Hampshire and Oregon recognize such marriages when one partner dies without a will or other estate plans.

Here's the interesting bit: if you and your man travel to common-law states and pass yourself off as husband and wife—for example, by registering at a hotel as Mr. and Mrs.—the non-common-law state may consider you married. States have a tradition of recognizing the laws that prevail in other states, which is why when Hawaii considered recognizing homosexual marriages, certain other states protested vigorously. In the case of an unmarried couple who over a fifteen-year period traveled two to three times a year to Washington, D.C., and registered as husband and wife, New York recognized their relationship as a common-law marriage and gave the woman the legal rights of a spouse. No wonder they say there's nothing like travel to solidify a relationship.

2. MAKE YOURSELF USEFUL.

A man cannot say to you, "You're terrific in bed, so move in with me so I can enjoy you regularly and I'll give you half my house [or buy you an apartment/jewelry/a cottage in the country, etc.]." Actually, he can say it, but no court will oblige him to make good on his promises. New York is one of several states in which you can't make an oral contract for illicit services. On the other hand, if he says, "You decorate like Martha Stewart and entertain like Ivana Trump. Move in and I'll hire you to fix up the house and throw parties, and in return I'll give you half my house [etc., etc.]," then you have a legal right to demand whatever was promised. There is no absolute guarantee that you will get it all, but you can at least have your day in court.

3. Get your name on the lease.

Have yourself listed as a tenant in a rent-controlled or rent-stabilized apartment. If your Significant Other dies, you won't be evicted. (If your name is not on the lease, you don't have any rights.)

4. Or find a way around the marriage issue.

If you have financial reasons for not marrying, you can ensure your security in a number of ways. You can be written into his will and/or be the beneficiary (or owner) of his life insurance. For true protection, the policy should be even larger than if you were married, since in your arrangement there is no marital exclusion that would let one of you inherit tax-free from the other—though the will can provide for the estate to pay the taxes.

You can also each sign a durable power of attorney and/or health care proxy that would give the other person the right to make financial and/or health care decisions depending on how it was filled out.

To keep things uncomplicated, don't buy anything together that can't be cut in half. Keep your bank accounts separate, and establish some kind of system for paying common bills. If you purchase real estate, write an agreement spelling out what happens if one person dies or the relationship is terminated, because otherwise the assumptions of the law prevail.

> *I bought a little house that we were going to work on together. He was very creative and experienced with this kind of project, so I was happy to have his help. I started law school, so over time I had less time to spend on the house and less money. He put money into the upkeep for a couple of years, but I held the mortgage. To make him feel good, though, I always referred to it as "our" house. When we separated, he asked for a half share. As a lawyer I knew he had an action for a "constructive trust." It requires that the two parties have a "confidential relationship" (an intimate relationship), that one makes a promise (I had called it "our" house), that the other relies on that promise, and that one party keeping it would be unjustly enriched.*—"Lorraine Baron," 45, matrimonial lawyer, married, two grown children

Even if you're not in a common-law state, you can have a matrimonial lawyer draw up a palimony or pre-living-together agreement that spells out each partner's rights and obligations. Like any other contract, it is likely to be enforced by courts, provided that the obligations are legitimate in the eyes of the law. (In other words, sexual services don't count.) However, any award would probably be treated as income and be subject to taxes.

An arrangement in which one party works and the other doesn't creates potential tax problems. Everything that the "have" gives to the "have-not" is either a gift or compensation for services and in either case is theoretically taxable. If you suspect this may apply, consult an attorney.

FOUR FINANCIAL REASONS FOR NOT GETTING MARRIED

1. Government entitlements based on your financial circumstances may be lost if you marry a person with some means.
2. Spousal Social Security benefits may be lost. A spouse who is entitled to benefits based on her former husband's employment may lose them if she remarries before age sixty (unless the second marriage is terminated before she reaches that age).
3. In general, marriage will increase your income taxes. For example, the $125,000 once-in-a-lifetime capital gains exclusion on the sale of a residence may be lost. If one of the parties in the marriage has already used this exclusion, it isn't available to the new spouse.
4. Tax rates may be higher if you file as a married couple.

IF YOU ARE WIDOWED

Much of what we have already covered in this book in terms of asset allocation and investments will apply to you in your new financial situation. But these are among the specific changes you might make or issues you will want to address:

INSURANCE

- If you are still working, consider taking out disability insurance to protect yourself and your wage-earning ability.
- If you have young children, take out or increase the amount of term insurance coverage on yourself to replace your income and/or to provide for child care in the event anything happens to you. You may be entitled to some medical coverage for a limited period of time from your husband's previous employer under the COBRA law. You will have to pay out of pocket for it, but at least you will be guaranteed an insurer for a while.

BENEFITS

- Check your Social Security benefits. Unmarried children whose parent has died can collect on that parent's account; so can widows and even ex-wives whose spouse has died.
- To find out what benefits you're entitled to from the company that employed your late husband, call the human resources person or the benefits person. If those resources aren't helpful, you can try the insurance company that the company uses.
- If he has died before receiving his 401(k) benefits, you get them. You can roll them over into an IRA or withdraw the money. If you withdraw, you will have to pay income taxes, but you won't have to pay an early withdrawal penalty.

ESTATE PLANNING

- Visit a lawyer immediately. Rewrite your will and change the beneficiaries on your life insurance, pension plans, annuities, living trusts, and IRAs.
- Report your widowed status to all credit givers.

At the beginning of this book, we talked about birth—the birth of our club and the birth of our financial self-awareness. And here, at the close, we are dealing with issues of death and widowhood. But despite the subject matter, our emphasis here as always is not on finality, but rather on new beginnings. For we believe that if you have absorbed the lessons of this book, read it carefully, and followed its suggestions, like our club members, you should be on the road to financial independence, competence, and self-sufficiency.

This in turn should help you face the prospect of being alone without being afraid. That is the gift we have given to ourselves and, we hope, to you. It is a gift more meaningful and valuable to all of us than any amount of worldly goods. Unlike them, it can never be taken away.

we are dealing with issues of death and widowhood. But despite the subject matter, our emphasis has [illegible] summary, and [illegible] on [illegible] beginnings. If we believe that [illegible] have absorbed the lessons of [illegible] carefully and followed its suggestions, like [illegible] [illegible] independence, [illegible] and self-sufficiency.

[illegible] should [illegible] face the prospect of being alone [illegible] one [illegible] the [illegible] have [illegible] and [illegible] we hope [illegible] and [illegible] fulfilling future [illegible] like [illegible]

RESOURCES

1. WHAT BELONGS IN YOUR HOME FINANCIAL FILES

Everything you need to know about your finances fits into one of the categories below. Details about the specific information and/or documents you need to gather, along with other information, are explained in the following pages.

Some documents should be duplicated and copies placed in a safe deposit box for protection in the event of a fire. We've marked those with an asterisk. Make a photocopy of these pages, fill them in, and distribute copies as needed.

MASTER LIST

Note: Photocopy this form every couple of years, bring it up to date, and send copies to your lawyer, executor, child(ren), and/or a trusted friend.

LAWYER:	Firm:
Address:	Phone:
ACCOUNTANT:	Firm:
Address:	Phone:
INSURANCE BROKER:	Firm:
Address:	Phone:
BANKER:	Bank:
Address:	Phone:
EXECUTOR:	Firm:
Address:	Phone:
EMPLOYEE BENEFITS MANAGER:	Firm:
Address:	Phone:
BROKER/FINANCIAL ADVISOR:	Firm:
Address:	Phone:

BANK ACCOUNT(S)			
Type of Account	***Bank***	***Branch***	***Account No.***

BROKERAGE ACCOUNT(S)		
Firm	*Branch*	*Account No.*

MONEY MARKET ACCOUNT(S)			
Type of Account	*Institution*	*Branch*	*Account No.*

Safe Deposit Box

Bank:	Address:
Box No.:	Deputy:

Social Security Numbers

Name:	Number:
Name:	Number:
Name:	Number:
Name:	Number:
Name:	Number:

Location of Other Papers

Other Home Financial Files:	
Current and past tax records:	
Canceled checks:	
Checkbooks, deposit slips, receipts:	
Home safe:	Combination:

Date completed:
Copies sent to:

DEATH- AND ESTATE-RELATED INFORMATION

Note: Use this checklist to gather information. Give a copy of the list and relevant documents to whoever will be handling your affairs.

DOCUMENTS

- ☐ Conformed copy of will. Original is held by: ___________.
- ☐ Copy of any other testamentary document (such as letter of instruction; see pages 208–210)
- ☐ Signed copy of power of attorney/durable power of attorney
- ☐ Signed copy of medical durable power of attorney/health care proxy
- ☐ Signed copy of living will

INSTRUCTIONS IN EVENT OF DEATH

- ☐ Funeral instructions. Do you wish cremation, memorial service, and/or funeral with open or closed casket?
- ☐ Special information in death notice in newspaper. Papers to contact.

- ☐ Instructions regarding memorial gifts:
  - Cemetery name: Address:
  - Plot number: Location of deed to plot:
- ☐ People/institutions to contact:
  - Employer:
  - Lawyer:
  - Insurance agent:
  - Mortgage holder:
  - Social Security office:

My friend's husband died suddenly, and she didn't know whether to have him buried in Chicago, where he came from, or Indianapolis, where they were living. People were coming to pay condolence calls and comfort her, and she couldn't even concentrate. The entire time she was out dealing with the cemetery plots. I've decided that my husband and I are going to sit down, make the decision, buy the plots—and then never talk about the thing again.—Carol Levin

- There should be only one signed copy of a will (see pages 210–211). If you change law firms, have the original attorney send the will to his or her successor. But your health care agent should have a signed copy of the health care proxy and living will.
- A safe deposit box is sealed when the bank learns of the owner's death, so the will—and any other papers that may be needed immediately after death—should be left elsewhere. Spouses with separate boxes should not keep each other's wills in them in the event of death in a common accident.

PERSONAL AND REAL PROPERTY

DOCUMENTS

- ☐ *Copy of deeds, titles, title insurance for home (original may be at bank if you have a mortgage).

- ☐ *Copy of deeds, titles, title insurance for any other property you own.
- ☐ *Copy of deeds, title, title insurance for car.
- ☐ *Copy of videotape inventory of house. Go through every room and closet. The video may help you file an insurance claim for theft or damage.
- ☐ *Receipts for big-ticket items (furs, furnishings) in case of insurance claims.

TAX INFORMATION NEEDED FOR EVENTUAL SALE OF HOME OR RENTAL PROPERTY

- ☐ Closing agreement regarding the purchase of your house.
- ☐ Form 2119—proceeds from the sale of any prior residence.
- ☐ File of receipts for any item or service you paid for that enhanced the value of your residence or kept it in good condition. (A checklist of over 200 items, including sewer connection, alarm system installation, driveway repair, and landscaping, is available from the National Council of Certified Public Accountants, 888-488-5400.) Total these expenses when you sell your house and deduct them from any profit in order to lower your capital gains tax.
- ☐ Expense records on rental properties to deduct from your profits at the time of the sale.
- Keep whatever you may need if you sell property or there is fire or theft damage that may be covered by insurance.

On the heels of a serious financial setback, we moved to a small apartment and rented out our house. After the move, I discovered all my jewelry was missing. Fifteen years later, I sold the house. As it was being cleared out, a workman brought me a paper bag that he had found in a deep closet. Inside was the "stolen" jewelry that I had obviously mislaid. Many people have told me similar stories. Always tell a child or a dear friend where you've hidden any of your precious things—or leave a letter with your will.—"Elizabeth Doyle," 65, retired museum administrator, widowed, two grown children

PERSONAL DOCUMENTATION

- ☐ List of credit cards and numbers (shortcut: take them all out of your wallet and photocopy back and front.)
- ☐ *Passport
- ☐ *College degree
- ☐ *Professional license
- ☐ *Marriage license
- ☐ *Separation/divorce papers
- ☐ *Copy of Social Security card (and updated entitlement forms; see pages 150–151)
- ☐ *Health information (vaccinations, hospitalizations, and so forth)
- ☐ *Military records

- If you apply for Social Security benefits and expect a check based on your spouse's earnings, you'll need a certified copy of your marriage license. Even after you divorce him, hang on to it. If you ever claim benefits based on an ex-spouse's earnings, you'll need to produce a certified copy of both the marriage license and the divorce papers.
- Check your credit rating every couple of years. Contact all three credit bureaus (TRW, Equifax, and Trans Union), or do one-stop shopping by contacting First America CRED-CO's Confidential Credit (800-441-9432). For $31.95 they'll send you a summary of your ratings in two weeks, along with detailed instructions about how to protest inaccurate information.

If you have been denied credit, the report from any of the credit bureaus is free. Just send a copy of the letter of denial along with the application. This service can come in very handy if you have been denied credit for a loan or a mortgage; you may be able to set things right very quickly with the information you get. Personnel at First America can even help you in foreign languages.

Ten years after a friend's husband resolved a credit problem, it was still appearing on all his credit records. The state attorney general's office provided an application to get it removed.

LIFE INSURANCE

- ☐ Life insurance policy(ies); a separate folder for each
- ☐ Employer life insurance policy
- ☐ Mortgage life and credit life insurance (which pay these bills in the event of your death)
- ☐ Insurance through credit card company

- Before you file away any insurance policies, go through every one with a highlighter pen and mark all the important points. You may find it helpful to summarize these points on a single sheet stapled to the front of the policy. If you have a question about the coverage, use a stick-on note reminding you to ask the agent about it at your next meeting.
- Check that the beneficiary is correct on your life insurance.
- Check the due date on the life insurance premium. Make sure it is paid every year.
- Check the cash value of any whole life policy. Ask if any loans have been made against it. Also use this opportunity to see if the policies have performed as promised and consider a change if necessary.
- Some credit card companies automatically bill you for flight insurance every time you charge an airline ticket. The chance of your dying this way is so small that the insurance is a waste of money. Call your credit card company to see if you have this insurance; if so, cancel it.

If you are looking for a lost policy:

- Start with your insurance agent.
- Check the canceled check stubs for the name of any insurance company to which payments were made.
- Contact the last employer to see if the company may have paid a premium or have insurance-related information in its files.
- The American Council of Life Insurance offers a free policy search. They will send you a questionnaire that is then circulated to about 100 companies. For more information, write to ACLI Policy Search Department, 1001 Pennsylvania Avenue, N.W., Washington, DC 20004.

HEALTH-RELATED INSURANCE

- □ Health and hospitalization policy
- □ Additional health and hospitalization policy
- □ Disability policy
- □ Long-term-care policy

PROPERTY INSURANCE

- □ *Homeowner's insurance
- □ Liability
- □ Auto

- Keep liability policies for the past three years. Someone may come out of the woodwork and sue you for an injury that happened a while ago. In case the company computers have gone amok and lost the data, you'll want to be able to prove you were insured back then.

RETIREMENT FUNDS

- □ *Keogh
- □ *IRAs
- □ *SEPs
- □ *401(k)
- □ *Other retirement information (deferred compensation, etc.)
- □ *Pension information
- □ *Profit-sharing plan

- Keep whatever the employer sends, especially annual statements on the status of pensions, profit-sharing plans, and so forth.
- Keep numbers and locations of all Keogh plans, IRAs, and tax-deferred annuities in a safe deposit box, but keep documents and other materials at home.

INVESTMENTS

- ☐ Confirmation of purchase(s) that show price, number of shares, and total cost including commissions as well as information regarding cost basis adjustments due to stock splits, mergers, or acquisitions (get from your broker).
- ☐ Confirmation of sales—date and price. Keep this and all above information for five years after the sale. Your broker will have this.
- ☐ Mutual fund prospectuses.
- ☐ Brokerage house statements. Monthly statements show trading activity and in the event of divorce may be useful, especially if your husband had input in making the decisions. Keep for five years.
- ☐ *Names of, original prospectuses, and sales materials for any limited partnerships.
- ☐ *List of any bonds and Treasury securities not held in street name.
- ☐ *List of savings bonds, their denominations, serial numbers, and issue.
- ☐ *Employment contract.
- ☐ *Photocopy of any stock certificates not held in street name.
- ☐ *Names and account numbers of any mutual funds and unit trusts not in street name.

- Although you will have separate confirmation of purchases and sales, we recommend that you keep summary sheets:

Stocks

Stock	Date Bought	No. of Shares	Cost per Share	Total Cost	Date Sold	Price per Share	Total Price

Bonds

Bond	Date Bought	Coupon Yield	Matures on	Callable?	Price Sold	Date Paid	Price

For stocks and/or bond mutual funds, you can call the mutual fund to ask for a printout of the history.

- When you sell a mutual fund, tell your accountant if you have made a practice of reinvesting the dividends. This means your actual cost will be higher than your original investment and may reduce your capital gains tax obligations.
- When you sell any inherited securities, tell your accountant. They are valued as of the date of death of the deceased person or six months later and are not based on the deceased's original cost.

MISCELLANEOUS ASSETS

- ☐ Certificates of deposit
- ☐ Passbooks
- ☐ Jewelry
- ☐ Collectibles
- ☐ Other

- Leave instructions for a potential executor about the best way to sell or preserve the collectibles. For example, offering Hummel figurines through the Hummel Collectors' Club will probably be a better way of selling them than offering them in bulk to a general antiques dealer.

OBLIGATIONS AND LIABILITIES

- ☐ Mortgages: loan agreement papers and a recent copy of statement
- ☐ Home equity loans
- ☐ Personal IOUs (payable); or a note indicating debt has been paid

- Keep copies of all obligations, whether you owe them individually or are jointly liable with your husband.
- If there is an estate to settle, heirs will need to know liabilities.

TAX RECORDS

- ☐ Past returns
- ☐ Canceled checks
- ☐ Checkbooks
- ☐ Deposit slips
- ☐ Receipts

- Keep at least three years' worth of receipts for business expenses, contributions, and other documentation for tax-deductible items in case of an audit.
- If you underreport your income by more than 25 percent, the IRS can ask you for records going back six years. If you're found guilty of fraud, it can ask you to produce material as far back as it wishes. For a small fee, the IRS will send you copies of your old tax forms going back as far as six years, but you won't get documentation. (And remember that if you file a year or two late, the three years from date of filing may mean you actually need records going back five years.)
- Keep at least the page of old returns that shows any carry-forward capital gain on your house or any contributions to an IRA that weren't tax-deductible. You can toss the rest, unless you think you may need them as proof you actually filed. To be on the safe side, keep the whole returns forever.
- For assets like real estate and stocks, keep the purchase records from the date bought through the date sold plus five years. For carry-forward losses, you need the records forever.
- If you bought a stock years ago and don't have the information, or haven't kept good records of dividend reinvestments, the company, your brokerage house, or accountant may be able to work out a reasonable estimate of cost. Otherwise the IRS may assume you paid the lowest possible price and tax you on the difference between that and the sales price—so you may pay a stiff tax.
- Keep all receipts until you're sure you won't have to return the item or, if the receipt is the warranty, until the warranty expires. But if you're using them for a tax-deductible item, keep them until you toss the return.

- Keep receipts for medical expenses for a year. If you spend more than 7.5 percent of your adjusted gross income on medical bills that aren't covered by insurance, you can deduct the excess. If you do, keep the bills until you toss the return.
- Keep receipts from charitable contributions along with your check for tax deductions until you toss the return.
- Keep only the canceled checks that:
  1. prove tax deductions were valid (though sometimes actual receipts may be required);
  2. prove you made alimony payments;
  3. prove you paid a bill (if proof may be necessary; i.e., to see that someone makes good on a warranty);
  4. prove you made permanent home improvements (see page 282);
  5. prove what you paid if you own property jointly with someone you're not married to.
- If you void a check, don't throw it out. Write "void," and include it with the month's statement.

II. WHAT BELONGS IN YOUR SAFE DEPOSIT BOX

A home safe should be fire-resistant enough to protect papers against high heat for a minimum of an hour. But a safe deposit box is probably a safer and more practical place than a home safe to keep important papers secure. Unless you've got a top-of-the-line security system, jewelry also is probably safest in the box, along with anything else you want to keep completely secure and private.

You can lease a safe deposit vault box from a bank for an annual rental fee. The amount depends on the size of the box. In some areas, safe deposit boxes are in short supply. You may get preferential treatment from a bank where you're a regular customer.

You can choose someone to be named a *deputy* with authorization to have access to your box. Both of you must fill out a signature card, which is checked when you visit the box.

You'll be assigned two keys. There is a small charge to replace one, but if you lose the second, the box will have to be drilled open, which may cost you $100 or more. To be on the safe side, have an extra key made for your deputy. Put the original key (or keys) in a safe place, such as in an envelope inside a marked folder. Don't put the name of the bank on the key envelope. If your wallet or purse is stolen, the thief has samples of your handwriting and may try to get access to your box.

When you visit the bank, you may take the box to a private room where you can go over the contents for as long as you like. (We know a couple who rented a safe deposit box just to have a private—if tiny—room for midday, midtown trysts. Added plus: a safe deposit box rental is tax-deductible.)

In many states, when the bank has been notified of a death the box is sealed and no deputy other than a spouse may have access. Tax inspectors seal the box in order to check inside in hopes of finding something—like a lot of cash or jewelry—that you may have neglected to mention on your tax returns or that will be taxable in your estate. More lenient states allow not only a spouse but also an executor in after your death. Others allow the bank to search a box for a will, a cemetery deed, or military discharge papers.

Can thieves break into a bank safe deposit box? Of course. Can you sue? Only if you prove negligence on the part of the bank. Can you recover? Only if you have receipts, photos, and appraisals of what you've lost. However, we wouldn't spend a lot of time worrying that your safe deposit box may be invaded by robbers. On the other hand, since boxes can be targeted, it is wise to keep the contents of the box to yourself.

Following is a list of what belongs in your safe deposit box. *Duplicate copies of starred items should also be in your home files for quick reference.* The reason for having a second copy of these items is that either they would be a nuisance to replace or they might be critical for an insurance claim in the event a fire destroyed your papers at home.

CHECKLIST FOR THE SAFE DEPOSIT BOX

REAL AND PERSONAL PROPERTY

- ☐ *Deeds, titles, title insurance for home
- ☐ *Deeds, titles, title insurance for any other property you own
- ☐ *Deeds, title, title insurance for auto
- ☐ *Videotape inventory of house
- ☐ *Copy of receipts for big-ticket items (furs, furnishings, etc.)
- ☐ *Copy of homeowner's insurance
- ☐ *Copy of receipts for home improvements
- ☐ *Coins, jewelry, etc.

FINANCIAL/BUSINESS

- ☐ *Copy of employment contract
- ☐ *Original stock certificates (if not in street name)
- ☐ *Original prospectuses and sales materials for any limited partnerships
- ☐ *Bonds and Treasury securities (if not in street name)
- ☐ *U.S. savings bonds

PERSONAL DOCUMENTATION

- ☐ Marriage certificate
- ☐ Birth certificate
- ☐ *Copy of passport
- ☐ *Copy of college degree
- ☐ *Copy of professional license
- ☐ *Copy of separation/divorce papers
- ☐ Social Security card
- ☐ *Copy of health information (vaccinations, hospitalizations)
- ☐ *Military records

III. STARTING YOUR OWN FINANCIAL SELF-HELP GROUP

If you don't want to start or join an investment club, then get yourself a buddy. Invest as a team, or give each other support. You can also get the family involved. Buy everyone stock in companies that appeal to them—perhaps Nike for the runner, Coca-Cola and Walt Disney for the preteens, AT&T and the Gap for the teenagers—to get them involved. Have little family financial sessions from time to time. However, if you can possibly pull it off, forming your own financial self-help group will be one of the best things you have ever done for yourself.

FINDING THE MEMBERS

You may be able to assemble a group of co-workers into a club that meets before or after work or at lunchtime in a space the company provides. This solves three problems: finding the people, finding the place to meet, and finding the time in your life to participate in a club.

Or follow the example of a group that meets in a local restaurant that caters a modestly priced buffet dinner. Food service begins at 5:30 P.M., and the meeting starts at 6:00.

Or transform an existing group into a club. For example, you and your bowling team could get together to hold a meeting an hour before your games begin.

You don't need to know everyone beforehand. In fact, meeting new people is one of the benefits of the club. If you're starting from scratch, post notices in your church, on your school bulletin board, at the health club, in the supermarket. Perhaps the local paper will run an announcement. Chances are that once the news gets out, you'll have more would-be members than you can handle.

Your membership will quickly thin out anyway. Your leader should stress the fact that membership involves a lot of time and energy, studying and research. You don't make investment choices by "listening to your gut." This will discourage anyone who has come just because a friend is joining or to get out of the house. Be very clear about your expectations about the amount of work, and have provisions for dealing with members who don't participate.

FINDING YOUR ADVISOR

The advisor may be a stockbroker, a certified financial planner, or an insurance agent. (If your advisor is other than a broker, he or she would have to set up a club trading account at a brokerage firm.) The person should be experienced, with good credentials. Even more important, you need someone who is willing to work with beginners and won't talk down to you or over your heads.

The financial advisor should make a commitment to attend most meetings and work closely with the club's treasurer, accountant, and lawyer (especially at the beginning), keep the group focused, organized, and informed, and provide a steady stream of educational materials. Finally, the advisor should be prepared to step aside quickly, allowing members to run their own show but clarifying or expanding as required.

There is a lot of work involved, but everyone in the group represents a potential client or friend, so you should be able to find several prospects to help you. Ask for recommendations from friends and other professionals. Lawyers and CPAs usually know many brokers and financial planners.

Take someone along to the interview. You'll need a second opinion about whether you've found the right person. (Use the Chapter 2 sections on "Sizing Each Other Up" and "Reviewing Your Impressions.")

GETTING IT ORGANIZED

If your advisor can't help you find a space to meet and there is no office available, see if a library, school, church, or Y will donate space. If necessary, advertise for space in a local paper.

The National Association of Investors Corporation (NAIC), a not-for-profit corporation, can provide a great deal of information about all aspects of organizing a club. Write them at P.O. Box 220, Royal Oak, MI

48068 or telephone 810-583-6242 from Monday through Friday, 8:30 A.M. to 5:00 P.M. ET.

A one-size-fits-all plan may not be sufficient. Since a club is an organization that is dealing with various people's money and we live in a very litigious society, we recommend that you hire both a lawyer and an accountant to give your club advice that suits its particular needs. At least two people (neither of whom made the recommendation) should interview prospects.

The accountant and lawyer will have to do some of the work before they are paid because, until the club is organized, you won't have any money. They may give you a preferred fee because club members represent potential new business, but don't expect them to work for free. There is simply too much to do.

The accountant must prepare the tax return for the partnership and the individual returns for each member, oversee the work of the treasurer, check the brokerage house statements, and prepare statements for members who are being bought out or coming in.

The attorney will have to spend time not only drawing up the papers but helping you come up with your own bylaws. Make them as comprehensive as possible. Though you will probably review and revise them after you are up and running, avoid having to make up rules on the spot. Oblige members to come to a certain number of meetings, and set up rules about payments.

Your own members will have to make a major time commitment, too. All of them will eventually have to spend some time as members of a stock selection committee and in following the existing stocks in the club's portfolio. In addition, officers who are members of the Executive Committee will have to work closely with the professionals in running the club. You will also need an administrative committee to handle such details as extra copies of the minutes.

FINDING YOUR WAY

Decide on your investment philosophy right away: do you want to make aggressive or conservative investments? Set realistic and long-term goals.

And have confidence in yourselves. If you are committed to making the club work, you can learn together and succeed together.

In the midst of organizing a club, my friend was becoming overwhelmed and frantic. I went around the room, closed all the books she was trying to read, and said, "You have a committed leader and an excellent advisor, an accountant, and a lawyer. That's all that you need. From there, just go with your gut. You are at the beginning of a wonderful journey."—Jane Bishop Shalam

ACKNOWLEDGMENTS

The authors wish to express their sincere appreciation to the securities, insurance, and legal professionals who gave so freely of their time and support. A book of this complexity could never exist without their collective skills. A particular thanks to the experts who were our primary sources of information and reviewed—and rereviewed—this material. We cannot fully express our gratitude for the support and enthusiasm of Gloria Gottlieb, RFC, of Glory Insurance Agency, Inc., an affiliate of American Insurance Consultants, Inc.; Carlyn McCaffrey of Weil, Gotshal & Manges LLP; Diane Steiner of Sheresky, Aronson & Mayefsky LLP, together with Ross Kass and Steve Greenberg of Jablon, Kass & Greenberg,

Certified Public Accountants, P.C.; and Steve Schanker of Schanker and Hochberg, P.C.

Thanks also to friends who had the kindness to look over our final draft to help up make sure we had the latest and most correct material. They include Deborah Baum of Guardian Life; Katie Behrens, Ph.D., of Madison Professional Planning; Mary Farrell, Ellen Harris, and Michael Stott of Paine Webber; Salvatore A. Mazzella of Concord Pension Consultants, Inc; Norman Sheresky of Sheresky, Aronson & Mayefsky LLP; and Christina Rizopoulos Valauri, senior equity analyst, Gruntal & Company.

Some very generous and encouraging publishing professionals helped bring this book from idea to reality: our agent, Pam Bernstein, who so capably helped us show others its potential; our talented editor, Fred Hills, and his assistant editor, Hilary Black; our supportive publisher, Michele Martin, and our enthusiastic publicist, Holly Zappala; and dedicated attorneys Bob Sugarman and Bernadette Ezring of Weil, Gotshal & Manges LLP.

Special thanks to our writer, Dale Burg, who shaped our thoughts into chapters, made order of it all, and captured the personality of our club in the pages that precede.

A deep-from-the-heart thanks to our cohorts in The Money Club, all of whom are a constant source of support, enthusiasm, and motivation, as you will have discovered in these pages. Second president Joann Jordan in particular worked with impressive dedication to bring the club to new heights.

Finally, our eternal gratitude to the club members and other friends, named and unnamed, who gave unstintingly of their time, opened their hearts, and shared their financial horror stories in the hopes that other women would learn from their experience. They were our greatest inspiration.

Personal acknowledgments from Marilyn: To my parents, Mary and Davy Crockett, who gave freely of their wisdom and love, supported my every adventure and enterprise, and let me soar. To my brother, John, a lifelong source of encouragement, stalwart supporter of this project, and dear friend, and his beloved wife, Maria, and son, Christopher. To Nancy McDonough and Stacy Williams, my friends and associates. To Dr. Richard Dolins, for always being there for me. And to Shelly Freeman and George Sula, for their belief in and support of my vision of women being financially independent.

Personal acknowledgments from Diane: To Derek Grover, who was as always there for me—and for everyone in our club—at every step, from inception to completion. To Ross Kass, who insisted that I would "get it" (and I got it!). To Ira Millstein, whose commitment to this project never waned, for which I am forever grateful. To my dear friend Joan Gelman, whose encouragement, support, and insightfulness cheered me from the start. To my best friend and daughter, Deborah Kerner, who shared my ongoing enthusiasm and helped me drive the book home. And to my husband, Marshall, who listened, listened, and listened, and who has maximized my potential in every way. I am blessed that you have all enriched my life and believed in me, and I want to say thank you from the bottom of my heart.

and George Soros, for their belief in and support of my vision of women being financially independent.

[illegible] acknowledgment [illegible] Dr. Dick Grover, who was [illegible] for me [illegible] everyone in our [illegible] every step, from [illegible] to completion. [illegible] who insisted that I would "get" [illegible] and [illegible] whose [illegible] project [illegible] were [illegible] my [illegible] friend [illegible] [illegible] from the [illegible] staggering [illegible] husband [illegible] and who [illegible] be [illegible] you have all [illegible] believed in me and I want to say thank you from the bottom of my heart.

INDEX

ABOUT THE AUTHORS

MARILYN HOPE CROCKETT is an expert on retirement planning, an authority on estate management, and a specialist in financial planning for women. She is a First Vice President, Investments, at a major New York firm, where she was appointed to the President's Council. Ms. Crockett is one of only thirty individuals licensed nationally by the National Center for Women and Retirement Research (Long Island University, Southampton, New York) to give Pre-Retirement and Planning (PREP) seminars on investing and financial management for women. She is the Financial Consultant/Manager for several corporate pension plans and several not-for-profit organizations and specializes in working with women business owners. Prior to joining her present firm, she was a Vice President, Private Client Group, at Smith Barney and a financial analyst with a private venture capital firm. She is an instructor at the Learning Annex and has led financial planning seminars for several cruise lines. Ms. Crockett's professional affiliations include American Women in Economic Development (AWED) and the National Association of Female Executives (NAFE). She is a member of the Daughters of the American Revolution, the Colonial Dames, and World Wings (former Pan American flight attendants). Her TV appearances include CNBC's *Money Bowl* (with the Beardstown Ladies), PBS's *Nightly Business Report,* and CNN's *Money Line.* She is single and lives in New York City.

DIANE TERMAN FELENSTEIN is president of Diane Terman Public Relations, founded in 1971, which specializes in lifestyle public relations and marketing. Her many clients have included Schrafft's, Seagrams, Salvador Dalí, *Self* magazine (Condé Nast), *European Travel and Life* (for Rupert Murdoch), Clairol, Prestige Cosmetics, Bob Hope Birthday Benefit, United Cerebral Palsy, Universal Motion Pictures, WMCA Radio and WNEW Radio, Ultra Slim-Fast, Colgate-Palmolive, and several book publishers. She is an accredited member of the Public Relations Society of America, Women Executives in Public Relations, the Fashion Group, and Cosmetic Executive Women. Ms. Felenstein is the cofounder of DayLight, the junior division of DayTop Village, and cofounder of Women's O.W.N., part of the Women's Health Institute of New York University, and has been a member of the board of several charitable foundations. She has lectured on the subject of public relations at Syracuse University, Cornell University, and New York University. Ms. Felenstein lives in New York City.

DALE BURG has written twelve books, seven long-running columns for magazines including *Family Circle, New Woman, First,* and *Woman's Day,* many articles and humorous essays on a variety of topics of interest to women, and software for Microsoft. She has also taught comedy writing at New York University. Ms. Burg lives in New York City.

Printed in the United States
By Bookmasters